ATLAS of the Bible and Christianity

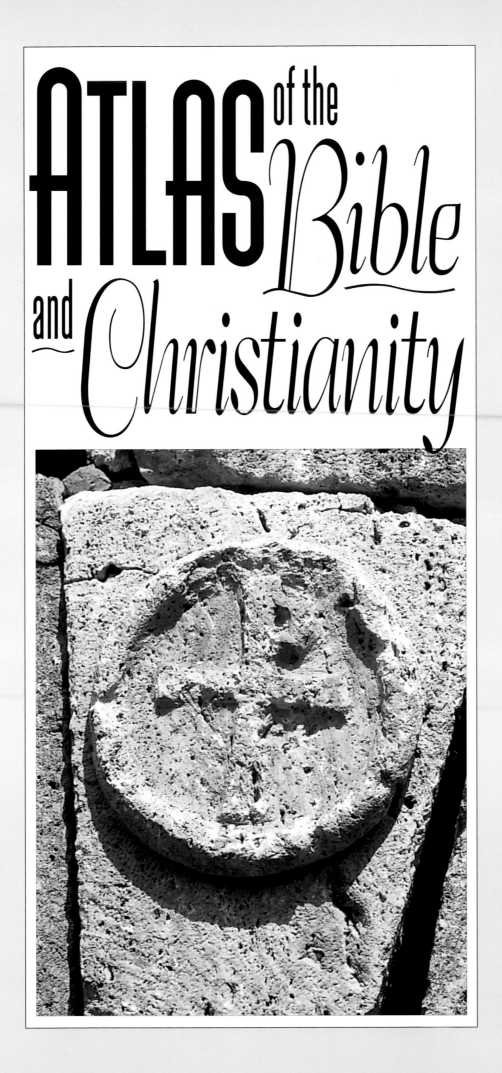

Copyright © 1997
Angus Hudson Ltd/Tim Dowley &
Peter Wyart trading as Three's
Company

First US edition published in 1997 by
Baker Books
a division of Baker Book House
Company
PO Box 6287, Grand Rapids, MI 48516-
6287

**Library of Congress Cataloging-in-
Publication Data** is on file at the
Library of Congress, Washington, DC.

ISBN 0-8010-2051-4

Designed by Peter Wyart,
Three's Company
Co-edition organised and produced by
Angus Hudson Ltd,
Concorde House,
Grenville Place,
Mill Hill,
London NW7 3SA

The maps in this atlas have been
computer generated by specialist
cartographers Hardlines for Three's
Company and Angus Hudson Ltd, who
are the copyright owners. The
cartographers and copyright owners
have made every effort to achieve
accuracy, but cannot be held responsible
for any errors or omissions.

Printed in Hong Kong

Cartography
by Hardlines, Charlbury,
Oxfordshire
Cartographer: Geoff Walker

Photographic Acknowledgments
Tim Dowley: pp. 11, 12, 18, 21, 32, 36, 38,
50, 57, 62, 63, 67, 71, 75, 87, 92, 97, 98,
102, 104, 107, 113, 120
FMB Southern Baptist Convention: p. 150
Andrew Holder: p. 109
Mig Holder: p. 109
Jamie Simson: p. 48
Peter Wyart: pp. 13, 17, 19, 26, 29, 55, 58,
60, 64, 72, 73, 78, 83, 87, 92, 93, 99, 102,
110, 116, 141

Illustrations
James Macdonald: pp. 27, 36, 44, 47, 50,
58, 68
Richard Scott: p. 37
Paul Wyart: p. 96

ATLAS of the Bible and Christianity

EDITOR: TIM DOWLEY

EDITORIAL CONSULTANTS:

Alan Millard
Rankin Professor in Hebrew and Ancient Semitic
Languages, University of Liverpool

David Wright
Senior Lecturer in Ecclesiastical History,
University of Edinburgh

Brian Stanley
Director of the North Atlantic Missiology Project
for the University of Cambridge, and Fellow
of St. Edmund's College

Research: Malcolm Day

INTRODUCTION

We believe that this atlas features several notable innovations. Chief among these is to combine an atlas of the Bible with an atlas of church history and of the development of Christianity in the two millennia since the birth of Christ. Moreover, a number of the maps of recent church history included in this atlas, particularly those covering the twentieth century, present material not previously available in this form. We have aimed to create a book that combines the accuracy and comprehensiveness required by the academic world with a clarity and interest that make it accessible to the general reader.

We believe this atlas breaks new ground too in being almost entirely computer-generated, with the enhanced accuracy and control that state-of-the-art technology affords. We have aided location finding by adding latitudes and longitudes to the maps, and by providing precise reference points in the exhaustive gazetteer at the back of the book.

This atlas, the end product of a number of years' intensive work, is the result of team effort. The original design work was by Tony Cantale of Tony Cantale Graphics, and the huge task of researching every map was completed by Malcolm Day. We are most grateful to the three specialist consultants, Professor Alan Millard, Mr David Wright and Dr Brian Stanley, for their advice and expertise at each stage in the development of the atlas. The page designs were created by Peter Wyart, and the boundary-expanding work of generating the finished maps by Geoff Walker and his team at Hardlines. The index and gazetteer were drawn up by Christopher Pipe. We are most grateful to them all.

Tim Dowley
St Nicholas' Day 1996

CONTENTS

LIST OF MAPS

THE GEOGRAPHY OF PALESTINE

When viewing the Holy Land from the air the eyes immediately slide down the long straight corridor that is the Jordan valley. It runs north-south the entire length of Palestine, from Mt Hermon to the Arabah. Although it meanders wildly along its lower course, unlike other rivers the River Jordan is constrained by high-sided valley walls which form part of the Great Rift Valley. This rift is part of a 6,500-kilometre (4,000-mile) geological fault that begins in Syria and ends in Mozambique.

Millions of years ago the subterranean plates, upon which the continents of Africa and Asia rest, shifted towards each other and caused the earth's crust to buckle and fracture. This produced the distinctive features of Palestine. Pressure between the two plates caused the sub-surface sediments to bulge and rise in the west, resulting in the Judean Hills. In Transjordan, the plate tilted upwards to produce the high Eastern Plateau. Between them the sediment dropped, with the result that the surface of the Dead Sea is some 400 metres (1,300 feet) below sea level, the lowest place on earth.

The consequence of this cataclysm for climate and vegetation in the region was huge. Although Palestine is only some 70 kilometres (45 miles) wide, altitudes range from over 1,000 metres (3,300 feet) in the Judean Mountains to minus 400 metres (1,300 feet) at the Dead Sea. Where the land is low lying, away from the coast, temperatures soar and desert conditions prevail. In the mountains temperatures are cooler and relief rainfall can support pastureland or cultivation. Since most of the land north of the Dead Sea is hilly, westerly winds coming off the Mediterranean Sea would bring rain which would support large areas of forest. South of the Dead Sea hot dry winds from Africa and Arabia produced deserts.

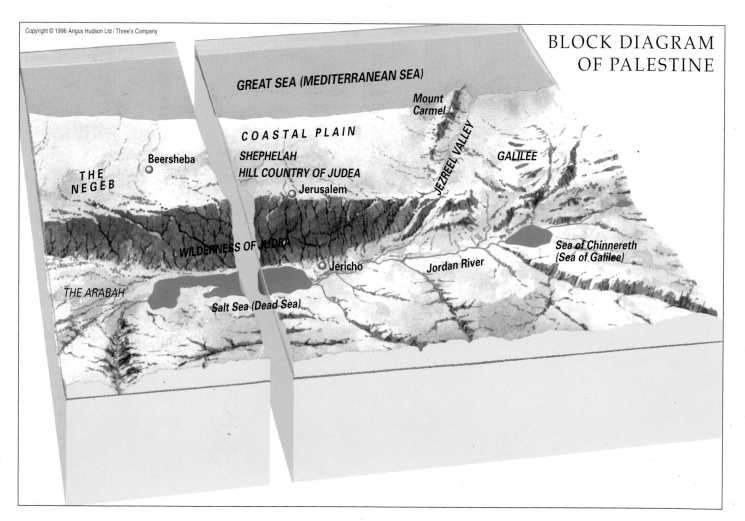

BLOCK DIAGRAM OF PALESTINE

GREAT SEA (MEDITERRANEAN SEA)

Mount Carmel

COASTAL PLAIN

SHEPHELAH

HILL COUNTRY OF JUDEA

Jerusalem

JEZREEL VALLEY

GALILEE

Beersheba

THE NEGEB

WILDERNESS OF JUDEA

Jericho

Jordan River

Sea of Chinnereth (Sea of Galilee)

THE ARABAH

Salt Sea (Dead Sea)

RELIEF MAP OF PALESTINE

Tyre

PLAIN OF PHOENICIA

Mt. Hermon
(9,232ft / 2,184m)

Dan

Lake Huleh

SYRIAN DESERT

ARAM

Acco

Hazor

SEA OF CHINNERETH
(SEA OF GALILEE)

GREAT SEA
(MEDITERRANEAN SEA)

Mt. Carmel
(1,732ft / 528m)

Tiberias

Yarmuk

Mt. Tabor
(1,929ft / 588m)

VALLEY OF JEZREEL

PLAIN OF SHARON

Megiddo

Mt. Gilboa
(1,630ft / 497m)

Pella

GILEAD

Jordan

Samaria

Mt. Ebal
(3,083ft / 940m)

Shechem
Mt. Gerizim
(2,889ft / 881m)

HILLS OF EPHRAIM

ISRAEL

THE ARABAH

Jabbok

AMMON

Joppa

Shiloh

Lod

Bethel

Gibeon

Gezer

Mt. of Olives
(2,723ft / 830m)

Jerusalem

Jericho

Heshbon

Ashkelon

Bethlehem

Mt. Nebo
(2,630ft / 802m)

SALT SEA (DEAD SEA)

SHEPHELAH

JUDAH

HILLS OF JUDEA

WILDERNESS OF JUDEA

Dibon

Gaza

Lachish

Hebron

Arnon

MOAB

Beersheba

THE NEGEB

THE ARABAH

Zered

EDOM

metres | feet
1,000 | 3,281
500 | 1,640
200 | 656
0 | 0
below sea level | below sea level

0   25   50 km
0   10   20   30 miles

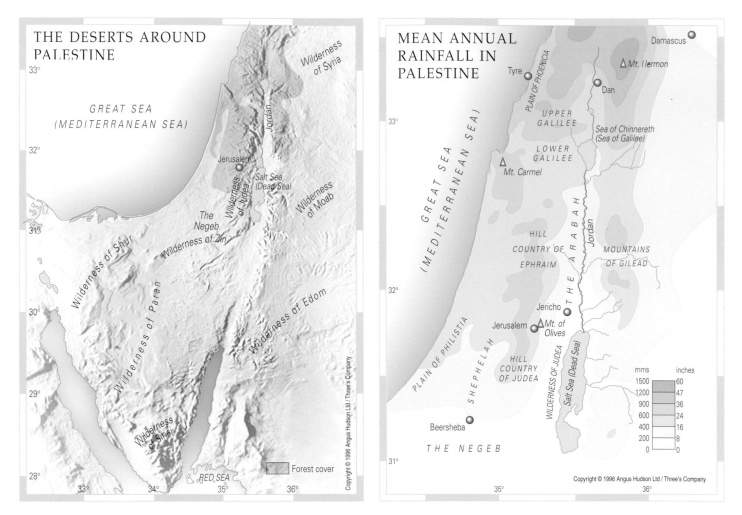

THE DESERTS AROUND PALESTINE

THE DESERTS AROUND
PALESTINE

33°

GREAT SEA
(MEDITERRANEAN SEA)

32°

Wilderness
of Syria

Jordan

Jerusalem

Salt Sea
(Dead Sea)

Wilderness
of Judea

The
Negeb

Wilderness
of Moab

31°

Wilderness of Shur

Wilderness of Zin

Wilderness of Paran

Wilderness of Edom

30°

29°

Wilderness
of Sinai

28°

33° 34° 35° 36°

RED SEA

Forest cover

MEAN ANNUAL RAINFALL IN PALESTINE

MEAN ANNUAL
RAINFALL IN
PALESTINE

Damascus

Tyre

Mt. Hermon

Plain of Phoenicia

Dan

33°

UPPER
GALILEE

Sea of Chinnereth
(Sea of Galilee)

LOWER
GALILEE

Mt. Carmel

HILL
COUNTRY OF
EPHRAIM

MOUNTAINS
OF GILEAD

GREAT SEA (MEDITERRANEAN SEA)

THE ARABAH

Jordan

32°

Jericho

Jerusalem

Mt. of
Olives

PLAIN OF PHILISTIA

SHEPHELAH

HILL
COUNTRY
OF JUDEA

WILDERNESS OF JUDEA

Salt Sea (Dead Sea)

mms	inches
1500	60
1200	47
900	36
600	24
400	16
200	8
0	0

Beersheba

THE NEGEB

31°

35° 36°

THE CLIMATE, VEGETATION AND ECONOMY OF PALESTINE

Warm air from the Mediterranean brings mild winters to the coastal zone, when over 90 per cent of the rainfall comes, but in the hills and mountains the temperature can drop below freezing and snow may fall in places such as Jerusalem. Summers, from May to September, are hot and dry, soaring to over 100°F/38°C in the Jordan Valley and beside the Dead Sea.

A transitionary steppe climate bridges the area between the mild Mediterranean zone and the harsh, arid conditions of the desert. In this zone, approximately between Hebron and Beersheba and on the western edge of the Transjordanian Plateau, 20-30 cm (8-10 in) of rain will fall in a year, while the desert areas beyond will generally have under 20 cm (8 in) per year.

It is sometimes suggested that the region has undergone a climatic change over time, and that this explains a change in the natural vegetation. However, there is virtually no archaeological evidence for this. More likely is that successive peoples over-exploited the natural resources, especially timber, causing soil erosion and a slow desertification of the region. The need of timber for building and fuel depleted what was a fairly extensive tree cover of oak, pine and acacia. (Since 1948 the Israeli government has undertaken a huge programme of tree-planting in an attempt to rectify this.) Uncontrolled grazing by sheep and goats also destroyed natural pasture, reducing large tracts of land to scrub. One exception to this deforestation is the centre of the Jordan Valley, which has remained a dense forest of tamarisk and thorn scrub, 'the jungle of the Jordan' (Jeremiah 12:5).

The traditional economy of Palestine was agricultural. Pastoralism predominated on the higher and poorer ground, while arable farming was practised in the valleys where at least 20 cm (8 in) of rain would fall annually. Rivalry for land was frequently a source of conflict in the Old Testament, as portrayed in the stories of Abraham and Lot, and may lie behind the confrontation between Cain and Abel.

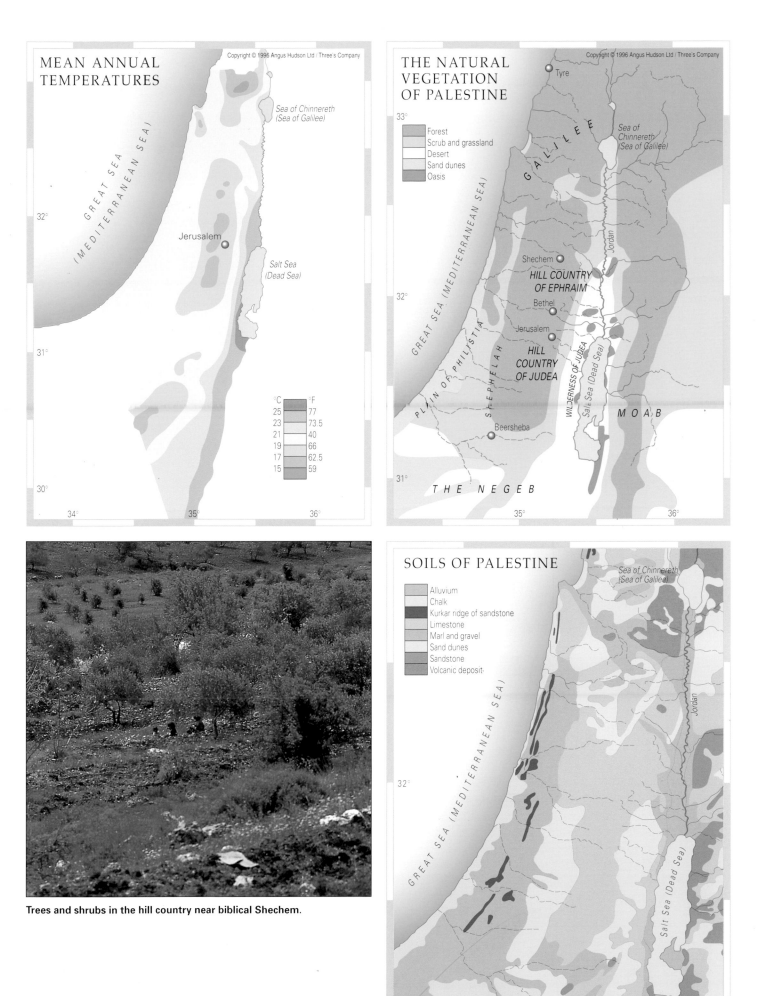

MEAN ANNUAL TEMPERATURES

Sea of Chinnereth
(Sea of Galilee)

GREAT SEA
(MEDITERRANEAN SEA)

Jerusalem

Salt Sea
(Dead Sea)

33°

32°

31°

30°

34°   35°   36°

°C	°F
25	77
23	73.5
21	40
19	66
17	62.5
15	59

THE NATURAL VEGETATION OF PALESTINE

Tyre

33°

Forest
Scrub and grassland
Desert
Sand dunes
Oasis

G A L I L E E

Sea of
Chinnereth
(Sea of Galilee)

GREAT SEA (MEDITERRANEAN SEA)

Shechem

HILL COUNTRY
OF EPHRAIM

32°

Bethel

Jordan

Jerusalem

HILL
COUNTRY
OF JUDEA

WILDERNESS OF JUDEA

Salt Sea (Dead Sea)

P L A I N O F P H I L I S T I A

S H E P H E L A H

M O A B

Beersheba

31°

T H E   N E G E B

35°   36°

Trees and shrubs in the hill country near biblical Shechem.

SOILS OF PALESTINE

Sea of Chinnereth
(Sea of Galilee)

Alluvium
Chalk
Kurkar ridge of sandstone
Limestone
Marl and gravel
Sand dunes
Sandstone
Volcanic deposit

GREAT SEA (MEDITERRANEAN SEA)

Jordan

32°

Salt Sea (Dead Sea)

35°

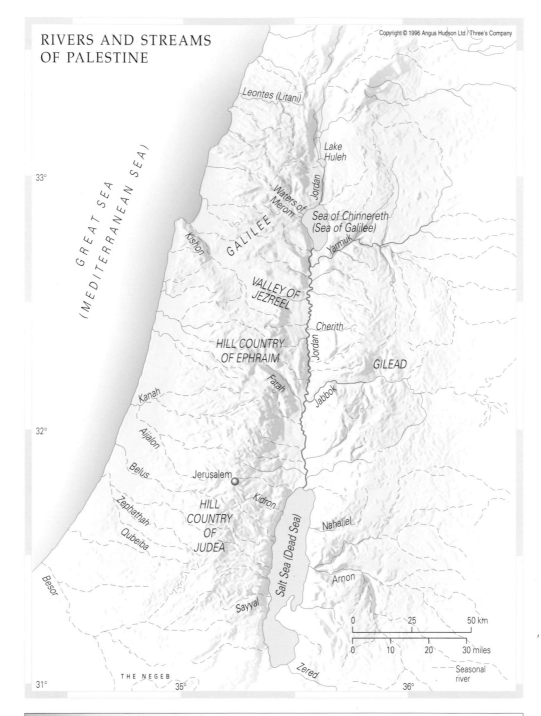

RIVERS AND STREAMS
OF PALESTINE

Copyright © 1996 Angus Hudson Ltd / Three's Company

Leontes (Litani)

Lake Huleh

Jordan

GREAT SEA (MEDITERRANEAN SEA)

33°

Waters of Merom

Sea of Chinnereth (Sea of Galilee)

GALILEE

Kishon

Yarmuk

VALLEY OF JEZREEL

Cherith

HILL COUNTRY OF EPHRAIM

Jordan

GILEAD

Farah

Jabbok

Kanah

32°

Ajjalon

Belus

Jerusalem

Kidron

Zephathah

HILL COUNTRY OF JUDEA

Nahaliel

Qubeiba

Salt Sea (Dead Sea)

Besor

Arnon

0   25   50 km

0   10   20   30 miles

Sayyal

Zered

Seasonal river

THE NEGEB

31°   35°   36°

The fast-flowing waters of the upper reaches of the River Jordan.

ATLAS of the Bible and Christianity

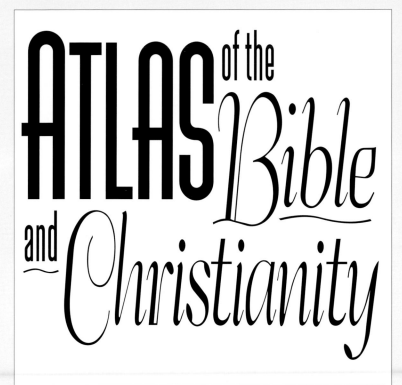

OLD TESTAMENT PERIOD

THE FERTILE CRESCENT

The Fertile Crescent is the arc of land running from the Gulf to the Nile Delta, hedged by mountains on the east and north and enclosing the deserts of central Syria and Arabia. Rainfall in those mountains and in the ranges along the Mediterranean coast (the Amanus and the Lebanon) fills the great Tigris and Euphrates rivers and the lesser Orontes and Jordan. The first two make farming possible in Babylonia and so enabled cities to arise there six thousand years ago. Rainfall in Ethiopia fills the Nile, giving life to Egypt.

The earliest farming consisted of grain production in the river countries, while grapes and olives were grown as well in the hilly regions such as Palestine. Animals grazed in the fields and hillsides, sheep being especially important in Babylonia, where their wool supplied a major textile trade (see Joshua 7:21). Horses were raised in the hills of Ararat (Eastern Turkey) and Iran. The usual animal for carrying loads was the donkey. From about 1200 BCE camel breeding began to be important in Arabia.

Copper was the major metal from about 5000 until 1000 BCE. Ores were found in the Arabah and smelted there. Copper was alloyed with tin to make bronze from about 2500 BCE onwards. Iron working developed late in the second millennium and the metal gradually replaced bronze for tools and weapons. Gold was brought from the Land of Punt, probably Somalia, to Egypt, and was also found in the south of Egypt itself. Solomon's source, Ophir, is unidentified. Gold was also panned from rivers in western Turkey. The Dead Sea was a major provider of salt, essential for preserving fish. Along the Mediterranean coast, as well as fishing, there was an important industry in dyeing cloth, notably with the Tyrian purple. Spices and incense came from southern Arabia, the Yemen, although balsam grew in the Jordan valley. Ivory from African and Syrian elephants was beautifully carved to make veneers and inlays for wooden furniture. This luxurious fashion was harshly condemned by the prophet Amos (3:15; 6:4).

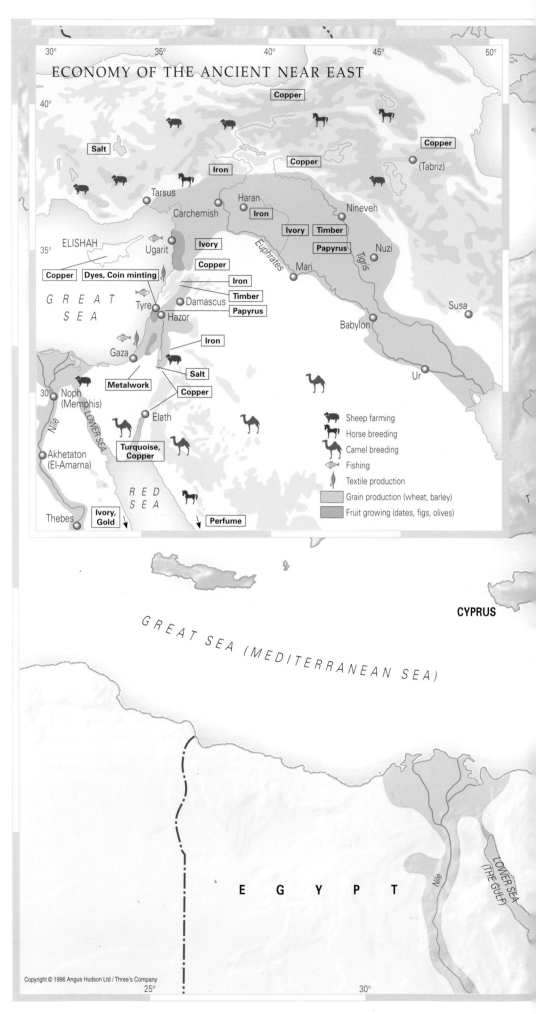

ECONOMY OF THE ANCIENT NEAR EAST

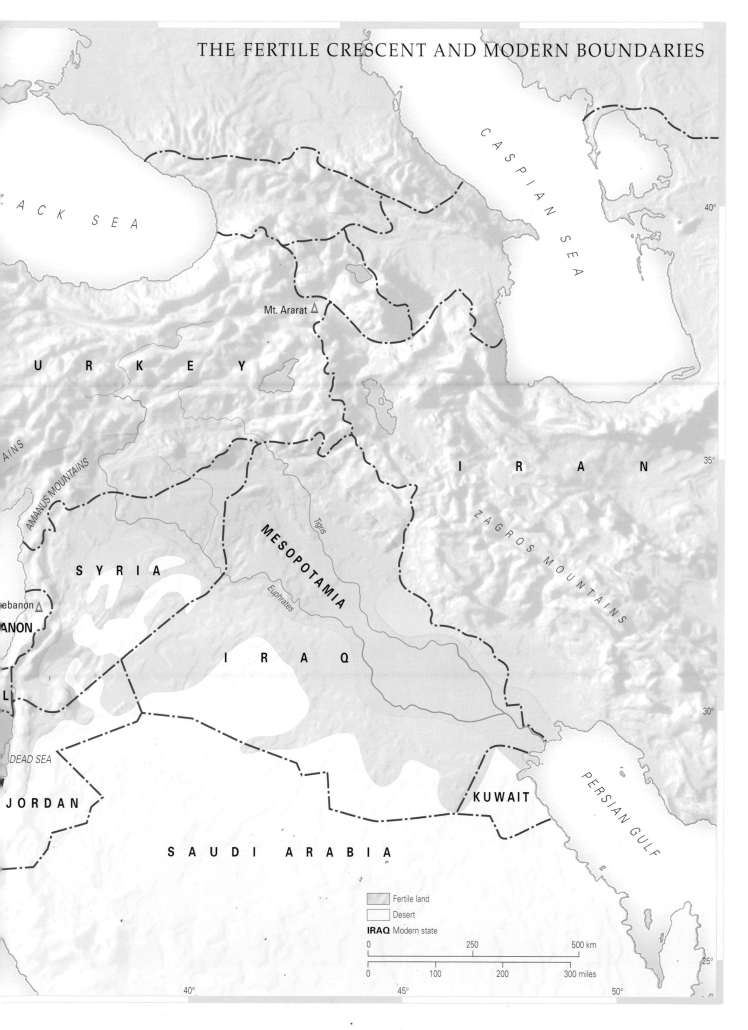

CASPIAN SEA

BLACK SEA

CASPIAN SEA

Mt. Ararat △

TURKEY

IRAN

AMANUS MOUNTAINS

AINS

SYRIA

ZAGROS MOUNTAINS

MESOPOTAMIA

Tigris

Euphrates

Lebanon △

ebanon

ANON

IRAQ

L

DEAD SEA

JORDAN

KUWAIT

PERSIAN GULF

SAUDI ARABIA

40°

35°

30°

25°

Fertile land
Desert
IRAQ Modern state

0		250		500 km

0	100	200	300 miles

40°

45°

50°

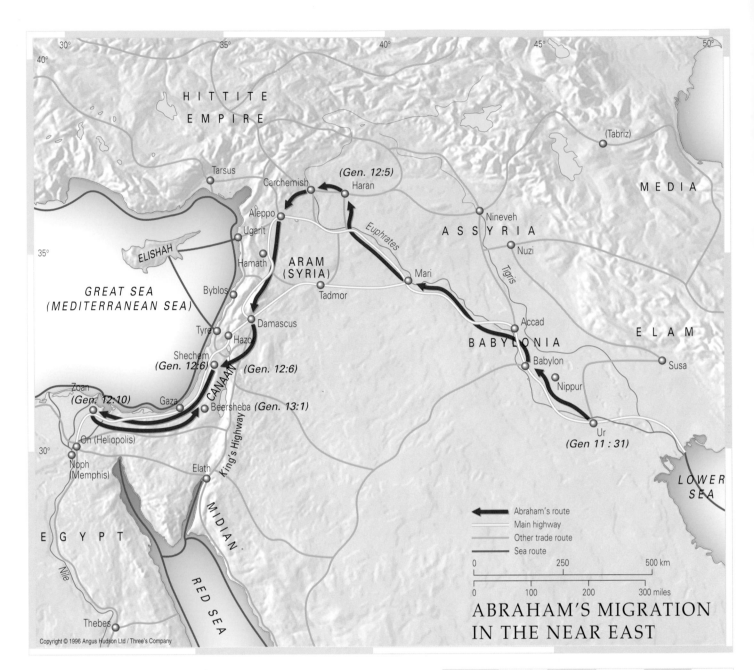

ABRAHAM'S MIGRATION
IN THE NEAR EAST

ABRAHAM'S JOURNEYS

Abraham's journeys began when his father took him from Ur of the Chaldees in southern Iraq. That was a major trading city and a centre for the worship of the moon-god Sin. The family made its home in Haran, another worship centre and city devoted to Sin. It was to this area that Abraham later sent Eliezer to find his son Isaac a wife, showing the importance of family ties for the Patriarchs.

By 2000 BCE there were both city-dwellers in Canaan and pastoralists who migrated in search of new pastures. Abraham never settled in a

city, but by purchasing the Cave of Machpelah as a burial place he made a claim to the land. Various tribes lived there, called generally Canaanites. Among them were the Hittites who sold Abraham the cave. They may have been linked to the powerful Hittites ruling Anatolia from about 1800 to 1200 BCE, but they may have been a separate group.

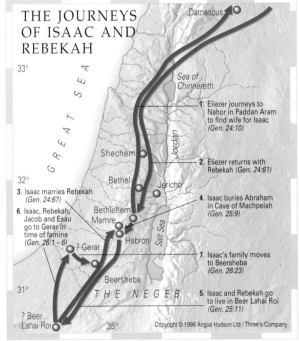

THE JOURNEYS
OF ISAAC AND
REBEKAH

1. Eliezer journeys to Nahor in Paddan Aram to find wife for Isaac (Gen. 24:10)

2. Eliezer returns with Rebekah (Gen. 24:61)

3. Isaac marries Rebekah (Gen. 24:67)

4. Isaac buries Abraham in Cave of Machpelah (Gen. 25:9)

5. Isaac and Rebekah go to live in Beer Lahai Roi (Gen. 25:11)

6. Isaac, Rebekah, Jacob and Esau go to Gerar in time of famine (Gen. 26:1–6)

7. Isaac's family moves to Beersheba (Gen. 26:23)

ABRAHAM IN CANAAN

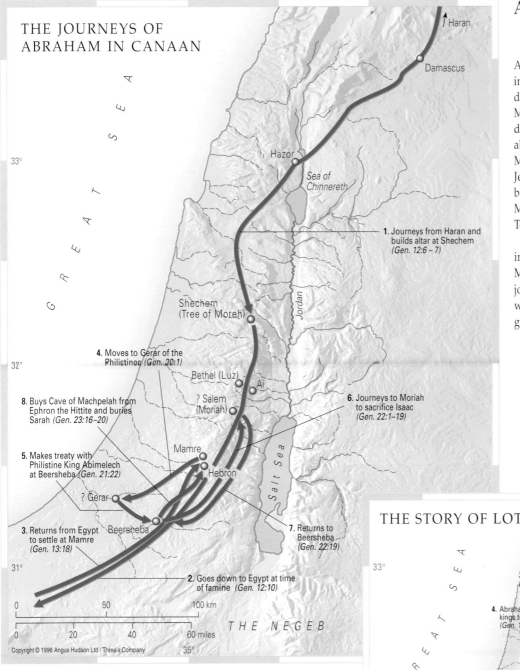

THE JOURNEYS OF ABRAHAM IN CANAAN

Haran

Damascus

Hazor

Sea of Chinnereth

1. Journeys from Haran and builds altar at Shechem *(Gen. 12:6 – 7)*

Shechem (Tree of Moreh)

4. Moves to Gerar of the Philistines *(Gen. 20:1)*

Bethel (Luz)

Ai

? Salem (Moriah)

8. Buys Cave of Machpelah from Ephron the Hittite and buries Sarah *(Gen. 23:16–20)*

6. Journeys to Moriah to sacrifice Isaac *(Gen. 22:1–19)*

Mamre

Hebron

5. Makes treaty with Philistine King Abimelech at Beersheba *(Gen. 21:22)*

Salt Sea

? Gerar

3. Returns from Egypt to settle at Mamre *(Gen. 13:18)*

Beersheba

7. Returns to Beersheba *(Gen. 22:19)*

2. Goes down to Egypt at time of famine *(Gen. 12:10)*

GREAT SEA

Jordan

33°

32°

31°

0   50   100 km
0   20   40   60 miles

THE NEGEB

Copyright © 1996 Angus Hudson Ltd / Three's Company

35°

Abraham's career made another place in Canaan important to his descendants. The blessing King Melchizedek gave him at Salem, and the divine intervention as Abraham was about to sacrifice Isaac on Mount Moriah, point to the later importance of Jerusalem in Jewish history, for Salem is believed to be Jerusalem and Mount Moriah the hill there on which the Temple stood.

Although Abraham spent many years in Canaan and never returned to Mesopotamia, he made one further journey, following the road to Egypt which the caravans travelled bearing goods from Syria.

The Cave of Machpelah, Hebron, traditionally the Patriarchs' burial place.

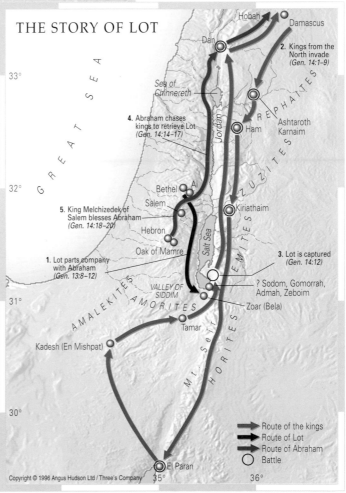

THE STORY OF LOT

Hobah

Damascus

Dan

2. Kings from the North invade *(Gen. 14:1–9)*

Sea of Chinnereth

REPHAITES

Ashtaroth Karnaim

4. Abraham chases kings to retrieve Lot *(Gen. 14:14–17)*

Ham

ZUZITES

Bethel

Ai

Salem

Kiriathaim

5. King Melchizedek of Salem blesses Abraham *(Gen. 14:18–20)*

Hebron

EMITES

3. Lot is captured *(Gen. 14:12)*

Oak of Mamre

1. Lot parts company with Abraham *(Gen. 13:8–12)*

Salt Sea

? Sodom, Gomorrah, Admah, Zeboim

VALLEY OF SIDDIM

Zoar (Bela)

Tamar

AMALEKITES

AMORITES

Mt. Seir

HORITES

Kadesh (En Mishpat)

GREAT SEA

Jordan

33°

32°

31°

30°

→ Route of the kings
→ Route of Lot
→ Route of Abraham
○ Battle

El Paran

35°   36°

Copyright © 1996 Angus Hudson Ltd / Three's Company

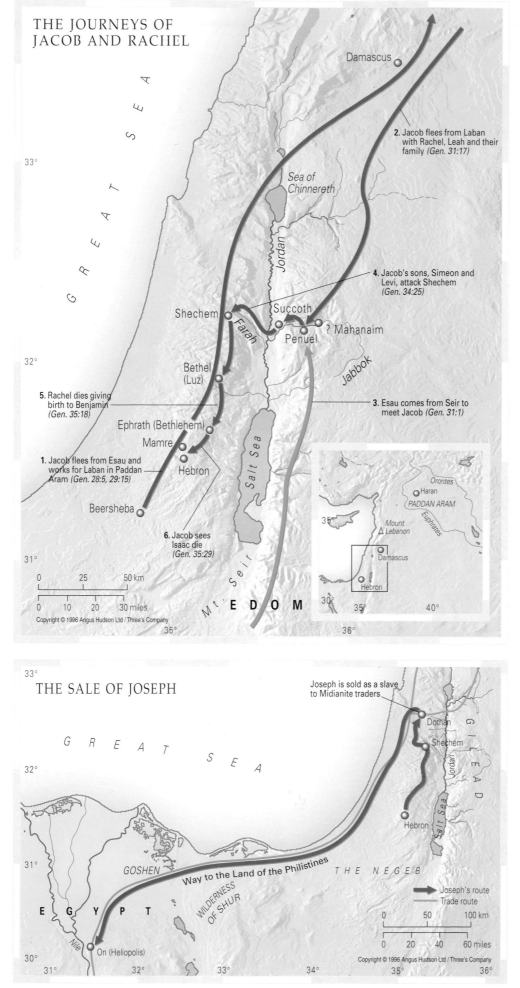

THE JOURNEYS OF JACOB AND RACHEL

Damascus

2. Jacob flees from Laban with Rachel, Leah and their family (Gen. 31:17)

G R E A T   S E A

Sea of Chinnereth

Jordan

4. Jacob's sons, Simeon and Levi, attack Shechem (Gen. 34:25)

Shechem   Succoth
        Farah
                Penuel   ? Mahanaim

Jabbok

Bethel (Luz)

5. Rachel dies giving birth to Benjamin (Gen. 35:18)

3. Esau comes from Seir to meet Jacob (Gen. 31:1)

Ephrath (Bethlehem)

Mamre

1. Jacob flees from Esau and works for Laban in Paddan Aram (Gen. 28:5, 29:15)

Hebron

Salt Sea

Beersheba

6. Jacob sees Isaac die (Gen. 35:29)

Mt. Seir   E D O M

0   25   50 km
0   10   20   30 miles

Copyright © 1996 Angus Hudson Ltd / Three's Company

Orontes
Haran
PADDAN ARAM
Euphrates
Mount △ Lebanon
Damascus
Hebron

THE SALE OF JOSEPH

Joseph is sold as a slave to Midianite traders

G R E A T   S E A

GILEAD

Dothan
Shechem

Jordan

Hebron

Salt Sea

GOSHEN
Way to the Land of the Philistines
THE NEGEB

WILDERNESS OF SHUR

E G Y P T

Nile
On (Heliopolis)

Joseph's route
Trade route

0   50   100 km
0   20   40   60 miles

Copyright © 1996 Angus Hudson Ltd / Three's Company

THE PATRIARCHS

During the Patriarchal period we begin to see tribal associations with particular areas. Abraham and Isaac stayed in southern Canaan, in the area of Hebron, where the family burial place was, and near the Philistines of Gerar. Esau settled in southern Transjordan, in the Mount Seir region of Edom. Abraham, Isaac and Jacob all maintained links with Haran far to the north.

It was, however, the visits of Jacob's sons to Egypt, and eventually of the patriarch himself, that transplanted the family from Canaan. The stories of Joseph and his brothers agree with other evidence for Semitic people living in the Nile Delta area, especially between about 2000 and 1550 BCE. The circumstances of that period agree better than any other with the way of life and events the Patriarchal narratives describe.

The Sphinx and the pyramids, Cairo, Egypt.

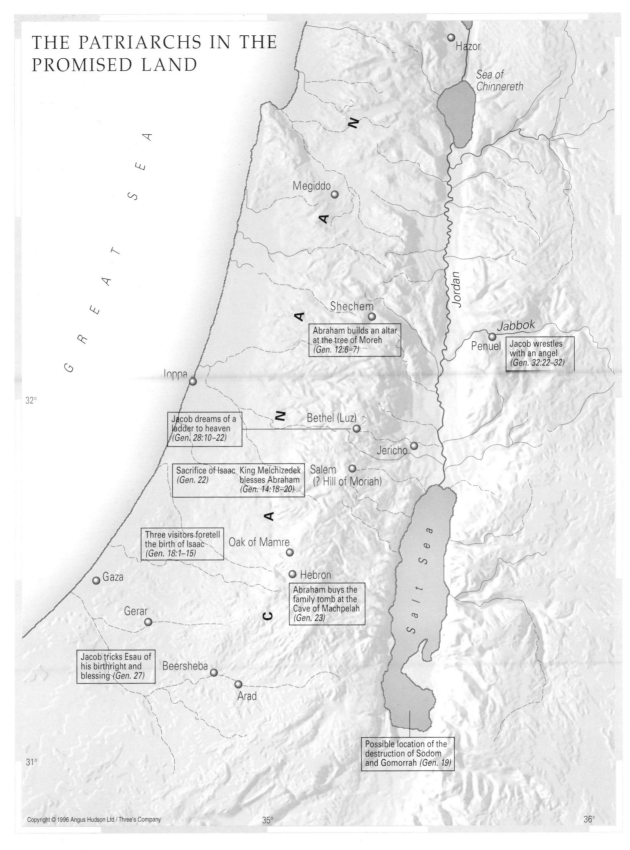

THE PATRIARCHS IN THE PROMISED LAND

Hazor

Sea of Chinnereth

G R E A T   S E A

Megiddo

N

A

Shechem

Abraham builds an altar
at the tree of Moreh
(Gen. 12:6–7)

Jabbok

Penuel

Jacob wrestles
with an angel
(Gen. 32:22–32)

Jordan

Ioppa

32°

N

Jacob dreams of a
ladder to heaven
(Gen. 28:10–22)

Bethel (Luz)

Jericho

Sacrifice of Isaac
(Gen. 22)

King Melchizedek
blesses Abraham
(Gen. 14:18–20)

Salem
(? Hill of Moriah)

A

Three visitors foretell
the birth of Isaac
(Gen. 18:1–15)

Oak of Mamre

S a l t   S e a

Gaza

Hebron

Abraham buys the
family tomb at the
Cave of Machpelah
(Gen. 23)

Gerar

C

Jacob tricks Esau of
his birthright and
blessing *(Gen. 27)*

Beersheba

Arad

Possible location of the
destruction of Sodom
and Gomorrah *(Gen. 19)*

31°

Copyright © 1996 Angus Hudson Ltd / Three's Company

35°

36°

Mamre, where Isaac's birth was foretold.

Sheep in the Judean wilderness.

19

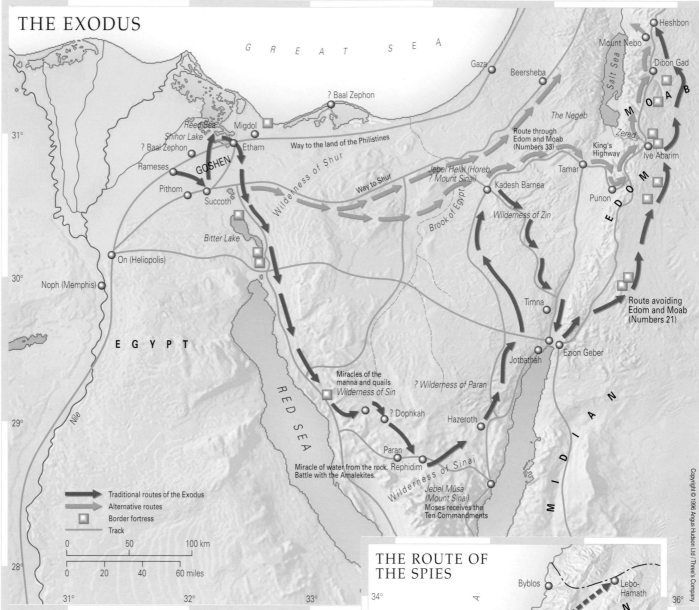

THE EXODUS

G R E A T   S E A

Heshbon
Mount Nebo
Dibon Gad
Gaza
Beersheba
M O A B
? Baal Zephon
Migdol
Reed Sea
Shihor Lake
The Negeb
Route through
Edom and Moab
(Numbers 33)
? Baal Zephon
Etham
Way to the land of the Philistines
Rameses
GOSHEN
Jebel Helal (Horeb,
? Mount Sinai)
Kadesh Barnea
Tamar
King's Highway
Iye Abarim
Pithom
Way to Shur
Wilderness of Shur
Succoth
Zered
Bitter Lake
Brook of Egypt
Wilderness of Zin
On (Heliopolis)
E D O M
Punon
Noph (Memphis)
E G Y P T
Timna
Route avoiding
Edom and Moab
(Numbers 21)
Ezion Geber
Jotbathah
Nile
Miracles of the
manna and quails
Wilderness of Sin
? Wilderness of Paran
R E D   S E A
? Dophkah
Hazeroth
Paran
M I D I A N
Miracle of water from the rock. Rephidim
Battle with the Amalekites.
Wilderness of Sinai
Jebel Mûsa
(Mount Sinai)
Moses receives the
Ten Commandments
M I D I A N

Traditional routes of the Exodus
Alternative routes
Border fortress
Track

0   50   100 km
0   20   40   60 miles

TOWARDS THE PROMISED LAND

On his return to Egypt from Midian, Moses led the Israelites out of
captivity (Exodus 12–13). The route taken is debated. The traditional
route runs from Rameses to Succoth, and then turns northwards to cross
the Reed Sea, a marshy lake. It is stated in Exodus 13:17-18 that the
Israelites did not take the direct route to Canaan, the 'Way to the Land
of the Philistines', which was heavily fortified. Instead, they turned
south, taking the desert route.

The locations of some of the places visited by the Israelites during the
wilderness period are uncertain. The traditional site of Mount Sinai is
Jebel Musa. However, an alternative opinion places it at Jebel Helal in
north Sinai. If this were so, the Israelites would have taken the Way to
Shur, a much shorter journey to Canaan, via Beersheba. The route of the
Israelites' wandering in the desert has two apparently conflicting
traditions. Once the Israelites had reached Kadesh-barnea, according to
Numbers 21 they were refused permission by border guards to pass
through Edom and Moab. They had to retrace their steps to Ezion-geber
and skirt the eastern border of Edom and Moab to Heshbon. But
Numbers 33 lists towns in Edom and Moab through which the Israelites
passed on their way to Mount Nebo. Many scholars think that this list
records a migration of tribes at a different time.

THE ROUTE OF
THE SPIES

Byblos
Lebo-Hamath
C A N A A N
Amorites
Damascus
G R E A T   S E A
Tyre
Hazor
Sea of Chinnereth
Canaanites
Jordan
Shechem
Amorites
Jebusites
? Valley of Eshcol
Jebus (Jerusalem)
Canaanites
Hittites
Hebron
Salt Sea
M O A B
THE
NEGEB
Arad
Brook of Egypt
Amalekites
Kadesh Barnea
E D O M

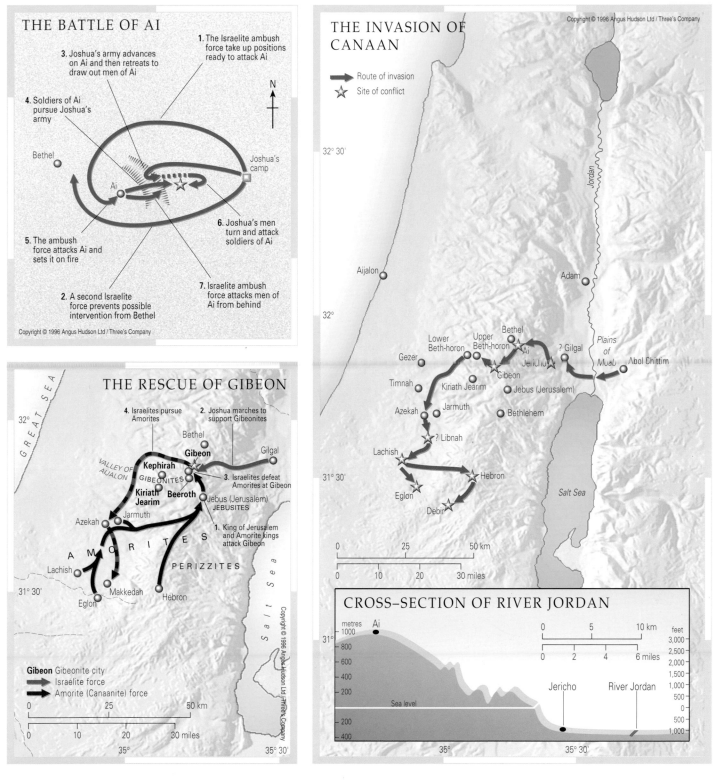

THE BATTLE OF AI

1. The Israelite ambush force take up positions ready to attack Ai

2. A second Israelite force prevents possible intervention from Bethel

3. Joshua's army advances on Ai and then retreats to draw out men of Ai

4. Soldiers of Ai pursue Joshua's army

5. The ambush force attacks Ai and sets it on fire

6. Joshua's men turn and attack soldiers of Ai

7. Israelite ambush force attacks men of Ai from behind

N

Bethel

Ai

Joshua's camp

Copyright © 1996 Angus Hudson Ltd / Three's Company

THE INVASION OF CANAAN

Copyright © 1996 Angus Hudson Ltd / Three's Company

→ Route of invasion
☆ Site of conflict

32° 30'

32°

31° 30'

31°

Jordan

Aijalon

Adam

Plains of Moab

Abel Shittim

Lower Beth-horon

Upper Beth-horon

Bethel

Ai

Jericho

? Gilgal

Gezer

Gibeon

Timnah

Kiriath Jearim

Jebus (Jerusalem)

Azekah

Jarmuth

Bethlehem

? Libnah

Lachish

Eglon

Debir

Hebron

Salt Sea

0   25   50 km

0   10   20   30 miles

35°   35° 30'

THE RESCUE OF GIBEON

GREAT SEA

32°

31° 30'

4. Israelites pursue Amorites

2. Joshua marches to support Gibeonites

Bethel

Gibeon

Kephirah

GIBEONITES

3. Israelites defeat Amorites at Gibeon

Gilgal

VALLEY OF AIJALON

Kiriath Jearim

Beeroth

Jebus (Jerusalem)
JEBUSITES

1. King of Jerusalem and Amorite kings attack Gibeon

Azekah

Jarmuth

A M O R I T E S

PERIZZITES

Lachish

Makkedah

Hebron

Eglon

Salt Sea

Copyright © 1996 Angus Hudson Ltd / Three's Company

Gibeon Gibeonite city
➡ Israelite force
➡ Amorite (Canaanite) force

0   25   50 km

0   10   20   30 miles

35°   35° 30'

CROSS–SECTION OF RIVER JORDAN

metres   Ai   0   5   10 km   feet
1000   3,000
800   2,500
600   2,000
400   1,500
200   1,000
Sea level   0   2   4   6 miles   500
200   Jericho   River Jordan   0
400   500
                                1,000

Jericho, the 'city of palms'.

THE INVASION OF CANAAN

Joshua led the Israelites across the River Jordan, opposite Abel-Shittim, and established camp at Gilgal (Joshua 4:19). From here, Joshua conducted his campaigns in the south of Canaan. After the capture of Jericho and Ai, the people of Gibeon signed a peace treaty with the Israelites. To counter this, the king of Jerusalem formed a coalition with the kings of Hebron, Jarmuth, Lachish and Eglon, and attacked Gibeon. Joshua's army supported Gibeon in the ensuing battle, and pursued the enemy as far as Makkedah. Many of the enemy soldiers were killed by huge hailstones, and after the battle the sun stood still in the middle of the sky for a full day (Joshua 10:1-15).

ISRAEL IN CANAAN

The most important battle in the conquest of northern Canaan was at Merom Waters (Joshua 11:1-11). A coalition of kings led by Jabin, the king of Hazor, was outwitted by Joshua's army; Hazor, the largest city in Canaan in this period, was burned.

The Israelites gradually took control of the highlands, and tended to settle there. The Canaanites, with their superior weaponry, especially the iron chariot, prevailed in the lowland areas. When the land was divided among the tribes of Israel, some towns remained unconquered, and the Israelites had to live alongside the Canaanites.

Part of the Israelite citadel at Hazor.

LAND ALLOCATED TO THE TRIBES OF ISRAEL

GREAT SEA

DAN
Dan (Laish)
Tyre
Kedesh
ASHER
NAPHTALI
33°
Sea of Chinnereth
Golan
ZEBULUN
MANASSEH
Shimron
Endor
Megiddo
ISSACHAR
Ramoth-gilead
MANASSEH
Jordan
Shechem
Succoth
Beth-dagon
EPHRAIM
Shiloh
GAD
32°
DAN
BENJAMIN
Gibeah
Jericho
Jebus (Jerusalem)
Heshbon
Bezer
JUDAH
REUBEN
Gaza
Hebron
Salt Sea
Beersheba
MOAB
SIMEON
E   D   O   M

| 0 | 25 | 50 km |
| 0 | 10 | 20 | 30 miles |

Brook of Egypt

—·—·— Probable boundary of tribe of Israel
➤ Migration of the tribe of Dan
◎ City of refuge

31°
34°
35°

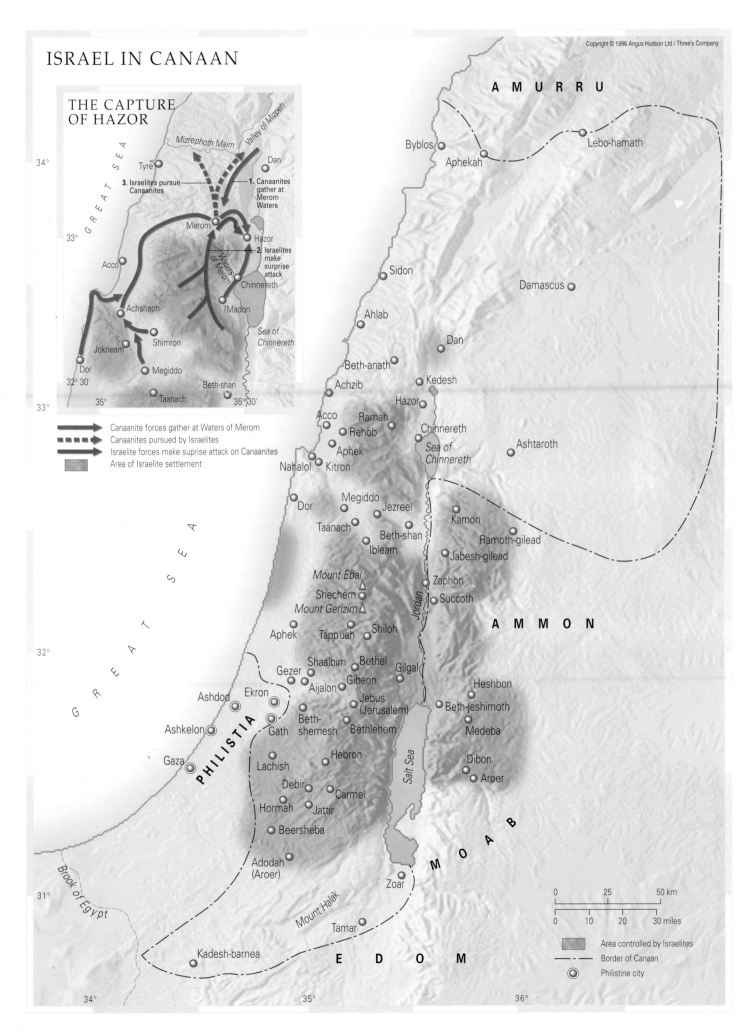

ISRAEL IN CANAAN

AMURRU

THE CAPTURE OF HAZOR

34°

Mizrephoth Maim

Valley of Mizpeh

Tyre

Dan

3. Israelites pursue Canaanites

1. Canaanites gather at Merom Waters

G R E A T   S E A

Merom

33°

Hazor

2. Israelites make surprise attack

Acco

Waters of Merom

Chinnereth

Achshaph

?Madon

Sea of Chinnereth

Joknean

Shimron

Dor

Megiddo

32° 30'

Beth-shan

Taanach

33°

35°

35° 30'

➡ Canaanite forces gather at Waters of Merom

▶▶▶ Canaanites pursued by Israelites

➡➡ Israelite forces make suprise attack on Canaanites

▨ Area of Israelite settlement

Byblos

Lebo-hamath

Aphekah

Sidon

Damascus

Ahlab

Dan

Beth-anath

Kedesh

Achzib

Hazor

Acco

Ramah

Chinnereth

Ashtaroth

Rehob

Sea of Chinnereth

Aphek

Nahalol

Kitron

Dor

Megiddo

Jezreel

Kamon

Taanach

Ramoth-gilead

Beth-shan

Jabesh-gilead

Ibleam

Mount Ebal

Zaphon

Shechem

Succoth

Mount Gerizim

Jordan

A M M O N

Aphek

Tappuah

Shiloh

Shaalbim

Bethel

Gilgal

Gezer

Aijalon

Gibeon

Heshbon

Ashdod

Ekron

Jebus (Jerusalem)

Beth-jeshimoth

Ashkelon

Beth-shemesh

Bethlehem

Medeba

PHILISTIA

Gath

Gaza

Hebron

Dibon

Lachish

Aroer

Salt Sea

Debir

Carmel

Hormah

Jattir

Beersheba

G R E A T   S E A

M O A B

Adodah (Aroer)

Zoar

Brook of Egypt

Mount Halak

Tamar

Kadesh-barnea

E D O M

34°

35°

36°

31°

32°

0		25		50 km

0	10	20	30 miles

▨ Area controlled by Israelites

▬ · ▬ Border of Canaan

◉ Philistine city

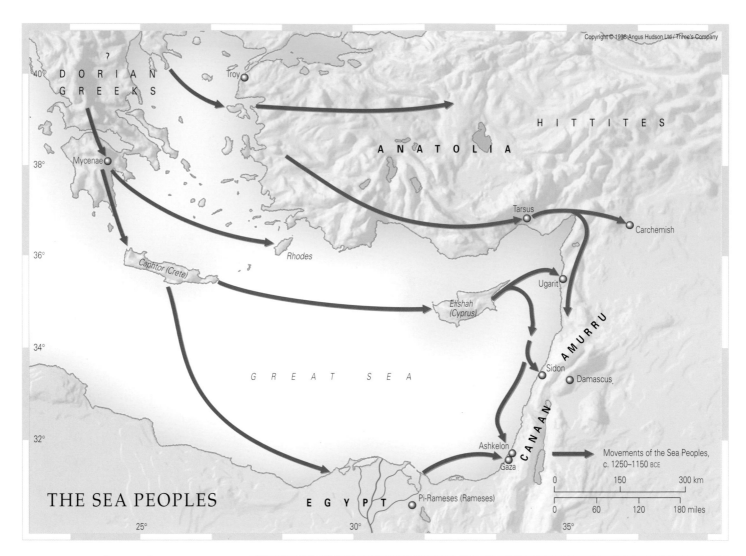

THE SEA PEOPLES

THE PHILISTINES

Large numbers of 'Sea Peoples', as the
Egyptians called them, including the
Philistines, migrated to the shores of
the eastern Mediterranean between
about 1250 and 1150 BCE. Ramesses III
tells how he repelled their forces from
the Nile delta in 1174 BCE and then they
settled along the coast of the southern
Levant, where they destroyed existing
Canaanite cities and built their own.

Archaeological finds include
distinctive Mycenaean-style pottery.
Indications of a well-organized
civilization support the Israelite notion
that the Philistines were powerful. Of
Israel's Judges, only Samson could
achieve temporary success against them
(Judges 13-16).

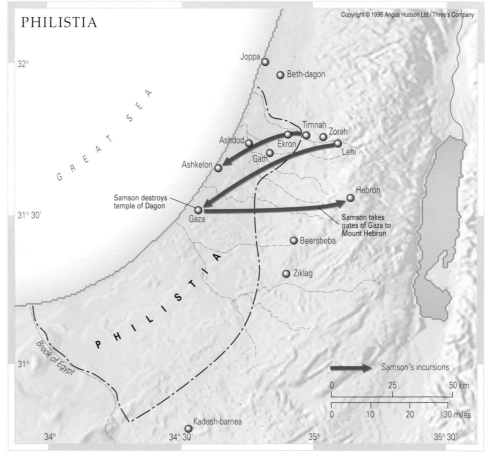

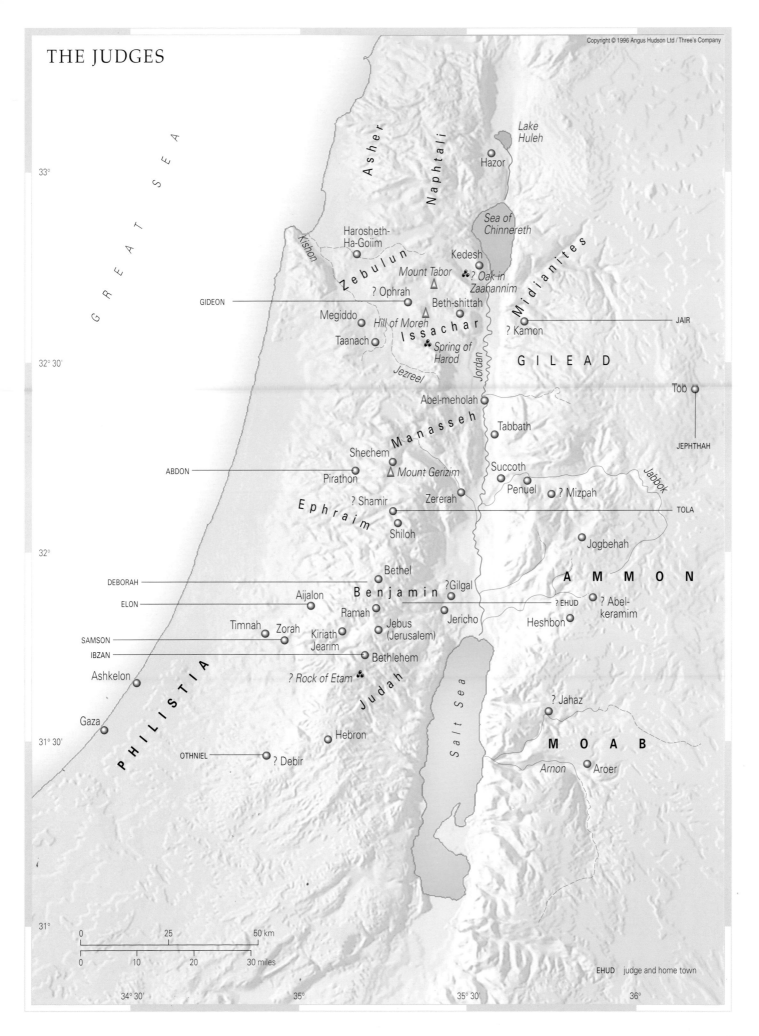

THE JUDGES

Lake Huleh

Hazor

33°

G R E A T   S E A

A s h e r

N a p h t a l i

Sea of Chinnereth

Harosheth-Ha-Goiim

Kishon

Kedesh

Z e b u l u n

Mount Tabor

? Oak in Zaahannim

GIDEON

? Ophrah

Beth-shittah

M i d i a n i t e s

JAIR

Megiddo

Hill of Moreh

I s s a c h a r

? Kamon

32° 30'

Taanach

Spring of Harod

G I L E A D

Jezreel

Jordan

Abel-meholah

Tob

JEPHTHAH

Tabbath

M a n a s s e h

Shechem

ABDON

Pirathon

△ *Mount Gerizim*

Succoth

Jabbok

? Shamir

Zererah

Penuel

? Mizpah

TOLA

E p h r a i m

Shiloh

Jogbebah

32°

Bethel

A M M O N

DEBORAH

?Gilgal

ELON

Aijalon

B e n j a m i n

? EHUD

? Abel-keramim

Ramah

Jericho

Heshbon

Timnah   Zorah

Jebus (Jerusalem)

SAMSON

Kiriath Jearim

IBZAN

Bethlehem

Ashkelon

? Rock of Etam

J u d a h

P H I L I S T I A

S a l t   S e a

? Jahaz

Gaza

31° 30'

Hebron

M O A B

OTHNIEL

? Debir

Arnon   Aroer

31°

0		25		50 km

0	10	20	30 miles

34° 30'   35°   35° 30'   36°

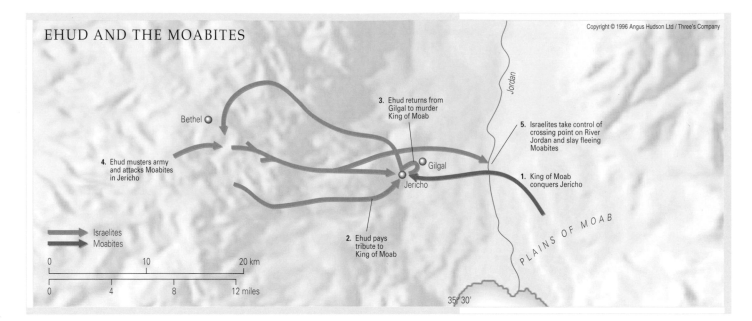

EHUD AND THE MOABITES

Copyright © 1996 Angus Hudson Ltd / Three's Company

Bethel ○

3. Ehud returns from Gilgal to murder King of Moab

5. Israelites take control of crossing point on River Jordan and slay fleeing Moabites

4. Ehud musters army and attacks Moabites in Jericho

Gilgal ○

Jericho ○

1. King of Moab conquers Jericho

2. Ehud pays tribute to King of Moab

PLAINS OF MOAB

→ Israelites
→ Moabites

0 — 10 — 20 km

0 — 4 — 8 — 12 miles

35° 30'

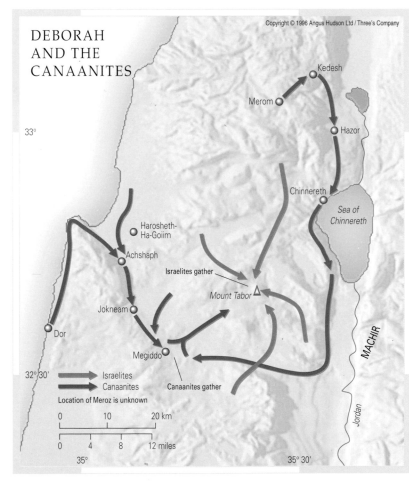

DEBORAH AND THE CANAANITES

Copyright © 1996 Angus Hudson Ltd / Three's Company

Kedesh ○

Merom ○

33°

Hazor ○

Chinnereth ○

Sea of Chinnereth

Harosheth-Ha-Goiim ○

Achshaph ○

Israelites gather

Mount Tabor △

Jokneam ○

MACHIR

Dor ○

Megiddo ○

32° 30'

Canaanites gather

→ Israelites
→ Canaanites

Location of Meroz is unknown

0 — 10 — 20 km

0 — 4 — 8 — 12 miles

35°   35° 30'

Jordan

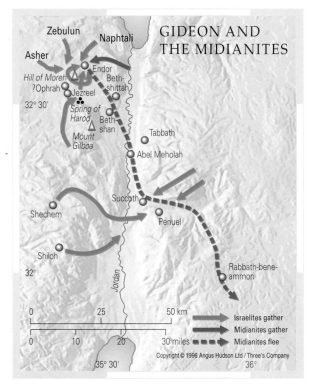

GIDEON AND THE MIDIANITES

Zebulun   Naphtali

Asher

Hill of Moreh — Endor — Beth-shittah

?Ophrah ○ — Jezreel

32° 30'

Spring of Harod

Beth-shan

Mount Gilboa △

Tabbath ○

Abel Meholah ○

Shechem ○

Succoth ○

Shiloh ○

Penuel ○

32°

Rabbath-bene-ammon

Jordan

0 — 25 — 50 km

0 — 10 — 20 — 30 miles

→ Israelites gather
→ Midianites gather
⇢ Midianites flee

Copyright © 1996 Angus Hudson Ltd / Three's Company

35° 30'   36°

Mount Tabor stands out prominently in the landscape.

THE JUDGES

Israelite Judges were charismatic military leaders, who were considered to be chosen by God. It is likely that they operated at a local level in skirmishes with territorial rivals. The Judges spanned the period from Joshua's settlement to the monarchy. From time to time there were leagues of tribes (Judges 4:5; 6:35; 20:1), but there was little political unity between north and south.

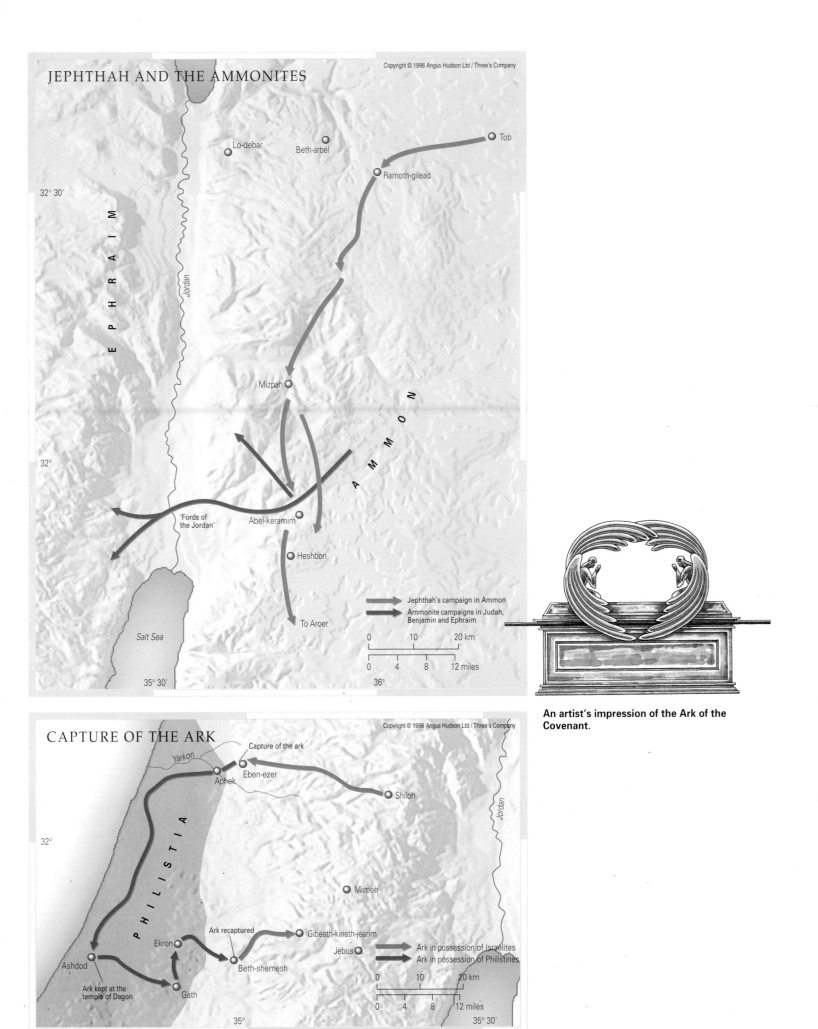

JEPHTHAH AND THE AMMONITES

Copyright © 1996 Angus Hudson Ltd / Three's Company

Tob

Lo-debar

Beth-arbel

Ramoth-gilead

32° 30'

E
P
H
R
A
I
M

Jordan

A
M
M
O
N

Mizpah

32°

'Fords of
the Jordan'

Abel-keramim

Heshbon

To Aroer

Salt Sea

Jephthah's campaign in Ammon

Ammonite campaigns in Judah,
Benjamin and Ephraim

| 0 | | 10 | | 20 km |

| 0 | 4 | 8 | 12 miles |

35° 30'

36°

An artist's impression of the Ark of the Covenant.

CAPTURE OF THE ARK

Copyright © 1996 Angus Hudson Ltd / Three's Company

Yarkon

Capture of the ark

Aphek

Eben-ezer

Shiloh

P
H
I
L
I
S
T
I
A

32°

Jordan

Mizpeh

Ekron

Ark recaptured

Gibeath-kiriath-jearim

Jebus

Ashdod

Beth-shemesh

Ark kept at the
temple of Dagon

Gath

Ark in possession of Israelites

Ark in possession of Philistines

| 0 | | 10 | | 20 km |

| 0 | 4 | 8 | 12 miles |

35°

35° 30'

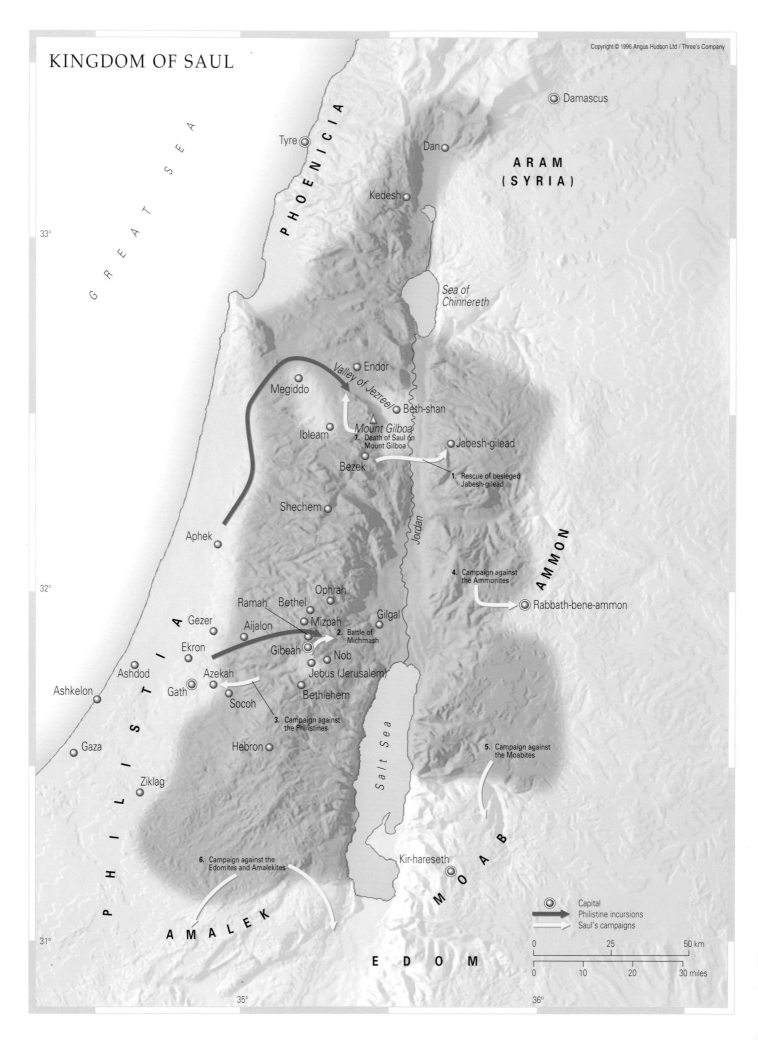

KINGDOM OF SAUL

Copyright © 1996 Angus Hudson Ltd / Three's Company

Damascus

PHOENICIA

Tyre

Dan

ARAM
(SYRIA)

33°

Kedesh

G R E A T   S E A

Sea of
Chinnereth

Endor

Valley of Jezreel

Megiddo

Beth-shan

Mount Gilboa

Ibleam

7. Death of Saul on
Mount Gilboa

Jabesh-gilead

Bezek

1. Rescue of besieged
Jabesh-gilead

Shechem

AMMON

32°

4. Campaign against
the Ammonites

Aphek

Ophrah

Rabbath-bene-ammon

Ramah   Bethel

Gezer

Mizpah

Gilgal

Aijalon

Ekron

2. Battle of
Michmash

Gibeah

Nob

Ashdod

Azekah

Jebus (Jerusalem)

Ashkelon

Gath

Socoh

Bethlehem

3. Campaign against
the Philistines

5. Campaign against
the Moabites

Hebron

Gaza

Salt Sea

Ziklag

MOAB

6. Campaign against the
Edomites and Amalekites

Kir-hareseth

31°

A M A L E K

Jordan

PHILISTIA

Capital

Philistine incursions

Saul's campaigns

0   25   50 km

0   10   20   30 miles

E   D   O   M

35°

36°

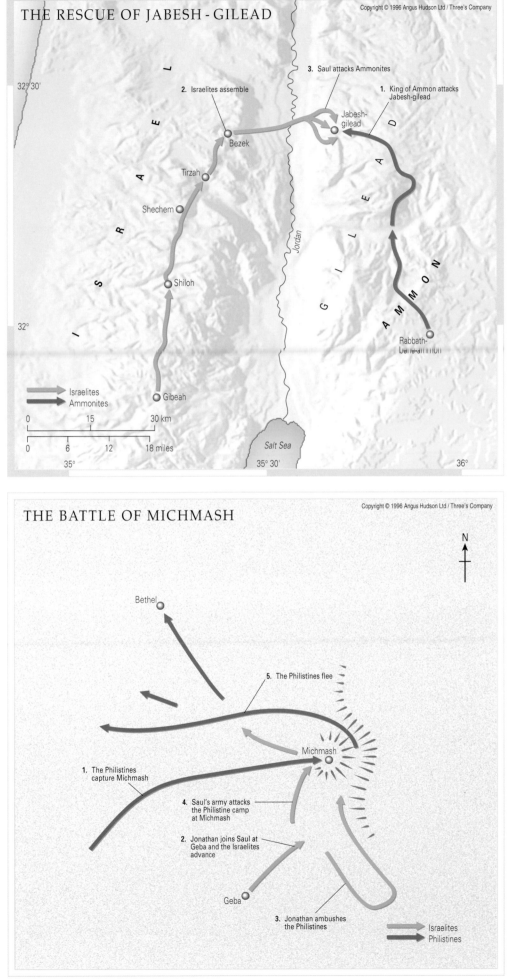

THE RESCUE OF JABESH-GILEAD

32° 30'

3. Saul attacks Ammonites

2. Israelites assemble

1. King of Ammon attacks Jabesh-gilead

I S R A E L

Bezek

Jabesh-gilead

G I L E A D

Tirzah

Shechem

Jordan

Shiloh

A M M O N

32°

Rabbath-bene-ammon

→ Israelites
→ Ammonites

Gibeah

| 0 | 15 | 30 km |
| 0 | 6 | 12 | 18 miles |

Salt Sea

35°   35° 30'   36°

THE BATTLE OF MICHMASH

N

Bethel

5. The Philistines flee

Michmash

1. The Philistines capture Michmash

4. Saul's army attacks the Philistine camp at Michmash

2. Jonathan joins Saul at Geba and the Israelites advance

Geba

3. Jonathan ambushes the Philistines

→ Israelites
→ Philistines

THE KINGDOM OF SAUL

Saul was made king of Israel by the prophet Samuel in response to popular clamour for a king (I Samuel 8:5). Neighbouring states were all kingdoms, and it was widely believed that Israel's military failures were due to her lack of leadership and unity.

Saul led Israel successfully against the Ammonites to relieve Jabesh-gilead, before being anointed king at Gilgal. In a concerted series of assaults on Philistine garrisons, the Israelites scored a number of victories over their old enemy 'from Michmash to Aijalon' (I Sam 14). With the help of his son Jonathan's ambush tactics, Saul recorded a famous victory at Michmash.

The hills near biblical Shiloh.

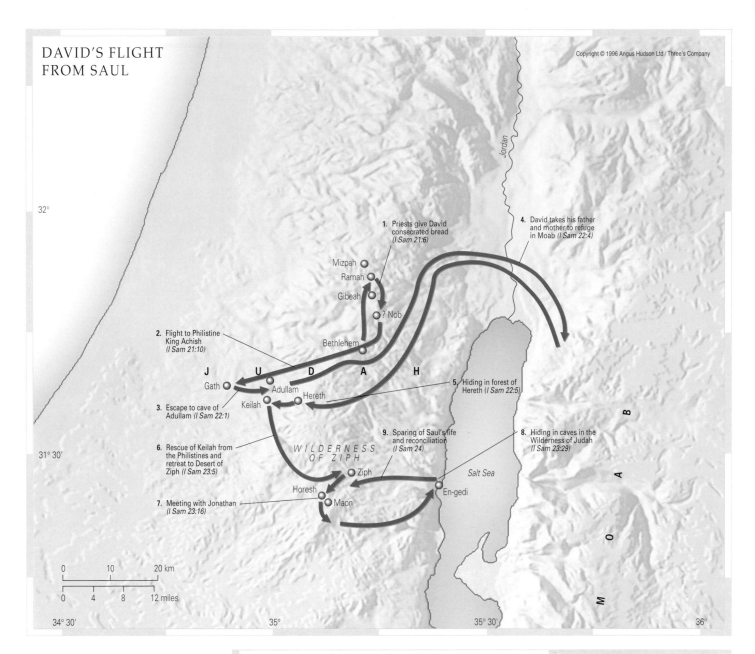

DAVID'S FLIGHT FROM SAUL

32°

1. Priests give David consecrated bread (I Sam 21:6)

4. David takes his father and mother to refuge in Moab (I Sam 22:4)

Mizpah
Ramah
Gibeah
? Nob
Bethlehem

2. Flight to Philistine King Achish (I Sam 21:10)

J U D A H

Gath
Adullam
Hereth
Keilah

5. Hiding in forest of Hereth (I Sam 22:5)

3. Escape to cave of Adullam (I Sam 22:1)

9. Sparing of Saul's life and reconciliation (I Sam 24)

8. Hiding in caves in the Wilderness of Judah (I Sam 23:29)

6. Rescue of Keilah from the Philistines and retreat to Desert of Ziph (I Sam 23:5)

31° 30'

WILDERNESS OF ZIPH

Ziph

Salt Sea

Horesh
Maon
En-gedi

7. Meeting with Jonathan (I Sam 23:16)

0 10 20 km
0 4 8 12 miles

34° 30'   35°   35° 30'   36°

Jordan

M O A B

THE DEATH OF SAUL

Successful campaigns to the south of the kingdom prepared the way for Saul's successor, David, to enlarge the realm. However, Saul's jealousy of David, even to the point of trying to kill him, marks the turn in Saul's fortunes. After consulting a 'witch' (medium) at Endor, he and Jonathan died when the Israelites were defeated by the Philistines at the Battle of Gilboa (I Samuel 31:1-6).

David was forced to flee from the murderous Saul and he sought refuge in many places, including the court of a Philistine king. After Saul's death, David was first crowned King of Judah, and then of all Israel, at Hebron (II Sam 2).

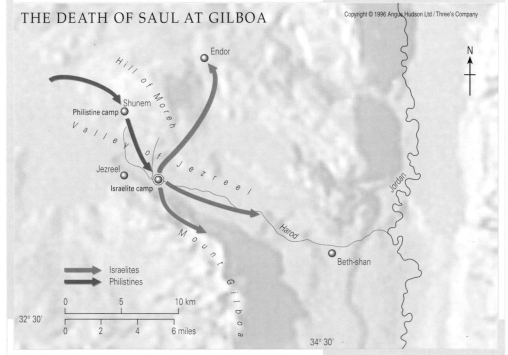

THE DEATH OF SAUL AT GILBOA

N

Endor

Hill of Moreh

Shunem
Philistine camp

Valley of Jezreel

Jezreel
Israelite camp

Jordan

Harod

Mount Gilboa

Beth-shan

→ Israelites
→ Philistines

0 5 10 km
0 2 4 6 miles

32° 30'   34° 30'

THE CAMPAIGNS OF DAVID

Damascus

ARAM
(SYRIA)

ZOBAH

Dan
Beth-rehob

8. Conquest of the
Arameans
(II Sam. 8:5–6)

Tyre

PHOENICIA

Helam

Sea of
Chinnereth

Acco

Edrei

G R E A T   S E A

Megiddo

Valley of
Jezreel

Beth-
shan

ISRAEL

AMMON

4. Conquest of the
Plain of Sharon
and Valley of
Jezreel

Shechem

Jordan

7. War against Ammon
(II Sam. 8:12)

Yarkon

Rabbah

Gath
(Metheg-
ammah)

3. Conquest of the
Philistines
(II Sam. 5 & 8)

Geba

Jericho

Heshbon

Gezer

Sorek

Jerusalem

Ashdod

Kidron

Medeba

Jarmuth

Valley of
Rephaim

Bethlehem

Valley of Elah

JUDAH

5. War against Moab
(II Sam. 8:12)

Keilah

2. Capture of
Jerusalem
(II Sam. 5)

Salt Sea

Gaza

Hebron

MOAB

Besor

Ziklag

Kir-hareseth

Gath

Beersheba

THE NEGEB

1. Conquest of the
Negeb (I Sam. 30)

6. War against Edom
(II Sam. 8:13–14)

EDOM

Brook of Egypt

Kadesh-barnea

THE ARABAH

? Sela

Campaign of David
Campaign of the Philistines
Coalition forces of Aram and Ammon

0   25   50   75 km

0   15   30   45 miles

Ezion-geber

David set about consolidating what Saul had begun: uniting his people, breaking the power of the Philistines, and expanding the frontiers of his kingdom over the Edomites, Ammonites, Moabites and Arameans. His capture of Jerusalem from the Jebusites completed the conquest of Canaan. Then the Ark of the Covenant (a cultic chest containing the sacred tablets of Moses) was ceremoniously brought up to the city which David made his capital (II Samuel 6).

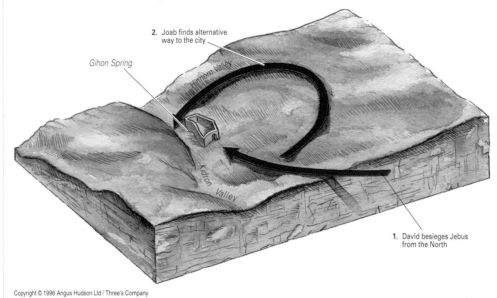

THE CAPTURE OF JERUSALEM

2. Joab finds alternative way to the city

Gihon Spring

Hinnom Valley

Kidron Valley

1. David besieges Jebus from the North

The Gihon spring flows through the Kidron valley and was the main source of water for ancient Jerusalem. It is thought that David captured the city by making a surprise attack via the Gihon spring. The cross-section shows the possible route referred to in II Sam 5:8, 'Anyone who conquers the Jebusites will have to use the water shaft . . .'. The vertical shaft is about nine metres (37 feet) deep.

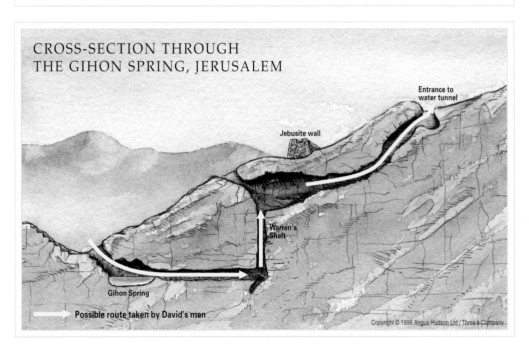

CROSS-SECTION THROUGH THE GIHON SPRING, JERUSALEM

Entrance to water tunnel

Jebusite wall

Warren's Shaft

Gihon Spring

→ Possible route taken by David's men

Part of the Kidron valley, Jerusalem, site of the Gihon spring.

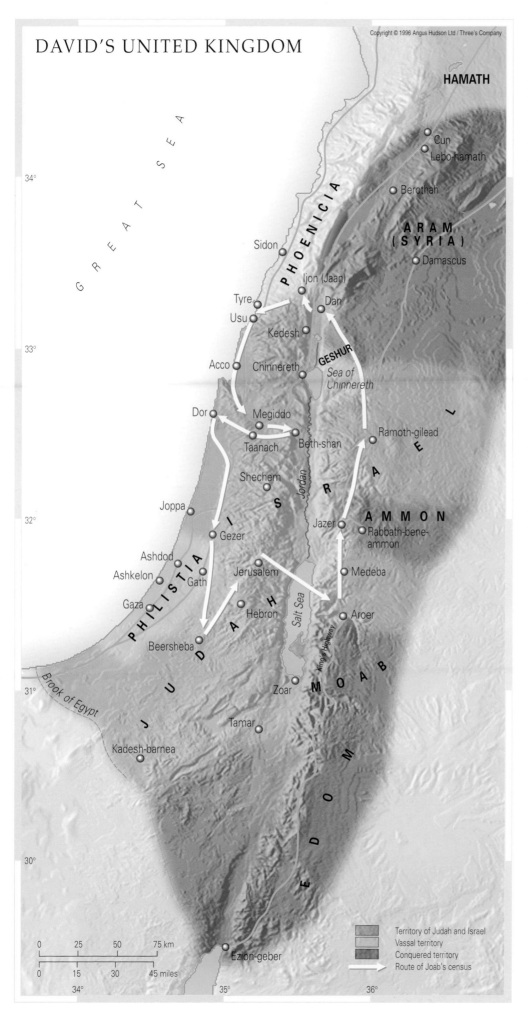

DAVID'S UNITED KINGDOM

Copyright © 1996 Angus Hudson Ltd / Three's Company

HAMATH

GREAT SEA

Cun
Lebo-hamath

Berothah

PHOENICIA

ARAM
(SYRIA)

Sidon

Damascus

Ijon (Jaan)

Tyre
Usu

Dan

Kedesh

GESHUR

Acco

Chinnereth

Sea of
Chinnereth

Dor

Megiddo

Ramoth-gilead

Taanach

Beth-shan

I S R A E L

Shechem

Jordan

Joppa

Gezer

AMMON

Jazer

Rabbath-bene-
ammon

Ashdod

Ashkelon
Gath

Jerusalem

Medeba

Gaza

Salt Sea

Hebron

Aroer

Beersheba

J U D A H

King's Highway

Zoar

M O A B

Tamar

Kadesh-barnea

E D O M

	Territory of Judah and Israel
	Vassal territory
	Conquered territory
→	Route of Joab's census

0   25   50   75 km
0   15   30   45 miles

Brook of Egypt

Ezion-geber

34° 35° 36°

DAVID'S KINGDOM

David extended his kingdom to include lands from Dan to the Brook of Egypt. His empire stretched much farther, to the Euphrates in the north and Ezion-geber on the Gulf of Aqabah in the south. The peoples of Edom, Moab, Ammon and Aram became his vassal states, and were subjected to paying tribute (II Samuel 8:2-14). This, together with the tax levied on the huge volume of trade which passed through the Levant, brought in a healthy income for the treasury. David was able to commission buildings, such as his own palace in Jerusalem, for which he used craftsmen from neighbouring states (II Samuel 5:11). David was careful to maintain peace treaties with his allies, the Philistines and the people of Hamath.

David and his generals managed to hold together the hegemony they had imposed on the Levant, in spite of two rebellions within Israel (one by his son Absalom, the other by Sheba the Benjaminite). At his death, c. 970 BCE, David handed over to his son Solomon an empire which, fifty years earlier, would have been unimaginable, and the size of which would not be seen again under Israelite rule.

SOLOMON'S KINGDOM

After winning a difficult succession struggle, Solomon was to reign for some forty years (c. 970-930 BCE). His strengths were administration and diplomacy. He married the daughters of neighbouring kings as a means of sealing diplomatic relations, and entered joint commercial enterprises with Hiram, the king of the Phoenician city of Tyre. His own kingdom he divided into twelve administrative districts (I Kings 4:7-19). This facilitated a nationwide building programme. Each district had an administrator responsible for organizing the corvée (forced labour) needed to quarry the hill country and produce masonry for building. Administrators in the lowlands would collect the levy, mainly from Canaanites.

Solomon developed a trade monopoly and exploited the natural resources in his empire. He built the Temple and other public buildings in Jerusalem, and fortified the cities of Hazor, Megiddo, Gezer, Lower Beth-horon, Baalath and Tamar in the Arabah (I Kings 6, 7, 9:15-18). He constructed smelting furnaces for his iron and copper mining enterprises, and made a naval base at Ezion-geber.

However, the extravagance of some of his schemes and the forced labour policy sowed the seeds of discontent which would result in the break up of the realm during the reign of his successor.

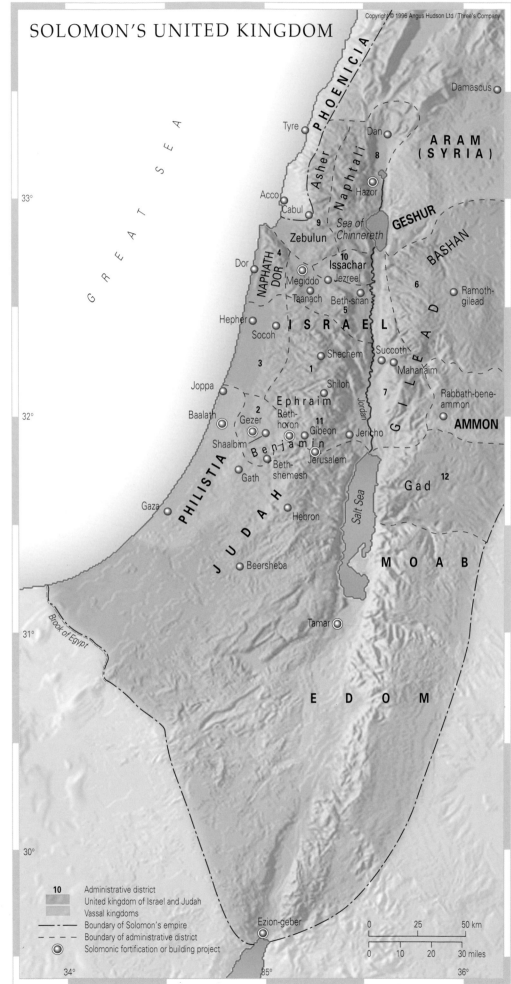

SOLOMON'S UNITED KINGDOM

Copyright © 1996 Angus Hudson Ltd / Three's Company

10	Administrative district
	United kingdom of Israel and Judah
	Vassal kingdoms
—·—	Boundary of Solomon's empire
— — —	Boundary of administrative district
◎	Solomonic fortification or building project

0   25   50 km
0 10 20 30 miles

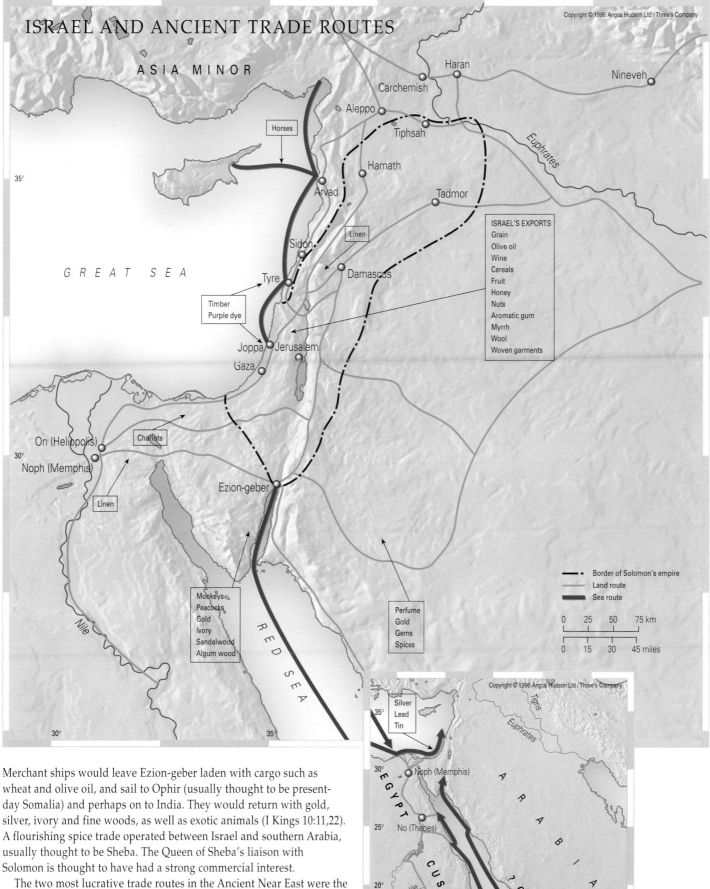

ISRAEL AND ANCIENT TRADE ROUTES

ASIA MINOR

Haran

Nineveh

Carchemish

Aleppo

Tiphsah

Horses

Hamath

35°

Tadmor

Arvad

Euphrates

Sidon

Linen

GREAT SEA

ISRAEL'S EXPORTS
Grain
Olive oil
Wine
Cereals
Fruit
Honey
Nuts
Aromatic gum
Myrrh
Wool
Woven garments

Tyre

Damascus

Timber
Purple dye

Joppa Jerusalem

Gaza

On (Heliopolis)

Charlots

30°

Noph (Memphis)

Ezion-geber

Linen

Border of Solomon's empire

Land route

Sea route

0   25   50   75 km

0   15   30   45 miles

Monkeys
Peacocks
Gold
Ivory
Sandalwood
Algum wood

Perfume
Gold
Gems
Spices

Nile

RED SEA

30°   35°

Silver
Lead
Tin

35°

Tigris

Euphrates

30°

Noph (Memphis)

E G Y P T

ARABIA

25°

No (Thebes)

OPHIR

20°

CUSH

Nile

15°

OPHIR

Meroe

SHEBA

To/from India

30°   35°   40°   50°

Merchant ships would leave Ezion-geber laden with cargo such as wheat and olive oil, and sail to Ophir (usually thought to be present-day Somalia) and perhaps on to India. They would return with gold, silver, ivory and fine woods, as well as exotic animals (I Kings 10:11,22). A flourishing spice trade operated between Israel and southern Arabia, usually thought to be Sheba. The Queen of Sheba's liaison with Solomon is thought to have had a strong commercial interest.

The two most lucrative trade routes in the Ancient Near East were the Way of the Sea, which linked Egypt with Asia, and the King's Highway, the main caravan route up from southern Arabia. Both of these were controlled by Israel at the time of the empire of David and Solomon. Solomon also controlled the maritime trade in a joint venture with King Hiram of Tyre: Hiram operated a coastal trade from Asia Minor which would link up with sea lanes from Ezion-geber to the Red Sea.

JERUSALEM

The Jebusite city that David captured was built on a spur of a hill to the north. Apart from its good defensive position, with high surrounding walls, this site was also chosen for its water supply, which lay at the foot of the eastern slope, and was known as the Gihon spring. There was limited space, and many houses had to be built on stone terraces on the slopes. As the city expanded in Solomon's time, so the centre shifted northwards to the flatter top of the hill. David selected an old Jebusite threshing-floor, reputedly the site of Isaac's sacrifice on Mt Moriah, as the place for the altar (II Samuel 24:18). It was here that Solomon built his Temple. He built a magnificent palace too, made of cedars from Lebanon, which served as an armoury and treasury; and also a judgement hall, and a palace for one of his wives, the daughter of the Pharaoh of Egypt.

The Temple Mount area, reputedly the site of Mount Moriah.

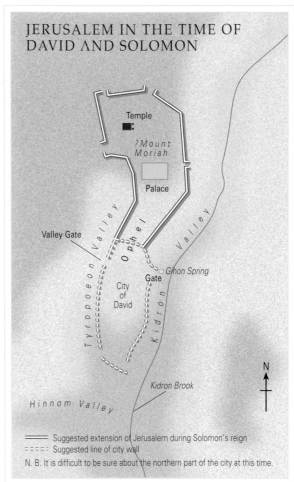

JERUSALEM IN THE TIME OF DAVID AND SOLOMON

Temple

?Mount Moriah

Palace

Valley Gate

Ophel

Tyropoeon Valley

Kidron Valley

Gihon Spring

Gate

City of David

Kidron Brook

Hinnom Valley

N

——— Suggested extension of Jerusalem during Solomon's reign
= = = = = Suggested line of city wall
N. B. It is difficult to be sure about the northern part of the city at this time.

MEGIDDO

Megiddo was a strategic city on the edge of the plain of Jezreel, guarding the Iron valley which passed through the Carmel range. The 'tell' (ruin mound) is some 20 metres (70 feet) high and the top covers more than 4 hectares (10 acres). Excavations have revealed that it was a Canaanite capital before Israelite settlement. Solomon fortified the gateway, but the stables were probably built in King Ahab's time.

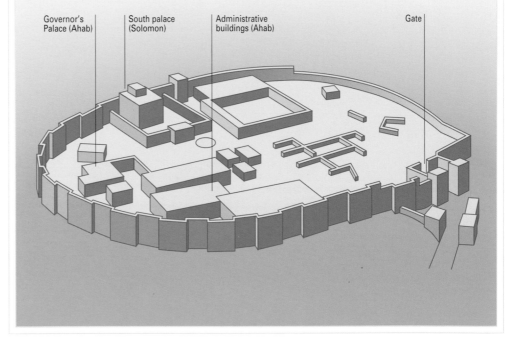

MEGIDDO IN THE TIME OF SOLOMON AND AHAB

Governor's Palace (Ahab)

South palace (Solomon)

Administrative buildings (Ahab)

Gate

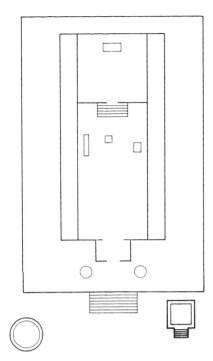

SOLOMON'S TEMPLE

Nothing remains of the Solomonic Temple. It is described in some detail in both I Kings and II Chronicles. Measurements are given and materials specified. Canaanite temple ruins have been excavated which are similar in style to the biblical description and may have provided a prototype for Solomon's Temple. The reconstruction (below) shows three main chambers – a porch, a main hall and the Holiest Place. The chief priest's ritual duties were performed in the main hall. The Holiest Place housed the Ark of the Covenant, which was guarded by two cherubim.

An artist's impression of Solomon's Temple.

Key to Plan

1 Holy Place
2 Ark of the
  Covenant
3 Altar of
  Sacrifice
4 Laver
5 Holiest Place
6 Jachin
7 Boaz

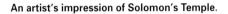

THE DIVISION OF THE KINGDOM

At Solomon's death, c. 930 BCE, his son Rehoboam was recognized as the new king in Judah, but was rejected by the elders of the northern tribes at the council of Shechem. They refused to accept him because he increased rather than lightened the taxation his father imposed. The northern tribes elected as their king Jeroboam, who had returned from Egypt, where he had found asylum in Solomon's reign.

Two kingdoms emerged, Israel in the north and Judah in the south, divided approximately along the traditional boundary between Ephraim and Benjamin (I Kings 12-13).

Conquered states broke away as civil war and diminishing control over trade routes weakened the two kingdoms. Syria, Ammon, Moab and the Philistines all reasserted their independence. Egypt, which for a long time had been unable to pursue her imperial ambitions into Asia, now took advantage of the situation and Pharaoh Shishak invaded Judah in the fifth year of Rehoboam's reign and his troops marched into Israel, in spite of Pharaoh's sheltering Jeroboam in his earlier exile.

An account of the invasion is recorded in the Temple at Karnak, in Egypt. More than 150 places were captured in Judah, the Negev, Israel and

The north gate of the excavated stronghold of Megiddo.

Transjordan. The speed and ferocity of Shishak's onslaught forced Rehoboam to surrender at Gibeon in order to prevent the inevitable destruction of Jerusalem. Shishak turned northwards and conquered Israel just as easily, Solomon's fortifications proving ineffective. One town after another was burned, including Megiddo.

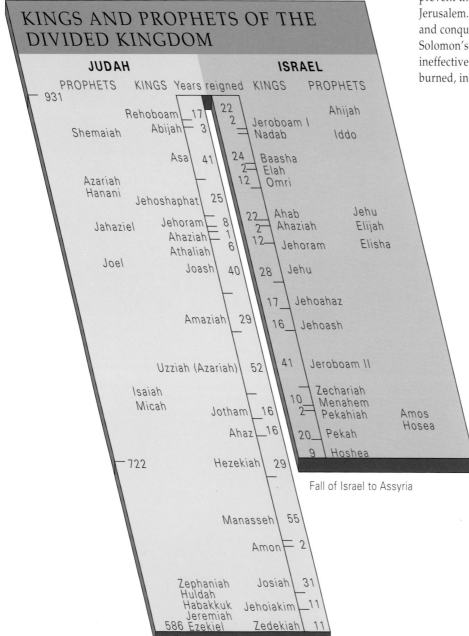

KINGS AND PROPHETS OF THE DIVIDED KINGDOM

JUDAH				ISRAEL	
PROPHETS	KINGS	Years reigned		KINGS	PROPHETS
931					
	Rehoboam	17	22		Ahijah
			2	Jeroboam I	
Shemaiah	Abijah	3		Nadab	Iddo
	Asa	41	24	Baasha	
			2	Elah	
Azariah			12	Omri	
Hanani					
	Jehoshaphat	25			
			22	Ahab	Jehu
Jahaziel	Jehoram	8	2	Ahaziah	Elijah
	Ahaziah	1	12	Jehoram	Elisha
	Athaliah	6			
Joel	Joash	40	28	Jehu	
			17	Jehoahaz	
	Amaziah	29	16	Jehoash	
	Uzziah (Azariah)	52	41	Jeroboam II	
Isaiah				Zechariah	
Micah			10	Menahem	
	Jotham	16	2	Pekahiah	Amos
	Ahaz	16	20	Pekah	Hosea
722	Hezekiah	29	9	Hoshea	

Fall of Israel to Assyria

	Manasseh	55	
	Amon	2	
Zephaniah			
Huldah	Josiah	31	
Habakkuk	Jehoiakim	11	
Jeremiah			
586 Ezekiel	Zedekiah	11	

Fall of Jerusalem to Babylon

THE KINGDOMS OF ISRAEL AND JUDAH

Copyright © 1996 Angus Hudson Ltd / Three's Company

Sidon

Damascus

Tyre

Dan

PHOENICIA

ARAM (SYRIA)

Hazor

Acco

GESHUR
Sea of Chinnereth

GREAT SEA

Dor

Megiddo

Shunem

Taanach

Beth-shan

Ramoth-gilead

Socoh

Auxiliary force of Shishak pursues
Jeroboam to Penuel and then rejoins
main army at Taanach

Shechem

I S R A E L

Shiloh

Penuel

AMMON

Bethel

Jordan

Aijalon

Rabbath-bene-ammon

Gezer

Gibeon

Gath

Jerusalem

Gaza

Hebron

Salt Sea

Auxiliary forces of
Shishak campaign in
southern Judah

Arad Rabbah

Beersheba

Kir-moab

PHILISTIA

M O A B

J U D A H

Tamar

Kadesh-barnea

E D O M

E G Y P T

◎ Capital

☆ Sanctuary city

International border

Route of invasion by Shishak of Egypt, *c.* 925 BCE

0   25   50   75 km

0   15   30   45 miles

39

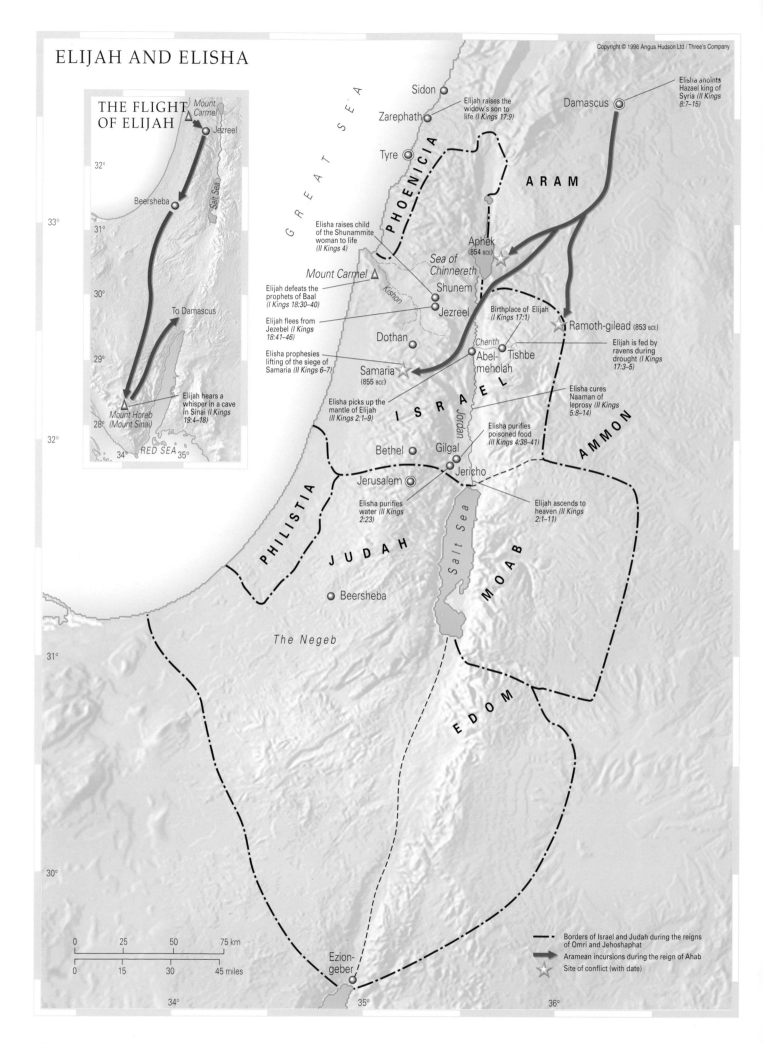

ELIJAH AND ELISHA

Copyright © 1996 Angus Hudson Ltd / Three's Company

THE FLIGHT OF ELIJAH

Mount Carmel

Jezreel

32°

Beersheba

To Damascus

Mount Horeb
(Mount Sinai)

Salt Sea

31°

33°

30°

29°

28°

32°

34° 35°

RED SEA

Elijah hears a whisper in a cave in Sinai (I Kings 19:4–18)

G R E A T   S E A

Sidon

Zarephath

Tyre

PHOENICIA

ARAM

Damascus

Elisha anoints Hazael king of Syria (II Kings 8:7–15)

Elijah raises the widow's son to life (I Kings 17:9)

Aphek (854 BCE)

Sea of Chinnereth

Elisha raises child of the Shunammite woman to life (II Kings 4)

Mount Carmel

Shunem

Kishon

Jezreel

Birthplace of Elijah (I Kings 17:1)

Ramoth-gilead (853 BCE)

Elijah defeats the prophets of Baal (I Kings 18:30–40)

Elijah flees from Jezebel (I Kings 18:41–46)

Dothan

Cherith

Tishbe

Elijah is fed by ravens during drought (I Kings 17:3–5)

Abel-meholah

Elijah prophesies lifting of the siege of Samaria (II Kings 6–7)

Samaria (855 BCE)

I S R A E L

Elisha cures Naaman of leprosy (II Kings 5:8–14)

AMMON

Elisha picks up the mantle of Elijah (II Kings 2:1–9)

Jordan

Elisha purifies poisoned food (II Kings 4:38–41)

Bethel

Gilgal

Jericho

Jerusalem

Elisha purifies water (II Kings 2:23)

Elijah ascends to heaven (II Kings 2:1–11)

PHILISTIA

JUDAH

Salt Sea

MOAB

Beersheba

The Negeb

31°

EDOM

30°

0   25   50   75 km

0   15   30   45 miles

Borders of Israel and Judah during the reigns of Omri and Jehoshaphat

Aramean incursions during the reign of Ahab

Site of conflict (with date)

Ezion-geber

34°   35°   36°

PROPHETS OF THE KINGDOMS
OF ISRAEL AND JUDAH

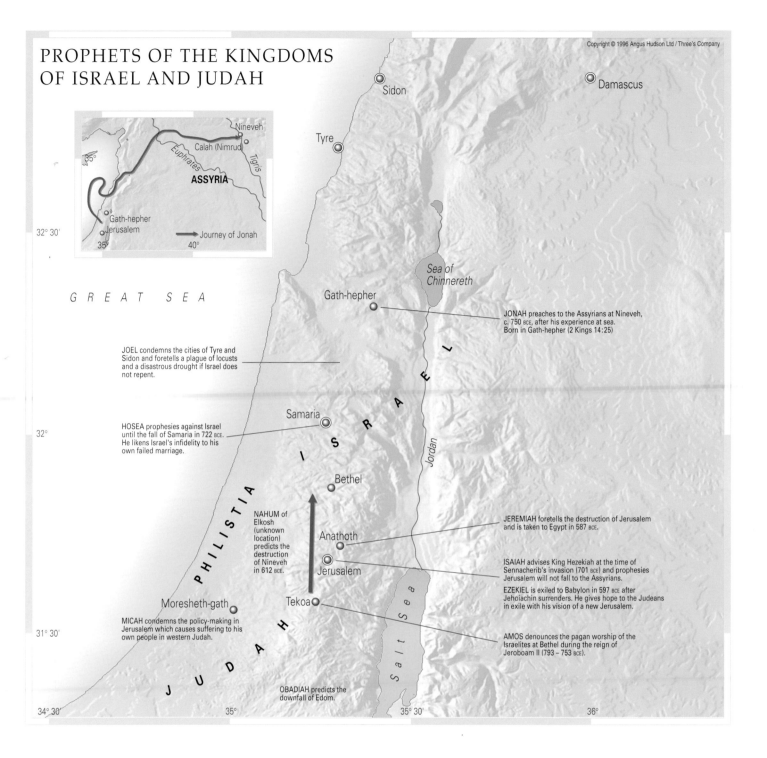

Copyright © 1996 Angus Hudson Ltd / Three's Company

Sidon

Damascus

Nineveh

Calah (Nimrud)

Euphrates

Tigris

ASSYRIA

35°

Gath-hepher

Jerusalem

35°

40°

→ Journey of Jonah

32° 30'

Tyre

GREAT SEA

Sea of Chinnereth

Gath-hepher

JONAH preaches to the Assyrians at Nineveh, c. 750 BCE, after his experience at sea. Born in Gath-hepher (2 Kings 14:25)

JOEL condemns the cities of Tyre and Sidon and foretells a plague of locusts and a disastrous drought if Israel does not repent.

HOSEA prophesies against Israel until the fall of Samaria in 722 BCE. He likens Israel's infidelity to his own failed marriage.

Samaria

32°

I S R A E L

Jordan

Bethel

P H I L I S T I A

NAHUM of Elkosh (unknown location) predicts the destruction of Nineveh in 612 BCE.

Anathoth

Jerusalem

JEREMIAH foretells the destruction of Jerusalem and is taken to Egypt in 587 BCE.

ISAIAH advises King Hezekiah at the time of Sennacherib's invasion (701 BCE) and prophesies Jerusalem will not fall to the Assyrians.

EZEKIEL is exiled to Babylon in 597 BCE after Jehoiachin surrenders. He gives hope to the Judeans in exile with his vision of a new Jerusalem.

Moresheth-gath

Tekoa

S a l t   S e a

MICAH condemns the policy-making in Jerusalem which causes suffering to his own people in western Judah.

AMOS denounces the pagan worship of the Israelites at Bethel during the reign of Jeroboam II (793 – 753 BCE).

31° 30'

J U D A H

OBADIAH predicts the downfall of Edom.

34° 30'

35°

35° 30'

36°

THE PROPHETS

Some fifty years after the separation of Israel from Judah, in the early ninth century BCE, Omri became king of Israel. He moved the capital to Samaria, and a period of relative peace and prosperity began. His son Ahab married Jezebel, the daughter of the king of Tyre. As a result Israel became more influenced by Phoenician culture, including the cult of Baal. It was Jezebel's sponsoring of Baal worship over that of Yahweh, the God of Israel,

which invoked the wrath of Israel's prophets, in particular Elijah (I Kings 18). Traditionally Israel's greatest prophet, Elijah single-handedly combatted the idolatry which threatened Israel's religious integrity.

Elisha continued Elijah's policies and, through his support for King Jehu, brought about the downfall of the House of Omri.

From the eighth century, the literary prophets arose, whose works are recorded in the Bible. They were enlightened individuals, often from within the priestly tradition, though not afraid to criticize it. As divine

messengers, they could foresee impending disasters, and counselled their people and leaders to change their ways in order to avoid the consequences. The greatest of these prophets were Isaiah, Jeremiah and Ezekiel.

JEROBOAM II AND UZZIAH

Israel and Judah became powerful and wealthy nations during the reigns of Jeroboam II and Uzziah in the eighth century. Once again Israel and Judah gained control of the commercial highways in the region. Jeroboam reigned in Israel from *c.* 789 to 748 BCE. He recovered lands taken earlier by the Arameans of Damascus now that their power had been broken by the Assyrians. He established control over a large area of Aram (II Kings 14:25). The prophets Amos and Hosea condemned the internal moral and religious corruption and materialistic life-style.

Uzziah reigned in Judah from *c.* 785 to 734 BCE. He pushed back the frontier with the Philistines and recovered the territory of Edom which King David had conquered. The port of Ezion-geber was rebuilt, giving a renewed outlet to the Red Sea.

Assyrian spearmen, from an Assyrian relief.

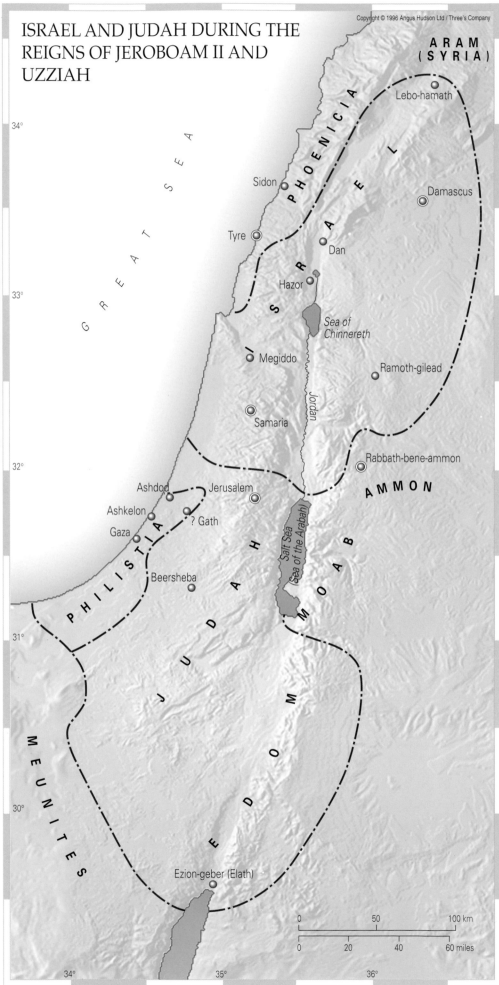

ISRAEL AND JUDAH DURING THE REIGNS OF JEROBOAM II AND UZZIAH

Copyright © 1996 Angus Hudson Ltd / Three's Company

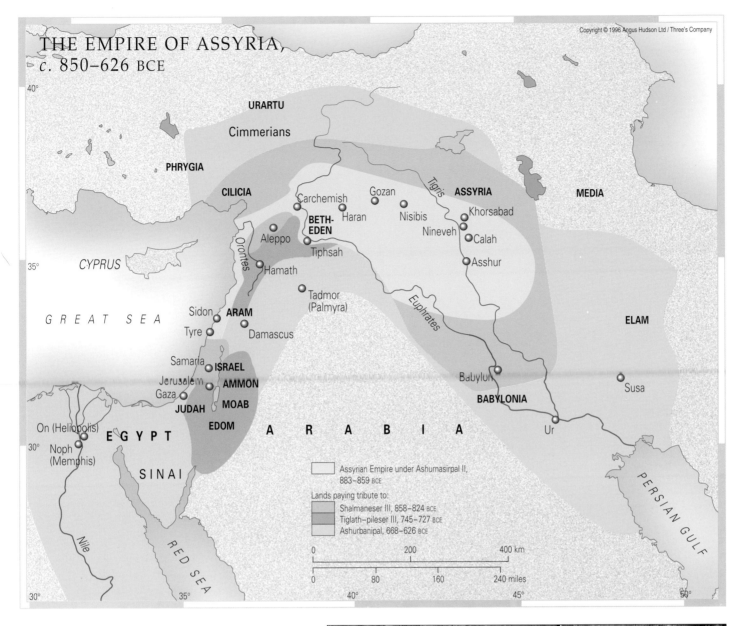

Copyright © 1996 Angus Hudson Ltd / Three's Company

THE EMPIRE OF ASSYRIA,
c. 850–626 BCE

URARTU

Cimmerians

PHRYGIA

CILICIA

Carchemish   Gozan   ASSYRIA   MEDIA

BETH-   Haran   Nisibis   Khorsabad
EDEN
Aleppo   Nineveh   Calah
Tiphsah
Hamath   Asshur

CYPRUS

Tadmor
(Palmyra)   ELAM

GREAT SEA   Sidon   ARAM
Tyre   Damascus

Samaria   ISRAEL
Jerusalem   AMMON   Babylon   Susa
Gaza   BABYLONIA
JUDAH   MOAB   Ur

On (Heliopolis)   EDOM   A R A B I A
EGYPT
Noph
(Memphis)

SINAI

	Assyrian Empire under Ashurnasirpal II, 883–859 BCE

Lands paying tribute to:
Shalmaneser III, 858–824 BCE
Tiglath-pileser III, 745–727 BCE
Ashurbanipal, 668–626 BCE

PERSIAN GULF

RED SEA   0   200   400 km
0   80   160   240 miles

THE ASSYRIAN EMPIRE

Detail from a relief at Nineveh: captured messengers from Urartu.

Assyria had been a force in Mesopotamia since the fourteenth century BCE. By *c.* 900 BCE it was expanding into an empire which, over the next 250 years, was feared throughout the ancient Near East. At its maximum extent the empire stretched from Egypt to the Persian Gulf, though Egypt was controlled only briefly. The capital of the empire shifted in different periods: Ashurnasirpal (883-859) moved it from Assur to Calah (modern Nimrud); Khorsabad was made capital briefly by Sargon II (721-705); his son Sennacherib moved it again to Nineveh, where it remained until the fall of the empire.

The first military involvement Israel had with Assyria was at the Battle of Qarqar, north of Hamath, when an alliance of twelve kings, including Ahab of Israel, checked the Assyrians' southward advance in 853 BCE. However, Assyria's victory at Damascus in 796 BCE was a portent of the military power they would demonstrate through the next century.

43

THE CAMPAIGNS OF TIGLATH-PILESER III

Copyright © 1996 Angus Hudson Ltd / Three's Company

Damascus

Ijon
Tyre
Abel-beth-maachah
Janoah
Kedesh
Hazor

ARAM (SYRIA)

33°

GREAT SEA

PHOENICIA

NAPHTALI

Sea of Chinnereth

Ashtaroth

VALLEY OF JEZREEL

Megiddo
Beth-shan

Ramoth-gilead

GILEAD

Samaria

ISRAEL

Mahanaim

Jordan

AMMON

32°

Gezer
Ashdod
Jerusalem

JUDAH

Rabbath-bene-ammon

Ashkelon

PHILISTIA

Gaza
Lachish

Salt Sea

MOAB

Beersheba

Kir-hareseth

Brook of Egypt

Tiglath-pileser's invasions in

→ 734 BCE
→ 733/32 BCE
·—·—· International border

0   25   50 km

0   10   20   30 miles

EDOM

34°   35°   36°

TIGLATH-PILESER III

From *c*. 740 BCE, the Assyrians put Israel and Judah under pressure. Until then the main purpose of Assyrian campaigns in the region had been to secure booty and tribute. With the accession of Tiglath-pileser III (745-727 BCE), Assyria began to assert more control over the states of the Levant, requiring regular tribute payments from loyal vassals; rebel kings were defeated and their realms often turned into Assyrian provinces.

Kings Pekah of Israel and Rezin of Damascus hoped to form a coalition against Assyria, but King Ahaz of Judah refused to join. They turned on Ahaz, who, against the advice of the prophet Isaiah, appealed to Tiglath-pileser for

help (II Kings 16:7). At high speed Tiglath-pileser campaigned down the western flank of the Levant in 734, destroying the major cities of Philistia, as far as the Brook of Egypt. A year later he concentrated on Israel, and took all of Galilee as far south as the Valley of Jezreel. A third campaign crushed Damascus and penetrated as far as Gilead. Pekah was assassinated and his replacement, Hoshea, was obliged to pay a heavy tribute as a vassal king to Assyria (II Kings 17:3).

The Assyrian king Ashurbanipal, from an Assyrian relief.

44

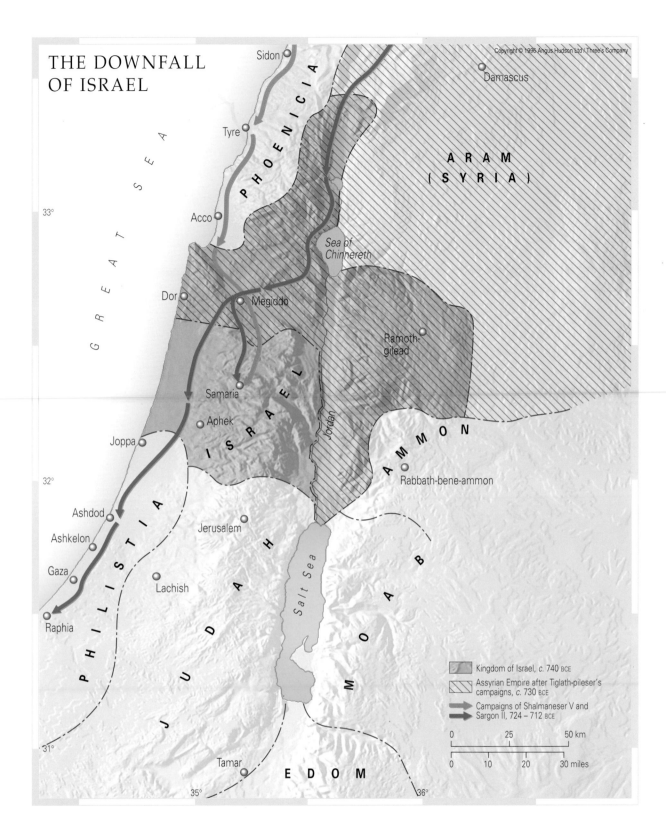

THE DOWNFALL OF ISRAEL

Sidon

Damascus

Tyre

P H O E N I C I A

A R A M
(S Y R I A)

33°

Acco

G R E A T   S E A

Sea of
Chinnereth

Dor

Megiddo

Ramoth-
gilead

I S R A E L

Samaria

Aphek

Joppa

J o r d a n

A M M O N

32°

Rabbath-bene-ammon

Ashdod

Jerusalem

Ashkelon

P H I L I S T I A

J U D A H

M O A B

Gaza

Salt Sea

Lachish

Raphia

Kingdom of Israel, *c.* 740 BCE

Assyrian Empire after Tiglath-pileser's
campaigns, *c.* 730 BCE

Campaigns of Shalmaneser V and
Sargon II, 724 – 712 BCE

0	25	50 km

0	10	20	30 miles

31°

Tamar

E D O M

35°

36°

THE FALL OF ISRAEL

Around 730 BCE, after Tiglath-pileser's campaigns, the administration of Israel was divided between Assyria and Israel. The northern and eastern parts conquered by Tiglath-pileser were made Assyrian provinces. Megiddo was rebuilt and became the administrative centre. Southern Israel was allowed to continue as a tribute-paying semi-autonomous state with its own king (at this time Hoshea), as long as it remained loyal to Assyria.

However, Hoshea tried to relieve his people of the heavy burden of tribute by turning to Egypt for military aid against Assyria. This prompted an attack from the new Assyrian king, Shalmaneser V, in 724 BCE. Hoshea was arrested and Samaria was besieged for three years before the city finally collapsed (II Kings 17:5-6). The inhabitants were deported to different parts of the Assyrian empire. A further campaign, under Sargon II, was launched in 720 BCE through the western region as far as Raphia, where the Assyrians were met by Egyptian forces.

SENNACHERIB

King Hezekiah of Judah saw the death of Sargon II (705 BCE) as an opportunity to rally potential allies against the mighty Assyria. He was promised support from the Cushites (Ethiopians) and Egyptians, though found only limited help in Philistia. He fortified some of the cities in western Judah and engineered underground water supplies in the event of siege. The Siloam tunnel into Jerusalem from the Gihon spring was one example.

The new Assyrian king, Sennacherib, invaded Phoenicia in 701 BCE and many city kings surrendered. The campaign continued southwards where Sennacherib defeated the Egyptian-Cushite force at Eltekeh. The chronology of events is uncertain, but at around the same time Sennacherib turned inland and, according to his Assyrian annals, sacked forty-six cities in western Judah, including the heavily fortified city of Lachish. The Assyrians marched on to Jerusalem. However, before the Assyrians could capture the city, their army was ravaged, perhaps by plague (the biblical author uses the term 'God's angel', II Kings 20:35), and they withdrew. Sennacherib did, though, extract a heavy tribute payment from Hezekiah.

The entrance to Hezekiah's Tunnel, which runs from the Gihon spring.

46

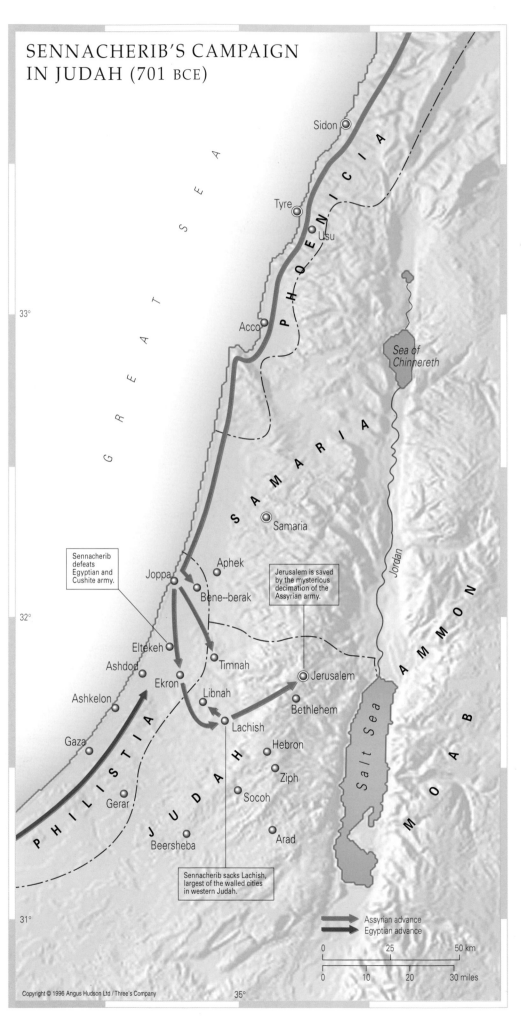

SENNACHERIB'S CAMPAIGN IN JUDAH (701 BCE)

Sidon

Tyre

Usu

PHOENICIA

Acco

G R E A T   S E A

33°

Sea of Chinnereth

SAMARIA

Samaria

Jordan

Aphek

Sennacherib defeats Egyptian and Cushite army.

Joppa

Bene–berak

Jerusalem is saved by the mysterious decimation of the Assyrian army.

32°

AMMON

Eltekeh

Timnah

Jerusalem

Ashdod

Ekron

Libnah

Bethlehem

Ashkelon

Lachish

Salt Sea

Gaza

Hebron

MOAB

Ziph

Gerar

Socoh

JUDAH

PHILISTIA

Beersheba

Arad

Sennacherib sacks Lachish, largest of the walled cities in western Judah.

31°

Assyrian advance
Egyptian advance

0 ——— 25 ——— 50 km

0 —— 10 —— 20 —— 30 miles

35°

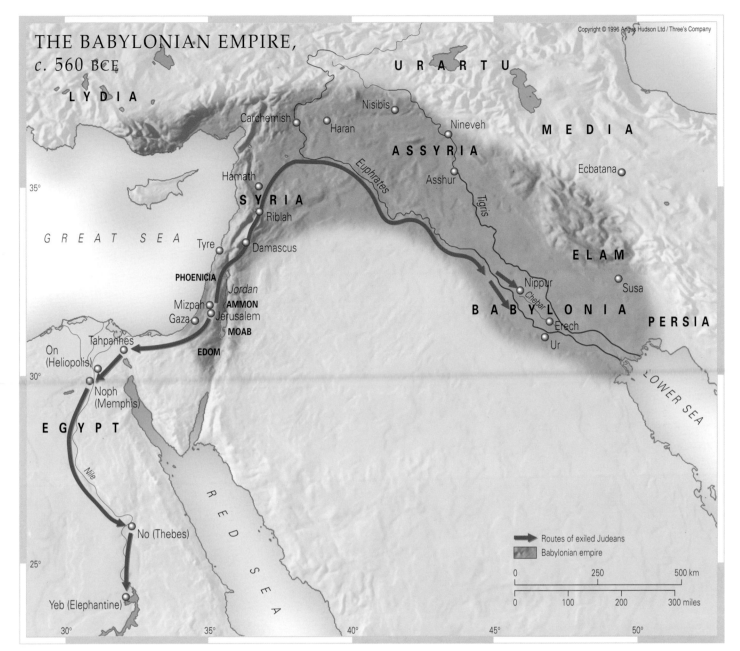

THE BABYLONIAN EMPIRE, c. 560 BCE

URARTU

LYDIA

Carchemish

Nisibis

Haran

Nineveh

MEDIA

ASSYRIA

Ecbatana

Hamath

Asshur

SYRIA

Riblah

GREAT SEA

Tyre

Damascus

ELAM

PHOENICIA

Jordan

Nippur

Susa

Mizpah

AMMON

Chebar

BABYLONIA

Gaza

Jerusalem

Erech

PERSIA

MOAB

Ur

Tahpanhes

EDOM

On (Heliopolis)

Noph (Memphis)

LOWER SEA

EGYPT

Nile

RED SEA

No (Thebes)

Yeb (Elephantine)

Copyright © 1996 Angus Hudson Ltd / Three's Company

→ Routes of exiled Judeans

Babylonian empire

| 0 | 250 | 500 km |
| 0 | 100 | 200 | 300 miles |

THE BABYLONIAN EMPIRE

The Assyrians were gradually conquered by the Babylonians, with help from the Medes, over a period from 626 to 612 BCE, in which year the capital Nineveh finally fell. Babylonia became the new threat and the Egyptians, fearing the danger, went to Assyria's aid. They were defeated by the Babylonians at the decisive Battle of Carchemish in 605. Jehoiakim of Judah, who had been put on the throne by the Egyptians, now had to pay tribute to Nebuchadnezzar of Babylon (II Kings 24:1).

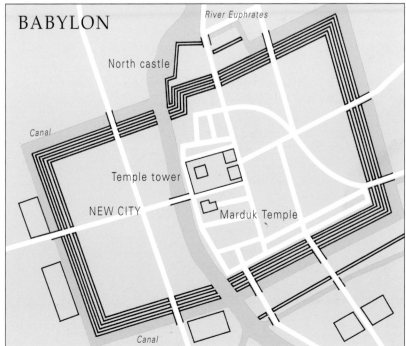

BABYLON

River Euphrates

North castle

Canal

Temple tower

NEW CITY

Marduk Temple

Canal

THE FALL OF JUDAH TO THE BABYLONIANS

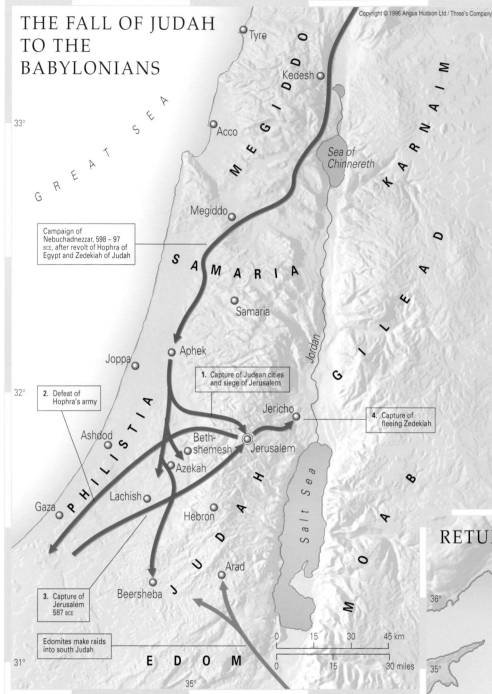

GREAT SEA

Tyre

Kedesh

MEGIDDO

Acco

Sea of Chinnereth

KARNAIM

Megiddo

Campaign of Nebuchadnezzar, 598 – 97 BCE, after revolt of Hophra of Egypt and Zedekiah of Judah

SAMARIA

Samaria

Aphek

Joppa

GILEAD

Jordan

1. Capture of Judean cities and siege of Jerusalem

2. Defeat of Hophra's army

Jericho

4. Capture of fleeing Zedekiah

Ashdod

Beth-shemesh

Jerusalem

Azekah

PHILISTIA

Lachish

Salt Sea

Gaza

Hebron

JUDAH

MOAB

Arad

3. Capture of Jerusalem 587 BCE

Beersheba

Edomites make raids into south Judah

EDOM

0   15   30   45 km

0   15   30 miles

THE FALL OF JUDAH

The Egyptians and Babylonians struggled for supremacy in the Near East. Egypt encouraged Judah to rebel against Babylonian control, which Jehoiakim did in 600 BCE by withholding his tribute. This provoked a Babylonian invasion of Judah in 598, as well as invasions from Judah's neighbouring enemies, in particular the Edomites to the south. The young Jehoiachin succeeded to the throne of Judah on his father's death and was unable to resist the Babylonian pressure. He surrendered Jerusalem in 597. He and many fellow Judeans were deported to Babylon, while a new puppet king, Zedekiah, replaced him (II Kings 24:18).

Once again, Judah was persuaded to rebel and Jerusalem was quickly under siege again in 589. Hophra of Egypt engaged the Babylonians in the west but was defeated. The siege of Jerusalem was renewed. In spite of holding out for nearly two years the city was finally burned in 586, and its inhabitants taken into exile (II Kings 25:1-12).

A mythical beast pictured on glazed tiles from the gate of ancient Babylon.

RETURN OF THE EXILES

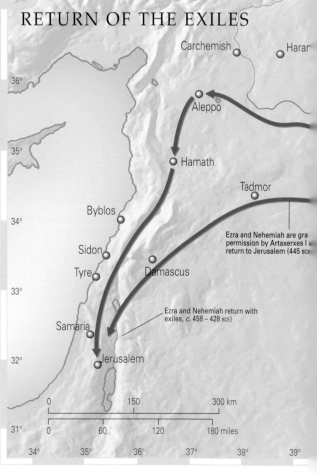

Carchemish

Harar

Aleppo

Hamath

Tadmor

Byblos

Ezra and Nehemiah are gra[nted] permission by Artaxerxes I [to] return to Jerusalem (445 BCE)

Sidon

Tyre

Damascus

Ezra and Nehemiah return with exiles, c. 458 – 428 BCE)

Samaria

Jerusalem

0   150   300 km

0   60   120   180 miles

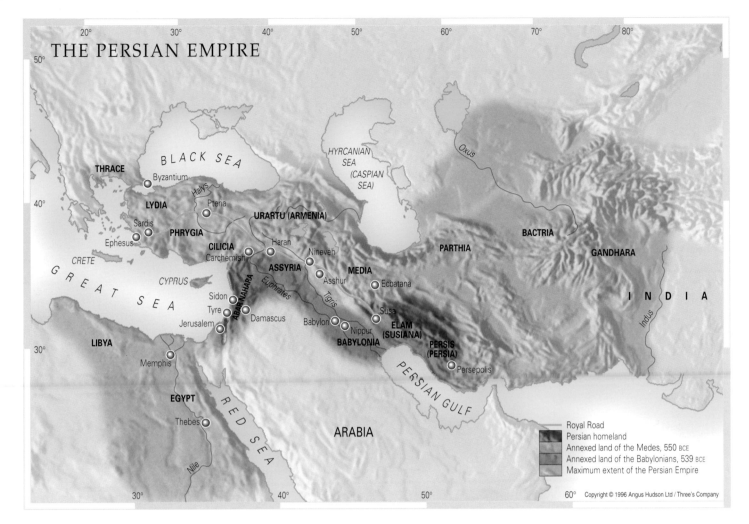

THE PERSIAN EMPIRE

20° 30° 40° 50° 60° 70° 80°

50°

THRACE
Byzantium

BLACK SEA

HYRCANIAN SEA (CASPIAN SEA)

Oxus

40°

LYDIA
Halys
Pteria
Sardis
PHRYGIA
Ephesus

URARTU (ARMENIA)

BACTRIA

GANDHARA

CRETE

CILICIA
Haran
Carchemish
Nineveh
ASSYRIA
Asshur

MEDIA
Ecbatana

PARTHIA

I N D I A

CYPRUS

G R E A T   S E A

Sidon
Tyre
ABAR NAHARA
Euphrates
Damascus
Jerusalem
Tigris
Babylon
Nippur
Susa
ELAM (SUSIANA)

Indus

BABYLONIA

PERSIS (PERSIA)

30°

LIBYA

Memphis

Persepolis

EGYPT

RED SEA

PERSIAN GULF

Thebes

Nile

ARABIA

Royal Road
Persian homeland
Annexed land of the Medes, 550 BCE
Annexed land of the Babylonians, 539 BCE
Maximum extent of the Persian Empire

30° 40° 50° 60° Copyright © 1996 Angus Hudson Ltd / Three's Company

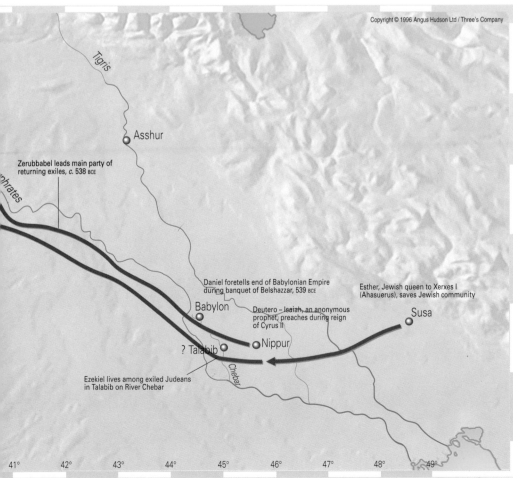

Copyright © 1996 Angus Hudson Ltd / Three's Company

Tigris

Asshur

Zerubbabel leads main party of
returning exiles, c. 538 BCE

Daniel foretells end of Babylonian Empire
during banquet of Belshazzar, 539 BCE

Esther, Jewish queen to Xerxes I
(Ahasuerus), saves Jewish community

Babylon
Deutero – Isaiah, an anonymous
prophet, preaches during reign
of Cyrus II

Susa

? Talabib
Nippur

Ezekiel lives among exiled Judeans
in Talabib on River Chebar

Chebar

41° 42° 43° 44° 45° 46° 47° 48° 49°

THE EXILE

The prophet Jeremiah records three
occasions of deportation: in 597, 586
and again in 582. The people were taken
to different parts of Babylonia but many
seem to have settled by the River
Chebar. Although Ezekiel and the
Psalms record their misery and great
sense of loss of homeland, conditions
were not harsh. They developed their
own farming communities and some
Judeans rose to high rank in the
Babylonian government. It was fifty
years, though, before the more
enlightened regime of the Persians
conquered Babylon, as foreseen by the
prophet Daniel at the banquet of
Belshazzar. The return to Palestine
happened in stages. The first, under
Zerubbabel, was permitted by decree of
the Persian emperor Cyrus the Great
(reigned 559-529 BCE), shortly after the
Persians took Babylon in 539 BCE. Later
returns took place under Ezra and
Nehemiah in the next century.

RETURN FROM EXILE

The initial enthusiasm of the returnees about rebuilding Jerusalem was gradually replaced by an anxiety over housing and feeding, and the hostility of neighbours who resented their immigration. The work of rebuilding the Temple lapsed. The prophets Haggai and Zechariah (*c.* 520 BCE) rebuked the Judeans for being more concerned about their own comfort than the restoration of their religious institutions. A spirited revival of interest brought completion of the Temple in 516 BCE.

Local opposition to the Judeans continued. Ezra travelled from Babylonia to Jerusalem in 458 to reinstate the Jewish Law, which was not being observed truly. In 445, Nehemiah was appointed governor of Judea by the Persian Emperor Artaxerxes I (464-423). His main task was to complete the rebuilding of Jerusalem's walls for greater protection against, among others, Sanballat, the governor of Samaria (Nehemiah 4). Most of the people of the Samaria region were brought there from other lands by the Assyrians after the fall of the northern kingdom in 721. They considered themselves Jews and the rightful inhabitants of all Palestine. Mutual resentment between the Jews from Babylon and the 'Samaritans' continued into New Testament times.

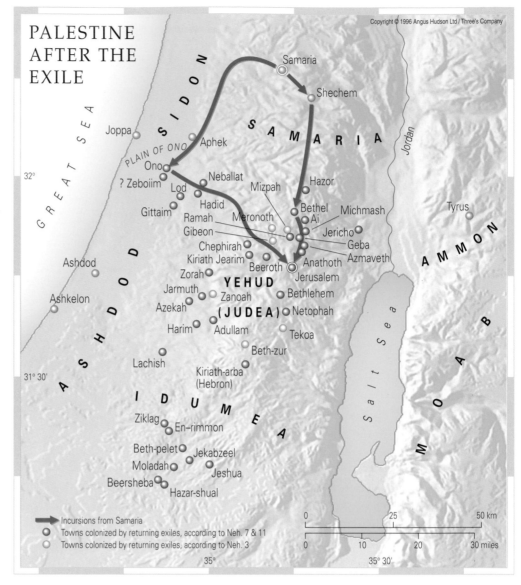

PALESTINE AFTER THE EXILE

Copyright © 1996 Angus Hudson Ltd / Three's Company

➤ Incursions from Samaria
◎ Towns colonized by returning exiles, according to Neh. 7 & 11
○ Towns colonized by returning exiles, according to Neh. 3

Section of the 'Broad Wall' in Jerusalem, possibly built in the late eighth century BCE.

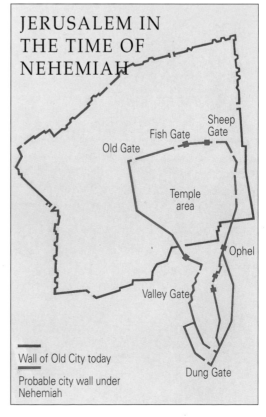

JERUSALEM IN THE TIME OF NEHEMIAH

Wall of Old City today

Probable city wall under Nehemiah

ALEXANDER THE GREAT'S CONQUESTS

Copyright © 1996 Angus Hudson Ltd / Three's Company

THRACE

MACEDONIA

Aegae
Pella

BLACK SEA

Sestus
Eleus
Zelea
Dascylium

AEGEAN SEA

MYSIA

Sardis

LYDIA

Athens

Ephesus

CARIA

Miletus

Halicarnassus

LYCIA

Sparta

Phaselis

Side

Perge

Sagalassus

PHRYGIA

Gordium

Ancyra

CAPPADOCIA

Cilician Gates

TAURUS MOUNTAINS

Issus

Tarsus

CILICIA

Myriandrus

Syrian Gates

SYRIA

PHOENICIA

Aradus

Byblos

Sidon

Tyre

Damascus

RHODES

CRETE

CYPRUS

MEDITERRANEAN SEA

Samaria

Jerusalem

JUDEA

→ Alexander's route
✕ Battle site

| 0 | 200 | 400 km |
| 0 | 80 | 160 | 240 miles |

EGYPT

ALEXANDER'S EMPIRE

MACEDONIA

BLACK SEA

ASIA MINOR

ARMENIA

CASPIAN SEA

MEDITERRANEAN SEA

Tigris

GAUGAMELA

Euphrates

Babylon

Alexander dies
323 BCE

Susa

Ecbatana

Rhagat

PARTHIA

Marakanda

HINDU KUSH

Taxila

EGYPT

Alexandria

PERSIA

Persepolis

THE GULF

Kandahar

Indus

GEDROSIA

INDIA

Nile

RED SEA

✕ Battle site

Copyright © 1996 Angus Hudson Ltd / Three's Company

ALEXANDER THE GREAT

Alexander the Great conquered Palestine in 332 BCE. His vast and rapidly acquired empire was divided up among his generals on his death in 323 BCE. Two opposing empires emerged – the Seleucids of Greece and western Asia, and the Ptolemies of North Africa. Palestine, as a land bridge between the two, became their battleground, and in different times the vassal state of one or the other. In 198 BCE, it became part of the Seleucid Empire.

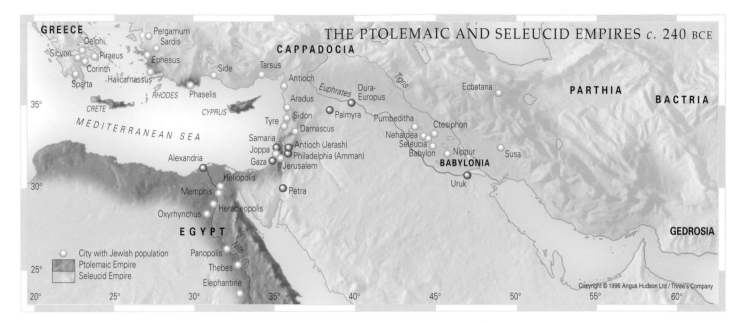

THE PTOLEMAIC AND SELEUCID EMPIRES *c.* 240 BCE

○ City with Jewish population
Ptolemaic Empire
Seleucid Empire

Copyright © 1996 Angus Hudson Ltd / Three's Company

THE MACCABEAN REVOLT

The Maccabean revolt broke out in 167 BCE when Mattathias openly rebelled against the Seleucid authorities by refusing to honour their pagan gods. Pagan worship had been instituted in Judea and Samaria as part of the process of hellenization that had crept through Jewish life ever since the Seleucids had come to power. Hellenized Jews from the high priestly families kowtowed to the excesses of the Seleucid ruler Antiochus IV Epiphanes, who even placed a statue of Zeus in the Temple and demanded sacrifices be made to it.

The Maccabee brothers led a series of campaigns against the Seleucid government which resulted in their eventual victory and establishment of the Hasmonean kingdom in 142 BCE (I Maccabees 13:41-42). This was an independent Jewish state. Traditional Jewish ritual was reinstated by descendants of the high-priestly family of Hashmon, who had always been critical of hellenizing tendencies in Judea. The kingdom reached its maximum extent under Alexander Janneus (103-76 BCE).

One of the reasons for the success of the Maccabees was the decline in power of the Seleucid Empire. The Parthians were hammering on their eastern front, while the Romans grew more powerful in the west. Athens fell in 86 BCE, and in 63 BCE the Roman general Pompey entered the Temple in Jerusalem and forced a settlement with the Hasmoneans by which Palestine became a Roman protectorate.

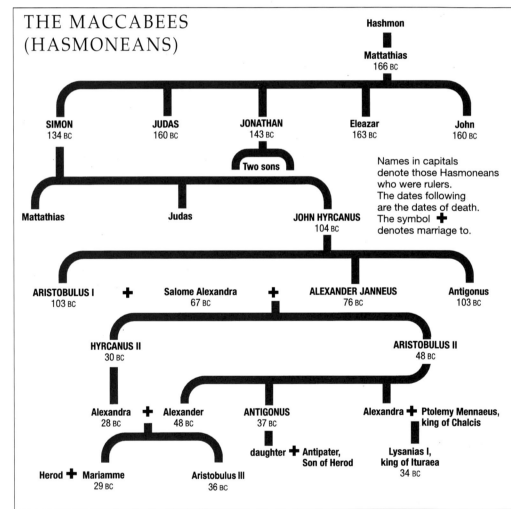

THE MACCABEES (HASMONEANS)

Names in capitals denote those Hasmoneans who were rulers. The dates following are the dates of death. The symbol ✚ denotes marriage to.

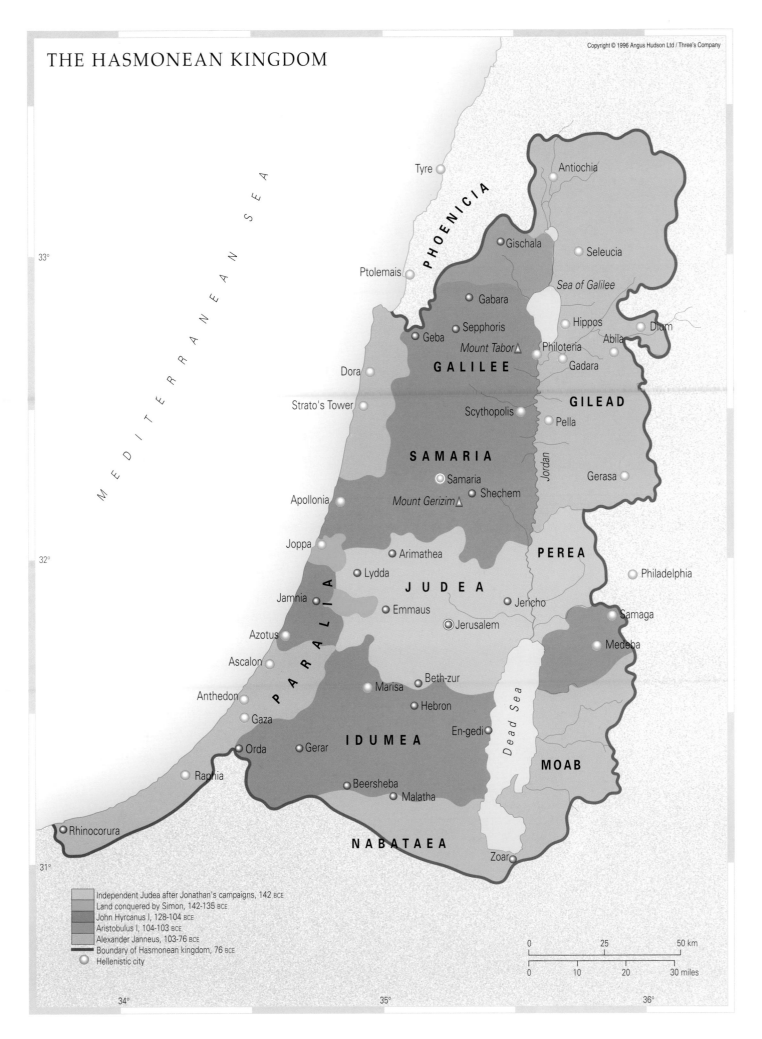

THE HASMONEAN KINGDOM

M E D I T E R R A N E A N   S E A

33°

P H O E N I C I A

Tyre

Antiochia

Gischala

Seleucia

Ptolemais

Sea of Galilee

Gabara

Hippos

Sepphoris

Abila

Dium

Geba

Mount Tabor △

Philoteria

G A L I L E E

Gadara

Dora

G I L E A D

Strato's Tower

Scythopolis

Pella

S A M A R I A

Samaria

Jordan

Gerasa

Mount Gerizim △

Shechem

Apollonia

Joppa

Arimathea

P E R E A

32°

Lydda

Philadelphia

J U D E A

Jamnia

Emmaus

Jericho

Samaga

Jerusalem

Azotus

Medeba

Ascalon

Beth-zur

P A R A L I A

Marisa

Anthedon

Hebron

En-gedi

Dead Sea

Gaza

Orda

Gerar

I D U M E A

M O A B

Raphia

Beersheba

Malatha

Rhinocorura

N A B A T A E A

Zoar

31°

Independent Judea after Jonathan's campaigns, 142 BCE
Land conquered by Simon, 142-135 BCE
John Hyrcanus I, 128-104 BCE
Aristobulus I, 104-103 BCE
Alexander Janneus, 103-76 BCE
Boundary of Hasmonean kingdom, 76 BCE
Hellenistic city

0   25   50 km

0   10   20   30 miles

34°   35°   36°

53

THE ECONOMY OF PALESTINE

Until Roman times Mediterranean trade had been controlled by the Phoenicians. But, with the Pax Romana, greater safety from pirates and bandits allowed more opportunities for commerce, both by sea and over land. The economy was still essentially agrarian: wheat was grown where possible in the valleys north of Jerusalem, giving way to barley in the south. The hill country provided pastureland for sheep and cattle. Vines, olives and dates were the main crops grown on the hillsides.

Metalwork in copper and iron thrived, and by this time there were organized potteries. Jerusalem was a major commercial centre, with 118 recorded luxury goods, such as jewellery and silk clothes. The Temple treasury drew annual tax payments from every Jew and was a source of great wealth. There was a system for banking, and money-changers would exchange foreign currencies for the shekel.

A half shekel coin struck during the Jewish Revolt, 66–70 CE.

54

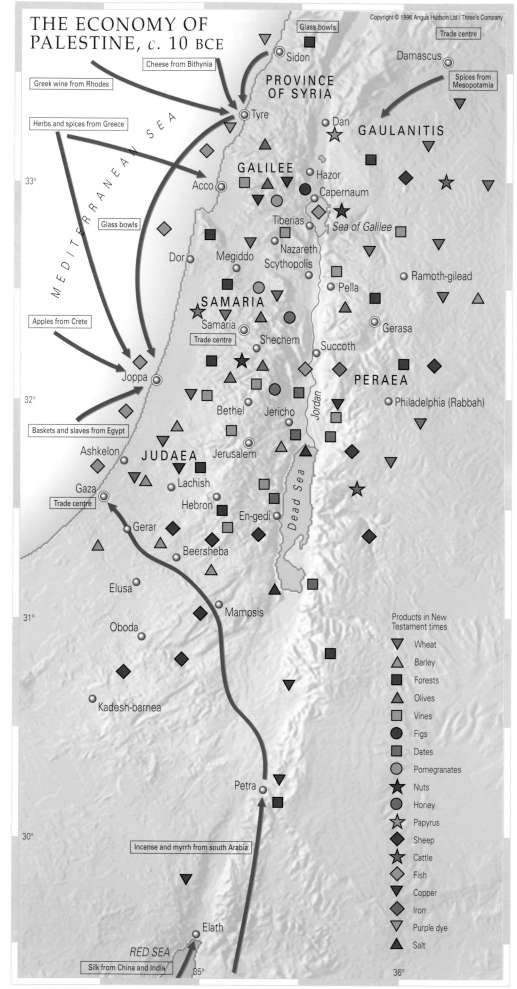

THE ECONOMY OF PALESTINE, *c.* 10 BCE

Copyright © 1996 Angus Hudson Ltd / Three's Company

Glass bowls

Trade centre

Cheese from Bithynia

Greek wine from Rhodes

Herbs and spices from Greece

Spices from Mesopotamia

Glass bowls

Apples from Crete

Trade centre

Baskets and slaves from Egypt

Trade centre

Incense and myrrh from south Arabia

Silk from China and India

MEDITERRANEAN SEA

PROVINCE OF SYRIA

GAULANITIS

GALILEE

SAMARIA

JUDAEA

PERAEA

Sea of Galilee

Dead Sea

Jordan

RED SEA

Sidon · Tyre · Dan · Damascus · Acco · Hazor · Capernaum · Tiberias · Nazareth · Scythopolis · Pella · Ramoth-gilead · Dor · Megiddo · Samaria · Shechem · Succoth · Gerasa · Bethel · Jericho · Philadelphia (Rabbah) · Jerusalem · Ashkelon · Lachish · Hebron · En-gedi · Gaza · Gerar · Beersheba · Elusa · Mampsis · Oboda · Kadesh-barnea · Petra · Elath

Products in New Testament times

- ▽ Wheat
- △ Barley
- ■ Forests
- ▲ Olives
- ▢ Vines
- ● Figs
- ▢ Dates
- ○ Pomegranates
- ★ Nuts
- ● Honey
- ☆ Papyrus
- ◆ Sheep
- ★ Cattle
- ◈ Fish
- ▽ Copper
- ◆ Iron
- ▽ Purple dye
- ▲ Salt

33°
32°
31°
30°
35°
36°

ATLAS of the Bible and Christianity

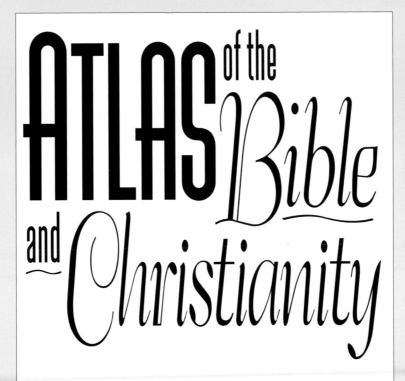

NEW TESTAMENT PERIOD

THE ROMAN EMPIRE

ATLANTIC

OCEAN

BRITANNIA

GERMANIA
INFERIOR

Rhine

LUGDUNENSIS

BELGICA

GERMANIA
SUPERIOR

RAETIA

Danube

NORICUM

AQUITANIA

PANNONIA

NARBONENSIS

ALPES POENINAE

ALPES
MARITIMAE

DALMATIA

MOESIA

ALPES
COTTIAE

Salonae

LUSITANIA

TARRACONENSIS

Rome

CORSICA

ITALIA

MACEDONIA

BAETICA

SARDINIA

Thess

EPIRUS

Corinth

Carthage

SICILIA

Syracuse

ACHA

MAURETANIA

AFRICA

M E D I T E R R

Cyrene

CYRENA

56

THE ROMAN EMPIRE

The Emperor Augustus brought peace, prosperity and stability to the Roman Empire. By the time of his death in 14 CE, the frontiers of the empire had been made secure: the River Danube became the northern frontier and a series of buffer states protected Asia Minor and east Mediterranean from the Parthians in the east. Some of these states were 'client' kingdoms, which acknowledged Roman dominance in return for their protection.

Further conquests by the Emperor Trajan (Dacia, Arabia, Armenia and Mesopotamia) expanded the imperial boundary to its maximum extent in 116 CE. An extensive programme of road building enabled a Roman citizen to travel safely and quickly; from Britain to Mesopotamia he needed no languages other than Latin and Greek, no passport and only the Roman denarius for currency.

The remains of the Forum of ancient Rome, the administrative centre of the Roman Empire.

57

QUMRAN

The Qumran region at the north-west end of the Dead Sea has become famous for the discovery in 1947 of ancient manuscripts, known as the Dead Sea Scrolls. They contain sections of the Bible and rules of communal discipline. They probably belonged to a monastic community living at Qumran, widely believed to have been the Essenes. The Scrolls were found in caves among the hills overlooking Qumran, where they had been hidden from the Romans during the Jewish War of 66-70 CE.

The settlement at Qumran probably dates from about 145 BCE, after the demise of Antiochus Epiphanes IV. The group may have arisen in opposition to the hellenization of Judaism during his reign. The community practised strict self-discipline and interpreted the Old Testament prophecies as referring to current events. They expected the imminent advent of a messianic figure, and as they considered themselves the remnant of the true Israel they believed they alone would win God's salvation.

The barren Judean Hills at Qumran. It was in caves in these cliffs that the Dead Sea Scrolls were discovered.

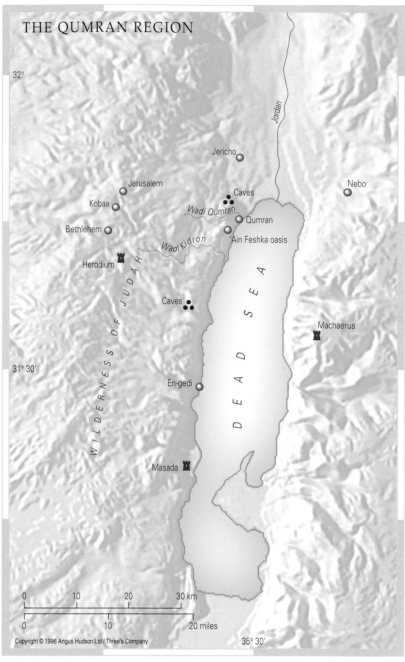

THE QUMRAN REGION

32°

Jordan

Jericho

Jerusalem

Caves

Nebo

Kobaa

Wadi Qumran

Qumran

Bethlehem

Wadi Kidron

'Ain Feshka oasis

Herodium

WILDERNESS OF JUDAH

Caves

DEAD SEA

Machaerus

31° 30'

En-gedi

Masada

| 0 | 10 | 20 | 30 km |
| 0 | | 10 | 20 miles |

Copyright © 1996 Angus Hudson Ltd / Three's Company

35° 30'

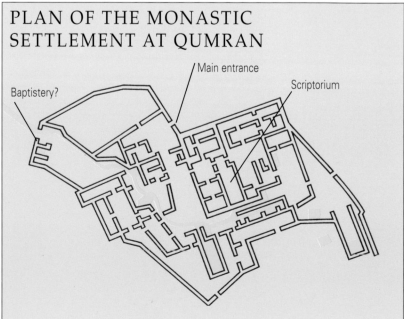

PLAN OF THE MONASTIC SETTLEMENT AT QUMRAN

Main entrance

Baptistery?

Scriptorium

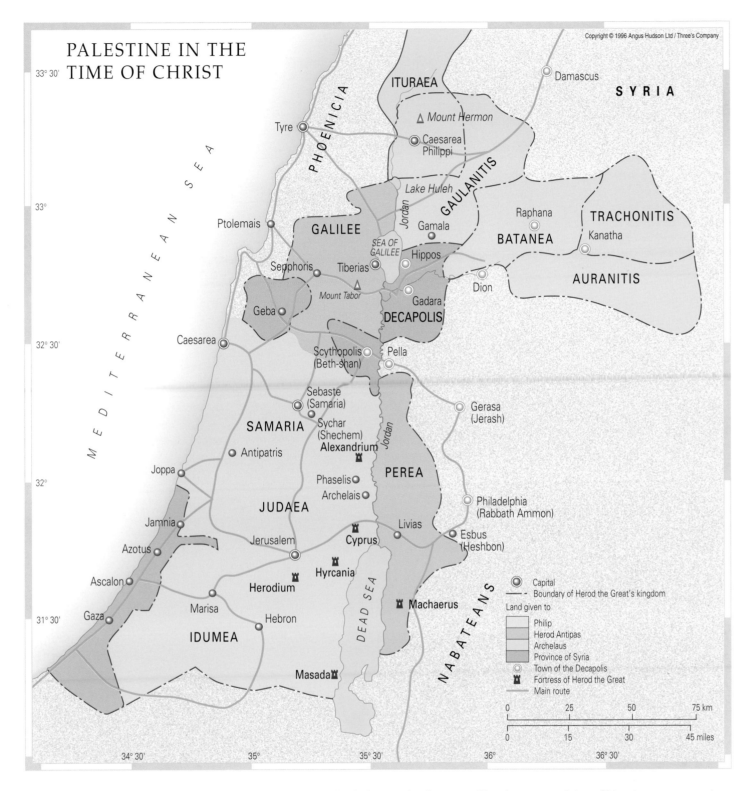

PALESTINE IN THE TIME OF CHRIST

33° 30'

33°

32° 30'

32°

31° 30'

SYRIA

Damascus

ITURAEA

△ Mount Hermon

Caesarea
Philippi

PHOENICIA

Tyre

GAULANITIS

Lake Huleh

GALILEE

Gamala

Raphana

BATANEA

TRACHONITIS

Kanatha

Ptolemais

SEA OF
GALILEE

Hippos

AURANITIS

Sepphoris

Tiberias

Mount Tabor △

Dion

Geba

Gadara

DECAPOLIS

Caesarea

Scythopolis
(Beth-shan)

Pella

Sebaste
(Samaria)

Gerasa
(Jerash)

SAMARIA

Sychar
(Shechem)

Alexandrium

Antipatris

PEREA

Joppa

Phaselis

Archelais

Philadelphia
(Rabbath Ammon)

JUDAEA

Jamnia

Livias

Azotus

Jerusalem

Cyprus

Esbus
(Heshbon)

Ascalon

Hyrcania

MEDITERRANEAN SEA

Jordan

Herodium

Marisa

Hebron

Machaerus

Gaza

DEAD SEA

IDUMEA

NABATEANS

Masada

Legend

◎ Capital
– · – Boundary of Herod the Great's kingdom
Land given to
　Philip
　Herod Antipas
　Archelaus
　Province of Syria
◎ Town of the Decapolis
🏰 Fortress of Herod the Great
— Main route

0   25   50   75 km
0   15   30   45 miles

34° 30'　　35°　　35° 30'　　36°　　36° 30'

PALESTINE IN THE TIME OF CHRIST

Herod the Great was appointed King of Judaea by the Roman senate in 40 BCE. The Parthians then invaded Syria and Palestine and installed their own choice of king, the Hasmonean Mattathias Antigonus. By 37 BCE, however, Herod had secured the throne for himself and he continued to reign until his death in 4 BCE, whereupon the kingdom was divided among his three sons. Herod was not popular with the Jews, despite his building of a new Temple in Jerusalem. His father was Idumaean (Edomite) and he was also very supportive of Roman policy, even erecting shrines to pagan gods.

Palestine now became a province ruled by tetrarchs (literally, ruler of a fourth part, but in practice a provincial ruler more subject to Rome than a king). Archelaus, called Herod the Ethnarch, ruled Judaea from 4 BCE to 6 CE. He was then sent into exile by the Romans after complaints of his mismanagement. A Roman governor then ruled Judaea until 41 CE. Herod Antipas ruled Galilee and part of Transjordan from 4 BCE to 39 CE; and Herod Philip ruled the northern regions until 34 CE.

The Decapolis was a confederation of ten cities formed after Pompey's campaign (65-62 BCE). It gave protection to its Gentile citizens, who were mainly Greek-speaking Roman soldiers, against militant Jews and Arabian tribes.

59

JESUS' CHILDHOOD

According to Luke's Gospel, a Roman census was conducted by Quirinius, governor of Syria. Everyone had to go to their native town to register. Thus, Joseph took Mary to his native town of Bethlehem, where she went into labour and bore Jesus (Luke 2:1-7). According to Matthew, visiting Magi from the east, who had followed a portentous star, visited King Herod asking to see the child who would be king of the Jews. Anxious about this new rival, Herod ordered the killing of all babies in Bethlehem. Joseph and Mary fled to Egypt to escape the slaughter (Matthew 2:1-18).

After Herod's death they went to Nazareth, their hometown, which was under the milder rule of Herod Antipas. Following tradition, Jesus was presented in the Temple at the age of twelve. After setting off on the return trip, his parents discovered that Jesus was not with them (presumably they were among a crowd and had not noticed). They went back to Jerusalem to find him debating with the elders (Luke 2:41-52). Finally they headed back to Nazareth. Jews travelling between Nazareth and Jerusalem would normally cross to the other side of the River Jordan in order to avoid Samaria. What would be a three-day journey on foot via Samaria was made twice as long by going through Transjordan.

A statue of the Holy Family in Nazareth.

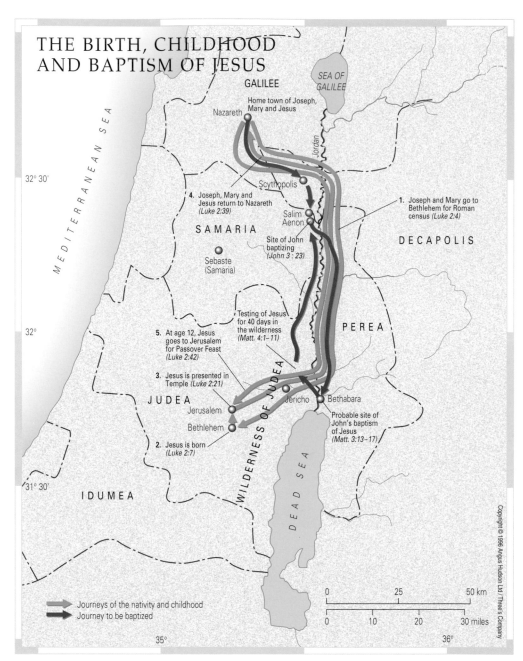

THE BIRTH, CHILDHOOD AND BAPTISM OF JESUS

GALILEE

SEA OF GALILEE

Nazareth — Home town of Joseph, Mary and Jesus

MEDITERRANEAN SEA

Jordan

Scythopolis

4. Joseph, Mary and Jesus return to Nazareth (Luke 2:39)

1. Joseph and Mary go to Bethlehem for Roman census (Luke 2:4)

Salim Aenon

SAMARIA

Site of John baptizing (John 3 : 23)

DECAPOLIS

Sebaste (Samaria)

Testing of Jesus for 40 days in the wilderness (Matt. 4:1–11)

PEREA

5. At age 12, Jesus goes to Jerusalem for Passover Feast (Luke 2:42)

3. Jesus is presented in Temple (Luke 2:21)

JUDEA

Jerusalem

Jericho

Bethabara

WILDERNESS OF JUDEA

Bethlehem

Probable site of John's baptism of Jesus (Matt. 3:13–17)

2. Jesus is born (Luke 2:7)

DEAD SEA

IDUMEA

0   25   50 km
0 10   20   30 miles

Journeys of the nativity and childhood
Journey to be baptized

THE FLIGHT INTO EGYPT

MEDITERRANEAN SEA

Jerusalem

Bethlehem

Jordan

Gaza

Pelusium

Flight of Joseph, Mary and Jesus to Egypt (Matt. 2:13–14)

Nile

E G Y P T

0   100   200 km
0 40 80 120 miles

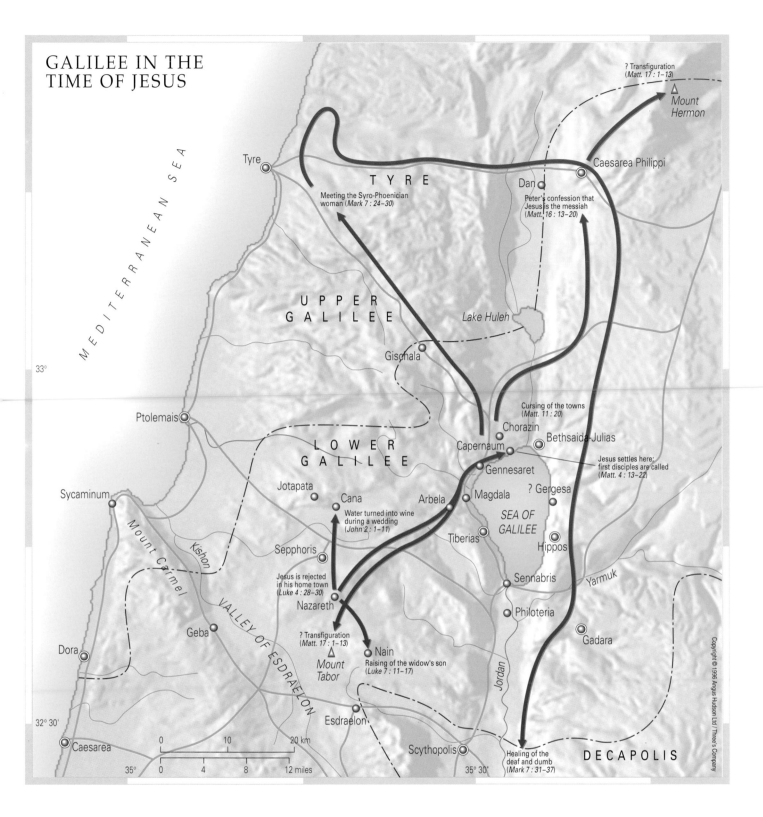

GALILEE IN THE TIME OF JESUS

? Transfiguration (*Matt. 17 : 1–13*)

△ *Mount Hermon*

MEDITERRANEAN SEA

Tyre

T Y R E

Caesarea Philippi

Dan

Meeting the Syro-Phoenician woman (*Mark 7 : 24–30*)

Peter's confession that Jesus is the messiah (*Matt. 16 : 13–20*)

UPPER GALILEE

Lake Huleh

33°

Gischala

Ptolemais

Cursing of the towns (*Matt. 11 : 20*)

L O W E R GALILEE

Chorazin

Bethsaida-Julias

Capernaum

Jesus settles here; first disciples are called (*Matt. 4 : 13–22*)

Gennesaret

Jotapata

Cana

Arbela

Magdala

? Gergesa

Water turned into wine during a wedding (*John 2 : 1–11*)

SEA OF GALILEE

Sycaminum

Sepphoris

Tiberias

Hippos

Jesus is rejected in his home town (*Luke 4 : 28–30*)

Mount Carmel

Kishon

Nazareth

Sennabris

Yarmuk

Geba

VALLEY OF ESDRAELON

? Transfiguration (*Matt. 17 : 1–13*)

△ *Mount Tabor*

Nain

Raising of the widow's son (*Luke 7 : 11–17*)

Philoteria

Dora

Gadara

Jordan

Esdraelon

32° 30'

Caesarea

| 0 | | 10 | | 20 km |
| 0 | 4 | 8 | | 12 miles |

35°

Scythopolis

Healing of the deaf and dumb (*Mark 7 : 31–37*)

DECAPOLIS

35° 30'

GALILEE IN JESUS' TIME

Galilee was much more prosperous as a region than Judea, and supported a large population. Galileans were generally despised by the religious leaders in Jerusalem. Many were not Jews by descent; their forebears had been forcibly converted by Alexander Jannaeus. Galileans were, though, probably more in touch with the daily reality of the Roman Empire, as Galilee lay on the great trade routes which crossed the Near East, and many foreigners would have passed through the region.

Jesus grew up in Nazareth, which was an unimportant small town. Rejected by its people (Luke 4:16-30), he moved to the vicinity of Lake Galilee. Archaeological excavations have revealed that there were twelve towns on the shores of the lake. The preservation of fish by salting and its export across the Roman Empire was a major industry. The city of Tiberias, built by Herod Antipas (*c.* 18 CE) in commemoration of the Roman emperor, was one of the main fishing centres.

CHRIST'S MINISTRY IN GALILEE

Most of the ministry of Jesus took place around Lake Galilee. He sometimes taught in a boat while the crowds watched from the shore. Crossings were frequently made 'to the other side', and Jesus' first apostles were local fishermen (Mark 1:14-20). The lake was large and subject to sudden squalls, as winds would swoop across the valley, hence the unexpected 'storm at sea' (Mark 4:35-41).

The location of the drowning of the Gadarene swine is disputed (Mark 5:1-20). It may have been at the foot of the hill descending from the inland village of Gadara at the southern end of Lake Galilee, or it may have been the traditional site at Kursi (perhaps Gergesa) which lay on the eastern shore. The lake is 21 km (13 miles) long and 11 km (7 miles) wide.

A view of Lake Galilee from the shore near Capernaum.

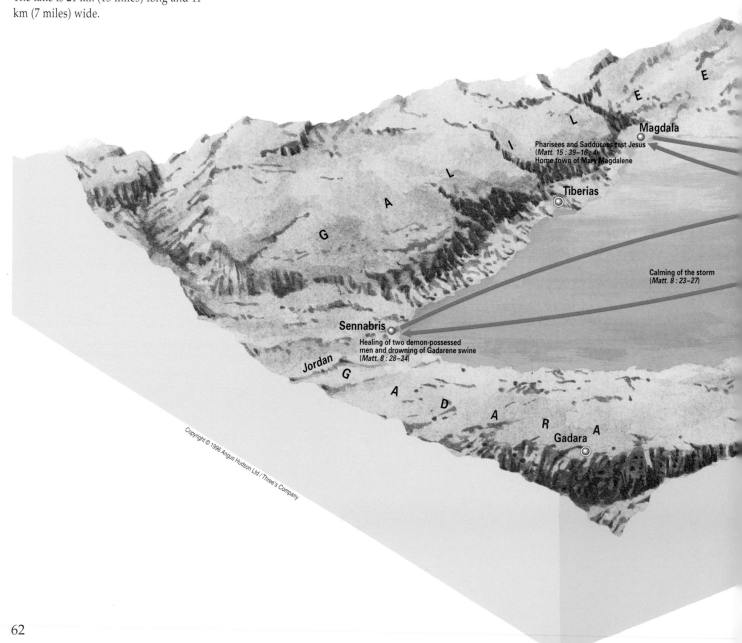

The partially reconstructed fourth-century synagogue at Capernaum.

The Mount of Beatitudes offers magnificent views over Lake Galilee.

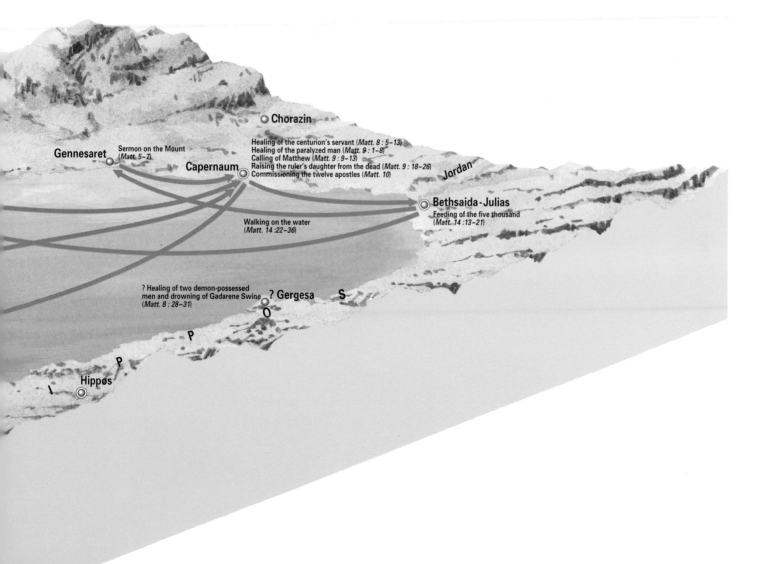

Chorazin

Gennesaret

Sermon on the Mount
(*Matt. 5–7*)

Capernaum

Healing of the centurion's servant (*Matt. 8 : 5–13*)
Healing of the paralyzed man (*Matt. 9 : 1–8*)
Calling of Matthew (*Matt. 9 : 9–13*)
Raising the ruler's daughter from the dead (*Matt. 9 : 18–26*)
Commissioning the twelve apostles (*Matt. 10*)

Jordan

Bethsaida-Julias
Feeding of the five thousand
(*Matt. 14 :13–21*)

Walking on the water
(*Matt. 14 :22–36*)

? Healing of two demon-possessed
men and drowning of Gadarene Swine
(*Matt. 8 : 28–31*)

? Gergesa

S

O

P

P

I

Hippos

JERUSALEM IN JESUS' TIME

Jesus visited Jerusalem several times during his three-year ministry, mainly to celebrate the festivals (John 2:13; 5:1; 7:10; 10:22-23). He stayed in Bethany at the house of Lazarus and his sisters, Mary and Martha (John 11).

As well as building cities and fortresses outside Jerusalem, Herod the Great made huge additions inside: the Temple Mount, the Antonia Fortress and the Upper Palace. The Upper City was the quarter of wealthy aristocrats. Herod's Palace was the residence of the Roman governors after Herod (6-41, 44-66 CE). It was most likely here, rather than at the Antonia Fortress, that Jesus was tried by Pontius Pilate (Matthew 27:11-26). It is also possible that he was tried at Herod Antipas' Palace.

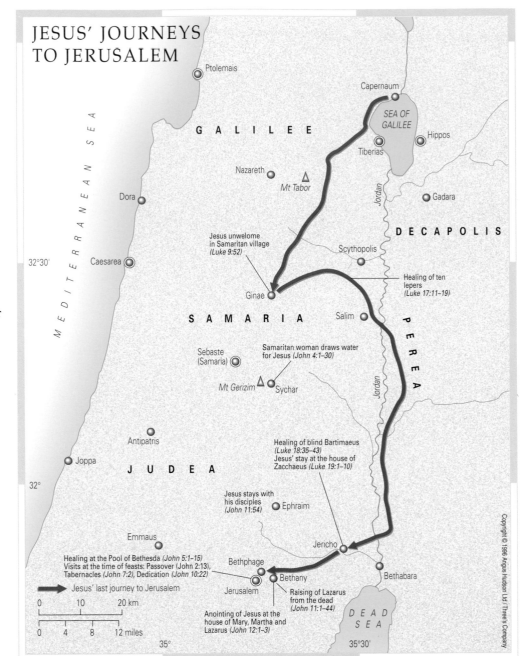

JESUS' JOURNEYS TO JERUSALEM

Ptolemais
Capernaum
SEA OF GALILEE
GALILEE
Hippos
Tiberias
Nazareth
Mt Tabor
Jordan
Gadara
Dora
DECAPOLIS
Jesus unwelome in Samaritan village (Luke 9:52)
Scythopolis
Healing of ten lepers (Luke 17:11–19)
Caesarea
Ginae
SAMARIA
Salim
P E R E A
Sebaste (Samaria)
Samaritan woman draws water for Jesus (John 4:1–30)
Mt Gerizim
Sychar
Jordan
Antipatris
Healing of blind Bartimaeus (Luke 18:35–43) Jesus' stay at the house of Zacchaeus (Luke 19:1–10)
Joppa
J U D E A
Jesus stays with his disciples (John 11:54) Ephraim
Emmaus
Jericho
Healing at the Pool of Bethesda (John 5:1–15) Visits at the time of feasts: Passover (John 2:13), Tabernacles (John 7:2), Dedication (John 10:22)
Bethphage
Bethany
Bethabara
→ Jesus' last journey to Jerusalem
Jerusalem
Raising of Lazarus from the dead (John 11:1–44)
Anointing of Jesus at the house of Mary, Martha and Lazarus (John 12:1–3)
DEAD SEA
0   10   20 km
0   4   8   12 miles
32°30'
32°
35°
35°30'

Part of the Western Wall consists of masonry from Herod's Temple.

The Citadel, Jerusalem, is on the site of Herod's Palace.

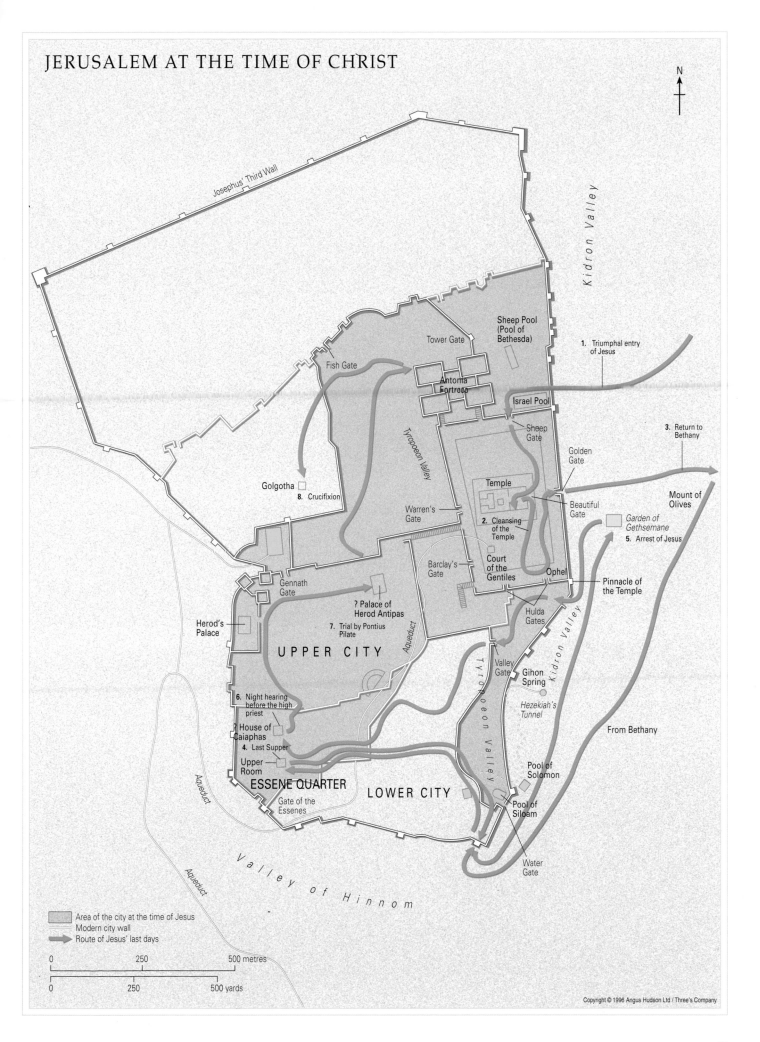

JERUSALEM AT THE TIME OF CHRIST

N

Josephus' Third Wall

Kidron Valley

Sheep Pool
(Pool of
Bethesda)

Tower Gate

1. Triumphal entry
of Jesus

Fish Gate

Antonia
Fortress

Israel Pool

Sheep
Gate

3. Return to
Bethany

Tyropoeon Valley

Golden
Gate

Temple

Mount of
Olives

Golgotha

Beautiful
Gate

8. Crucifixion

Warren's
Gate

2. Cleansing
of the
Temple

*Garden of
Gethsemane*

5. Arrest of Jesus

Barclay's
Gate

Court of
the
Gentiles

Ophel

Pinnacle of
the Temple

Gennath
Gate

**? Palace of
Herod Antipas**

Hulda
Gates

7. Trial by Pontius
Pilate

Aqueduct

Herod's
Palace

UPPER CITY

Valley
Gate

Gihon
Spring

Tyropoeon Valley

Kidron Valley

From Bethany

*Hezekiah's
Tunnel*

6. Night hearing
before the high
priest

**? House of
Caiaphas**

4. Last Supper

Upper
Room

Pool of
Solomon

ESSENE QUARTER

LOWER CITY

Pool of
Siloam

Gate of the
Essenes

Water
Gate

Aqueduct

V a l l e y   o f   H i n n o m

Aqueduct

Area of the city at the time of Jesus
Modern city wall
Route of Jesus' last days

0   250   500 metres

0   250   500 yards

Copyright © 1996 Angus Hudson Ltd / Three's Company

65

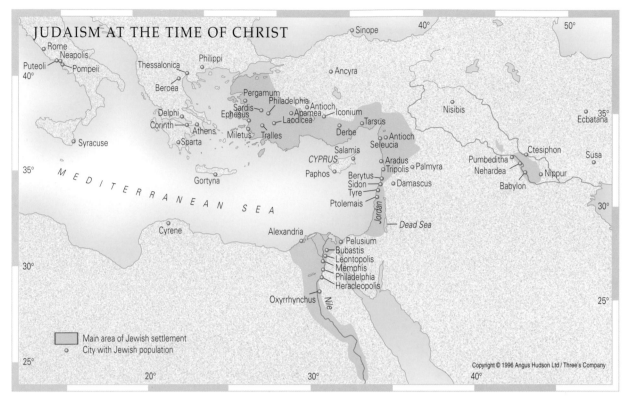

JUDAISM AT THE TIME OF CHRIST

With the coming of the Roman Empire and the Pax Romana, the movement of peoples across the Mediterranean world was made easier. Jews were beginning to spread to the west, beyond Italy. They were also able to spread eastwards through the Parthian Empire, and a sizeable community had established themselves in Babylonia. The main areas of concentration, though, remained in Judaea, Syria, western Asia Minor and Egypt, where Alexandria had become a major centre of Greco-Jewish culture.

JESUS' RESURRECTION

'Christ . . . was raised on the third day according to the Scriptures, and . . . he appeared to Peter, and then to the Twelve. After that, he appeared to more than five hundred of the brothers at the same time, most of whom are still living . . . Then he appeared to James, then to all the apostles, and last of all he appeared to me . . .'
(Paul: 1 Corinthians 15:4-8)

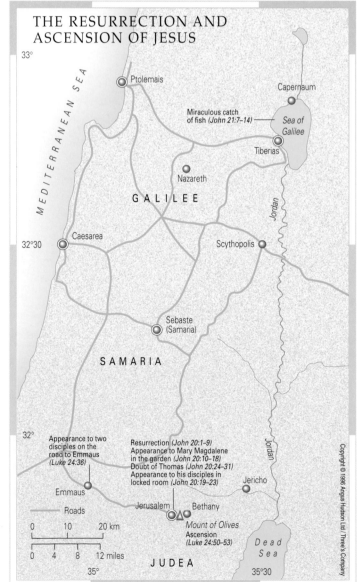

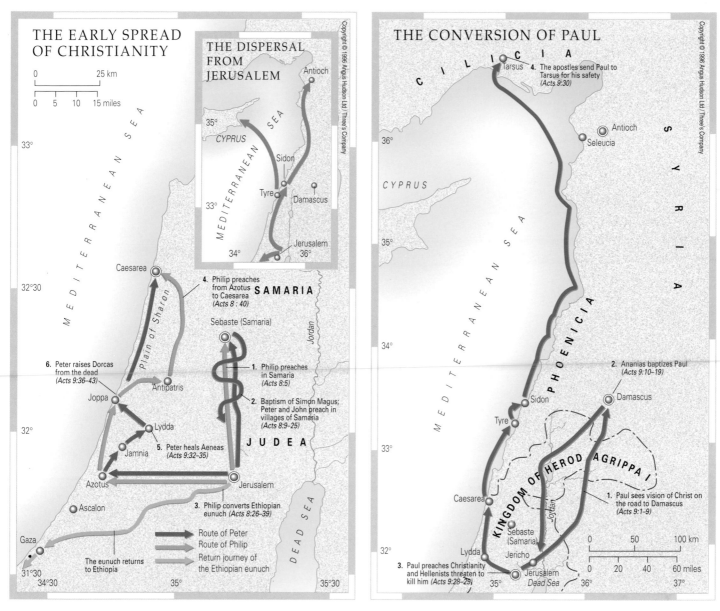

THE EARLY SPREAD OF CHRISTIANITY

0 ————— 25 km
0 5 10 15 miles

THE DISPERSAL FROM JERUSALEM

CYPRUS

MEDITERRANEAN SEA

Antioch

Sidon

Tyre

Damascus

Jerusalem

35°
33°
34°
36°

MEDITERRANEAN SEA

33°

32°30

32°

31°30

34°30   35°   35°30

Caesarea

Plain of Sharon

4. Philip preaches from Azotus to Caesarea (Acts 8 : 40)

SAMARIA

Sebaste (Samaria)

Jordan

1. Philip preaches in Samaria (Acts 8:5)

6. Peter raises Dorcas from the dead (Acts 9:36–43)

Antipatris

2. Baptism of Simon Magus; Peter and John preach in villages of Samaria (Acts 8:9–25)

Joppa

Lydda

JUDEA

Jamnia

5. Peter heals Aeneas (Acts 9:32–35)

Azotus

Jerusalem

Ascalon

DEAD SEA

3. Philip converts Ethiopian eunuch (Acts 8:26–39)

Gaza

Route of Peter
Route of Philip
Return journey of the Ethiopian eunuch

The eunuch returns to Ethiopia

THE CONVERSION OF PAUL

CILICIA

Tarsus   4. The apostles send Paul to Tarsus for his safety (Acts 9:30)

36°

Antioch
Seleucia

SYRIA

CYPRUS

35°

MEDITERRANEAN SEA

34°

PHOENICIA

2. Ananias baptizes Paul (Acts 9:10–19)

Sidon

Damascus

Tyre

33°

KINGDOM OF HEROD AGRIPPA I

1. Paul sees vision of Christ on the road to Damascus (Acts 9:1–9)

Caesarea

Jordan

Sebaste (Samaria)

32°

Lydda

Jericho

3. Paul preaches Christianity and Hellenists threaten to kill him (Acts 9:28–29)

Jerusalem
Dead Sea

35°   36°   37°

0   50   100 km
0   20   40   60 miles

Copyright © 1996 Angus Hudson Ltd /Three's Company

Copyright © 1996 Angus Hudson Ltd /Three's Company

CHRISTIANITY BEFORE PAUL

After the martyrdom of Stephen on the charge of 'blasphemy' (Acts 6:11), many of the apostles left Jerusalem and preached elsewhere. Philip, Peter and John all made conversions in Samaria (Acts 8), a 'no-go' area for religious (or 'strict') Jews. The coastal plain of Judaea, as far as Caesarea, was also evangelized by Peter and Philip. As the persecution of Christians by Jews in Jerusalem became more evident, so Jewish Christians dispersed northwards. They had reached as far as Antioch, third largest city in the Roman Empire, by the time Paul embarked on his missionary journeys (Acts 13).

PAUL'S JOURNEY TO DAMASCUS

Some time after Stephen's death, while Paul (then Saul) was still a Pharisee, he got permission from the Temple authorities to go to Damascus to search out Christians (Acts 9:1-2). It was on the way there that he received his blinding vision of the risen Christ. After regaining his sight in Damascus with the help of Ananias in Straight Street, Paul became a Christian and was himself forced to flee for his life back to Jerusalem (Acts 9:23-26). He was soon in danger again, from Hellenistic Jews, and departed for his home town of Tarsus via Caesarea.

By tradition, Stephen was martyred outside this gate into Jerusalem.

PAUL'S MISSIONARY JOURNEYS

Barnabas, who was preaching in Antioch, went to Tarsus and brought Paul back with him to Antioch. After a brief trip to Jerusalem they, together with Mark, set out on the first of three missionary journeys. Paul and his companions got a mixed reception. When they performed miracle cures they were sometimes treated as gods. At the other extreme, their preaching sometimes caused great offence to traditional Jews and on occasions they were thrown out of town.

The first journey established new churches in Galatia (Acts 13-14). It was probably to these communities that Paul addressed his Letter to the Galatians. The second journey took the gospel into Macedonia, and churches were founded at Philippi and Thessalonica (Acts 15:36 –18:22). Many women were baptized. Women in Greek society had greater freedom than they had in Palestine. They were allowed, for instance, to attend synagogue alongside the men, and so could have heard Paul's preaching. In Achaia, Paul founded the church at Corinth, which was to cause him so much trouble, and he presented his teaching at the highest philosophical court in the Western world: the Areopagus in Athens (Acts 17:19-34).

Roman corn ship from North Africa, on a coin of the Emperor Commodus.

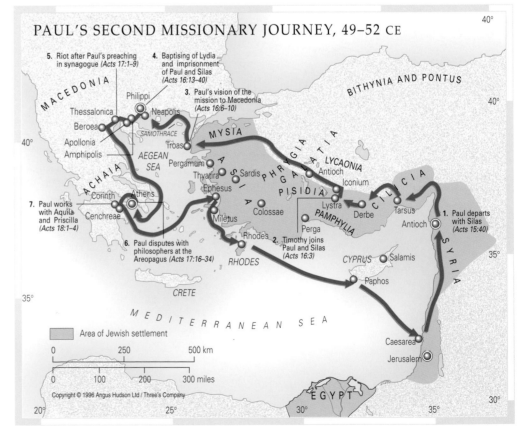

PAUL'S FIRST MISSIONARY JOURNEY, 46–48 CE

3. Paul and Barnabas are mistaken for gods after Paul's healing of a lame man (*Acts 14:8–13*)

2. Elymas the sorcerer is blinded (*Acts 13:6–12*)

1. Paul and Barnabas set sail for Cyprus (*Acts 13:4*)

Area of Jewish settlement

Copyright © 1996 Angus Hudson Ltd / Three's Company

PAUL'S SECOND MISSIONARY JOURNEY, 49–52 CE

5. Riot after Paul's preaching in synagogue (*Acts 17:1–9*)

4. Baptising of Lydia and imprisonment of Paul and Silas (*Acts 16:13–40*)

3. Paul's vision of the mission to Macedonia (*Acts 16:6–10*)

7. Paul works with Aquila and Priscilla (*Acts 18:1–4*)

6. Paul disputes with philosophers at the Areopagus (*Acts 17:16–34*)

2. Timothy joins Paul and Silas (*Acts 16:3*)

1. Paul departs with Silas (*Acts 15:40*)

Area of Jewish settlement

Copyright © 1996 Angus Hudson Ltd / Three's Company

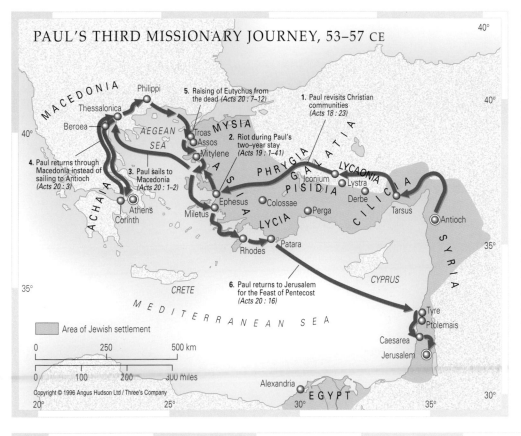

PAUL'S THIRD MISSIONARY JOURNEY, 53–57 CE

MACEDONIA

Philippi

5. Raising of Eutychus from the dead *(Acts 20 : 7–12)*

1. Paul revisits Christian communities *(Acts 18 : 23)*

Thessalonica

Beroea

AEGEAN SEA

MYSIA

Troas

Assos

Mitylene

2. Riot during Paul's two-year stay *(Acts 19 : 1–41)*

PHRYGIA

GALATIA

LYCAONIA

Iconium

4. Paul returns through Macedonia instead of sailing to Antioch *(Acts 20 : 3)*

3. Paul sails to Macedonia *(Acts 20 : 1–2)*

PISIDIA

Lystra

Derbe

CILICIA

ACHAIA

Athens

Corinth

Ephesus

Colossae

Perga

Tarsus

Miletus

LYCIA

Antioch

Rhodes

Patara

SYRIA

6. Paul returns to Jerusalem for the Feast of Pentecost *(Acts 20 : 16)*

CYPRUS

CRETE

Tyre

Ptolemais

M E D I T E R R A N E A N   S E A

Caesarea

Jerusalem

Area of Jewish settlement

0   250   500 km

0   100   200   300 miles

Alexandria

EGYPT

Copyright © 1996 Angus Hudson Ltd / Three's Company

On the third journey, Paul stayed more than two years at Ephesus, building an important Christian community there (Acts 19). Christianity spread out generally in western Asia Minor, reaching Colossae and Laodicea. When he returned to Jerusalem his enemies provoked a riot in the Temple area, which brought about his arrest and trial in Caesarea before the Roman authorities (Acts 21-26).

The voyage to Rome undertaken by Paul in order to have his case heard by the Roman Emperor resulted in a period of house arrest of two years (Acts 28:30). According to tradition he was freed and he then visited Troas, Miletus and Corinth again. Further tradition maintains that he was executed in Rome during the Great Fire in 64 CE.

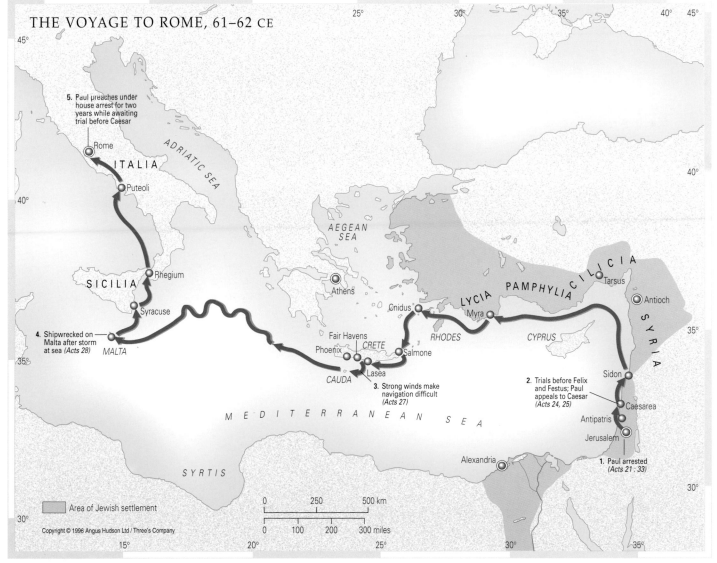

THE VOYAGE TO ROME, 61–62 CE

5. Paul preaches under house arrest for two years while awaiting trial before Caesar

Rome

ITALIA

ADRIATIC SEA

Puteoli

AEGEAN SEA

SICILIA

Rhegium

CILICIA

Athens

Cnidus

PAMPHYLIA

LYCIA

Tarsus

Syracuse

Myra

Antioch

4. Shipwrecked on Malta after storm at sea *(Acts 28)*

MALTA

Fair Havens

RHODES

CYPRUS

SYRIA

Phoenix

CRETE

Salmone

Phoenix

Lasea

CAUDA

Sidon

2. Trials before Felix and Festus; Paul appeals to Caesar *(Acts 24, 25)*

3. Strong winds make navigation difficult *(Acts 27)*

Caesarea

M E D I T E R R A N E A N   S E A

Antipatris

Jerusalem

Alexandria

1. Paul arrested *(Acts 21 : 33)*

SYRTIS

Area of Jewish settlement

0   250   500 km

0   100   200   300 miles

Copyright © 1996 Angus Hudson Ltd / Three's Company

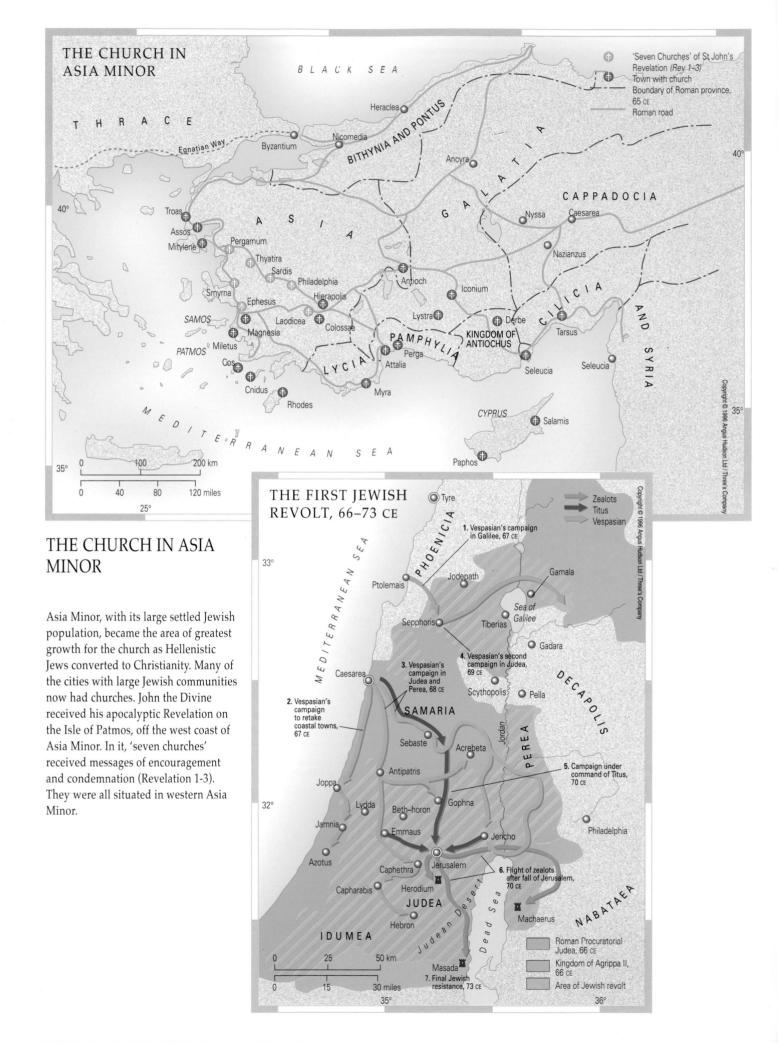

THE CHURCH IN ASIA MINOR

THE CHURCH IN ASIA MINOR

Asia Minor, with its large settled Jewish population, became the area of greatest growth for the church as Hellenistic Jews converted to Christianity. Many of the cities with large Jewish communities now had churches. John the Divine received his apocalyptic Revelation on the Isle of Patmos, off the west coast of Asia Minor. In it, 'seven churches' received messages of encouragement and condemnation (Revelation 1-3). They were all situated in western Asia Minor.

Map legend (The Church in Asia Minor):
'Seven Churches' of St John's Revelation (Rev 1–3)
Town with church
Boundary of Roman province, 65 CE
Roman road

Copyright © 1996 Angus Hudson Ltd / Three's Company

Map legend (The First Jewish Revolt, 66–73 CE):
Zealots
Titus
Vespasian

1. Vespasian's campaign in Galilee, 67 CE
2. Vespasian's campaign to retake coastal towns, 67 CE
3. Vespasian's campaign in Judea and Perea, 68 CE
4. Vespasian's second campaign in Judea, 69 CE
5. Campaign under command of Titus, 70 CE
6. Flight of zealots after fall of Jerusalem, 70 CE
7. Final Jewish resistance, 73 CE

Roman Procuratorial Judea, 66 CE
Kingdom of Agrippa II, 66 CE
Area of Jewish revolt

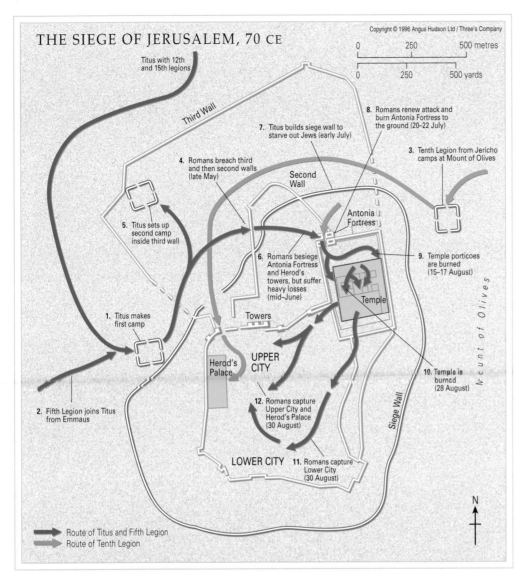

THE SIEGE OF JERUSALEM, 70 CE

Copyright © 1996 Angus Hudson Ltd / Three's Company

0   250   500 metres
0   250   500 yards

Titus with 12th and 15th legions

Third Wall

8. Romans renew attack and burn Antonia Fortress to the ground (20–22 July)

7. Titus builds siege wall to starve out Jews (early July)

3. Tenth Legion from Jericho camps at Mount of Olives

4. Romans breach third and then second walls (late May)

Second Wall

Antonia Fortress

5. Titus sets up second camp inside third wall

6. Romans besiege Antonia Fortress and Herod's towers, but suffer heavy losses (mid–June)

9. Temple porticoes are burned (15–17 August)

Temple

1. Titus makes first camp

Towers

Mount of Olives

Herod's Palace

UPPER CITY

10. Temple is burned (28 August)

2. Fifth Legion joins Titus from Emmaus

12. Romans capture Upper City and Herod's Palace (30 August)

Siege Wall

LOWER CITY   11. Romans capture Lower City (30 August)

N

Route of Titus and Fifth Legion
Route of Tenth Legion

THE FIRST JEWISH REVOLT

From 44 CE, Judaea was under the control of Roman procurators. Since the days of Herod, the Zealot party had been in revolt against Rome. Now, with increasing intolerance towards the Jews, the Roman authorities had caused the Pharisees to join ranks with the Zealots.

Once the revolt had sparked, it spread quickly through most of Judea and Galilee. The Roman general Vespasian arrived in Caesarea and set up his base at Ptolemais. He soon recaptured Galilee and the Golan in 67 CE, before turning south. In spite of the Jews' general hatred of the Romans, the war occasioned a good deal of factional fighting, which the Romans were able to exploit. The Jews' lack of unity resulted in the relentless re-occupation by the Romans of Samaria, Peraea and Judaea.

In spite of some fierce defence by the Zealots, Titus, Vespasian's son, did not take long to capture Jerusalem. He built a siege wall in order to starve out the inhabitants. Within three months of the beginning of the siege, the Temple had been burned and the other buildings destroyed.

Relief of the Romans in procession; another part shows them carrying the sacred vessels of the Temple in triumph after the destruction of Jerusalem, from Titus' Arch, Rome.

THE FALL OF MASADA

Masada is a massive outcrop of rock in the Judaean Desert. Herod the Great built a palace complex on the top. After the fall of Jerusalem a Zealot group under Eleazar took refuge there. With plenty of food and water, they were able to withstand the Roman offensive until 73 CE.

The Romans first built a siege wall around the rock to prevent the supply of more rations. They then built an earthen ramp up to the west side of the rock. On that, a base of wood and iron supported a siege tower. The Romans then had a vantage point from which to breach, with a battering ram, the main wall that surrounded the summit of the rock. Realising their hopeless plight, the 960 refugee Jews committed suicide overnight while waiting for the final assault.

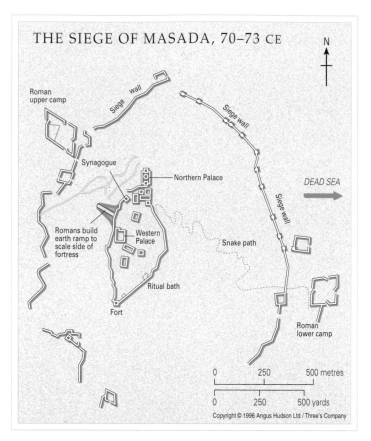

THE SIEGE OF MASADA, 70–73 CE

N

Roman upper camp

Siege wall

Siege wall

Synagogue

Northern Palace

DEAD SEA

Romans build earth ramp to scale side of fortress

Western Palace

Snake path

Siege wall

Ritual bath

Fort

Roman lower camp

| 0 | 250 | 500 metres |
| 0 | 250 | 500 yards |

Copyright © 1996 Angus Hudson Ltd / Three's Company

Replica of a Roman siege-engine, designed to catapult stones into a besieged stronghold such as Masada.

This view of Herod's Masada stronghold shows clearly the ramp constructed by the Romans to force their way in.

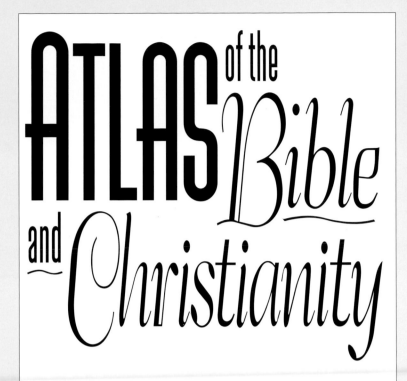

ATLAS of the Bible and Christianity

THE EARLY CHURCH

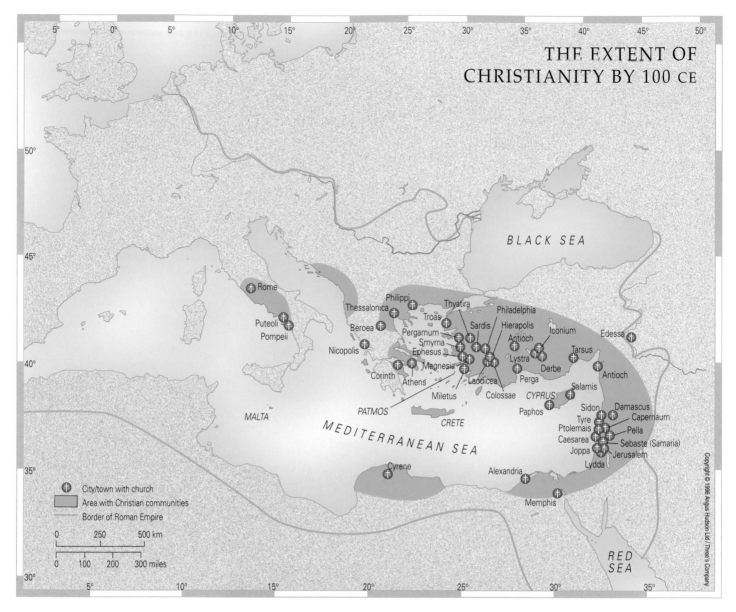

Legend:
- City/town with church
- Area with Christian communities
- Border of Roman Empire

0   250   500 km

0   100   200   300 miles

THE SPREAD OF CHRISTIANITY BY 100 CE

Paul and his fellow Jewish apostles carried the gospel to regions beyond Palestine. With the express purpose of evangelizing the Gentiles, they travelled extensively in Asia Minor and Greece. They visited synagogues in the Jewish Diaspora and talked with Gentiles in the marketplaces. Behind them they left small, uncertain groups of Christians whose faith was nurtured in subsequent visits and in the letters we know from the New Testament.

By the end of the first century Christianity was still virtually confined to the eastern Roman Empire, except for the communities in Rome, Puteoli and those around the Bay of Naples. The only possible church known outside the empire was at Edessa. Names of cities with Christians are known from the New Testament, such as the seven churches of Revelation, and from contemporary correspondence. Ignatius tells of churches in Magnesia and Tralles, and later writers of Alexandria, the home of Paul's helper, Apollos.

Patmos, the Aegean island to which John the Divine was exiled.

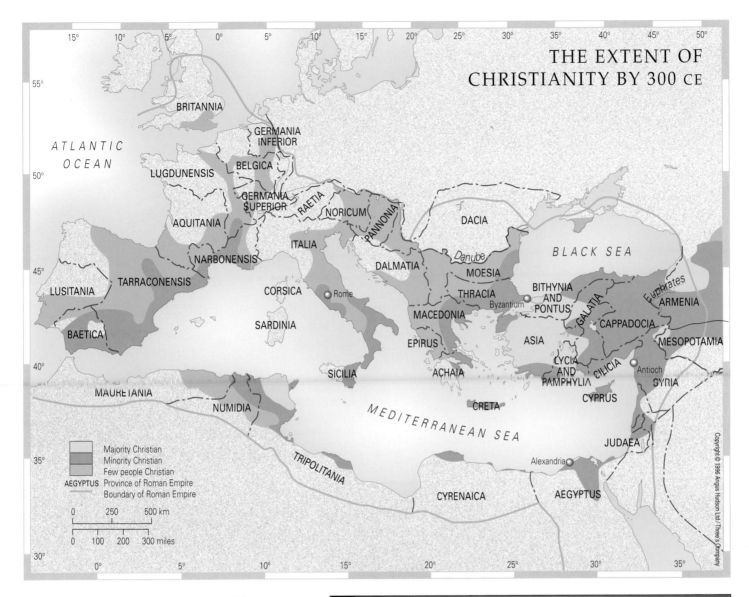

Majority Christian
Minority Christian
Few people Christian
AEGYPTUS Province of Roman Empire
Boundary of Roman Empire

0   250   500 km

0 100 200 300 miles

THE SPREAD OF CHRISTIANITY BY 300 CE

By the end of the third century the complexion of the Christian world was quite different. In the changes following the failure of the Jewish revolts, the Church and Judaism had increasingly gone their separate ways, and Christianity had become largely a religion of the Gentiles. With the expansion of the Church westwards as far as Roman Britain, its informal centre had shifted from Jerusalem to Rome. The scene was set for the Emperor Constantine to embrace Christianity around 312 CE. By the end of the fourth century it would be the official religion of the empire.

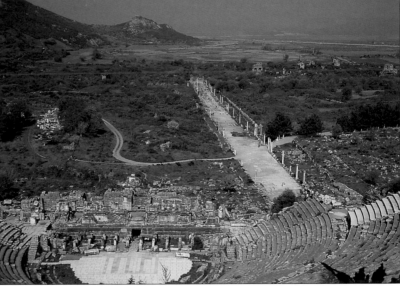

The view from the great theatre at Ephesus, an important Christian centre.

75

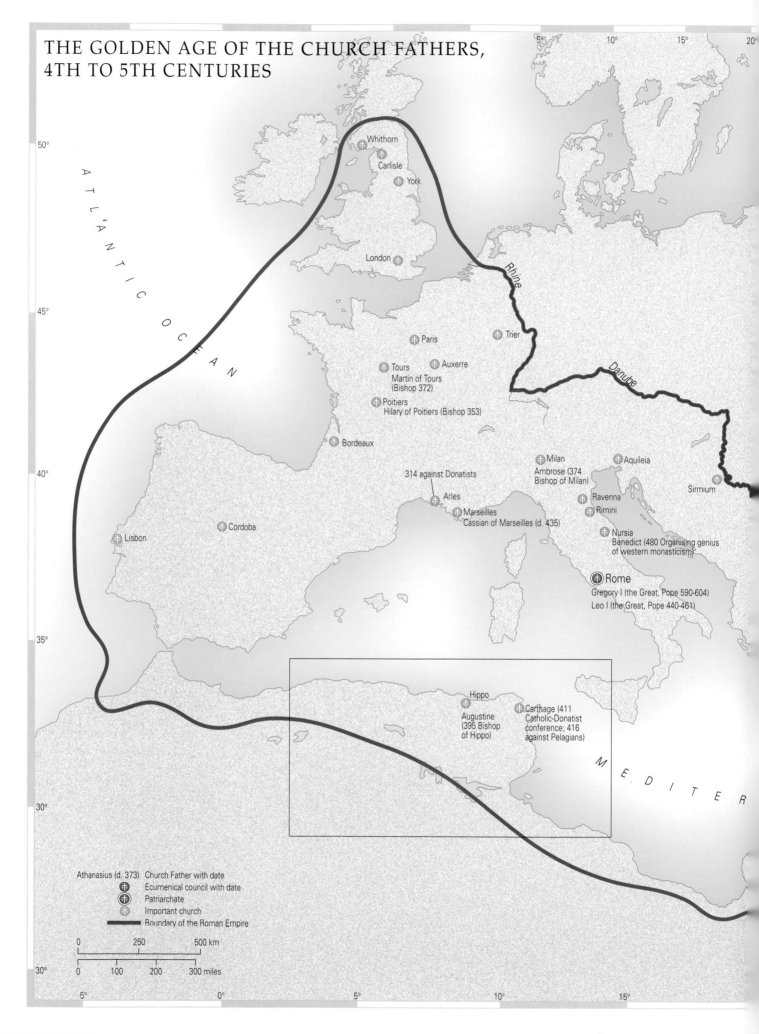

THE GOLDEN AGE OF THE CHURCH FATHERS, 4TH TO 5TH CENTURIES

ATLANTIC OCEAN

Whithorn

Carlisle

York

London

Rhine

Paris

Trier

Tours
Martin of Tours
(Bishop 372)

Auxerre

Poitiers
Hilary of Poitiers (Bishop 353)

Danube

Bordeaux

314 against Donatists

Milan
Ambrose (374
Bishop of Milan)

Aquileia

Arles

Ravenna

Sirmium

Marseilles
Cassian of Marseilles (d. 435)

Rimini

Cordoba

Nursia
Benedict (480 Organising genius
of western monasticism)

Lisbon

Rome
Gregory I (the Great, Pope 590-604)
Leo I (the Great, Pope 440-461)

Hippo
Augustine
(395 Bishop
of Hippo)

Carthage (411
Catholic-Donatist
conference; 416
against Pelagians)

MEDITER

Athanasius (d. 373)   Church Father with date
Ecumenical council with date
Patriarchate
Important church
Boundary of the Roman Empire

0   250   500 km

0   100   200   300 miles

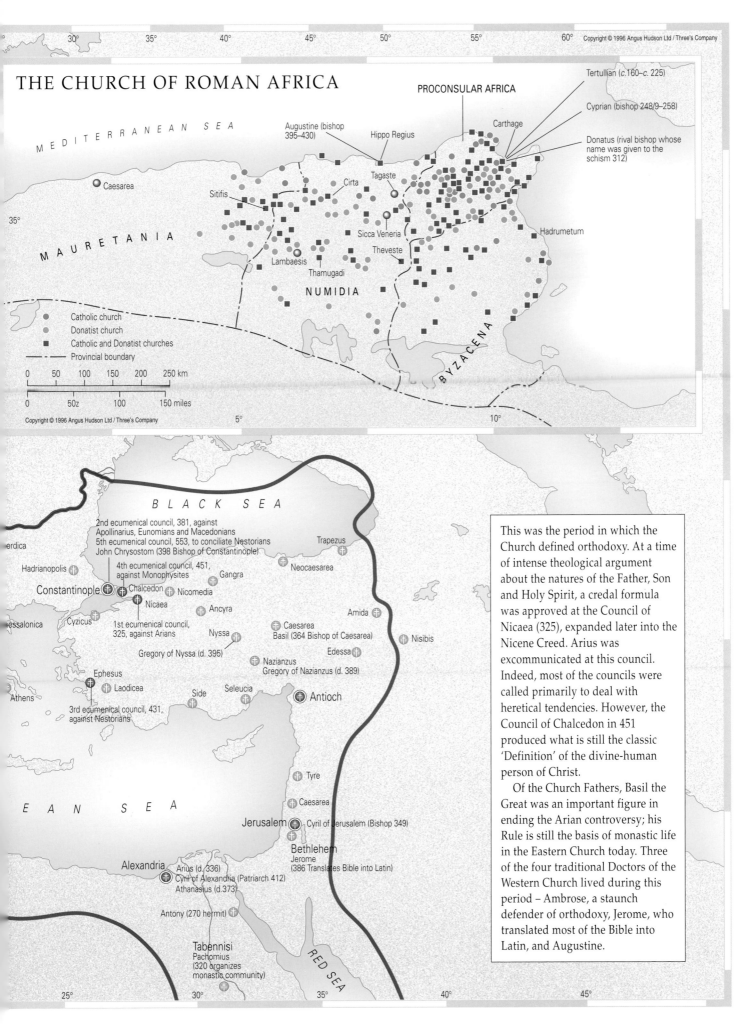

THE CHURCH OF ROMAN AFRICA

MEDITERRANEAN SEA

PROCONSULAR AFRICA

Tertullian (c.160–c. 225)

Cyprian (bishop 248/9–258)

Donatus (rival bishop whose name was given to the schism 312)

Carthage

Augustine (bishop 395–430)

Hippo Regius

Caesarea

Cirta

Tagaste

Sitifis

MAURETANIA

Hadrumetum

Sicca Veneria

Lambaesis

Theveste

Thamugadi

NUMIDIA

BYZACENA

- ● Catholic church
- ● Donatist church
- ■ Catholic and Donatist churches
- —·— Provincial boundary

0 50 100 150 200 250 km

0 50z 100 150 miles

Copyright © 1996 Angus Hudson Ltd / Three's Company

BLACK SEA

erdica

2nd ecumenical council, 381, against Apollinarius, Eunomians and Macedonians
5th ecumenical council, 553, to conciliate Nestorians
John Chrysostom (398 Bishop of Constantinople)

Trapezus

Hadrianopolis

4th ecumenical council, 451, against Monophysites

Gangra

Neocaesarea

Constantinople

Chalcedon

Nicomedia

Cyzicus

Nicaea

Ancyra

Amida

essalonica

1st ecumenical council, 325, against Arians

Caesarea
Basil (364 Bishop of Caesarea)

Nyssa

Nisibis

Gregory of Nyssa (d. 395)

Edessa

Nazianzus
Gregory of Nazianzus (d. 389)

Ephesus

Laodicea

Athens

Side

Seleucia

3rd ecumenical council, 431, against Nestorians

Antioch

EAN SEA

Tyre

Caesarea

Jerusalem

Cyril of Jerusalem (Bishop 349)

Bethlehem
Jerome
(386 Translates Bible into Latin)

Alexandria

Arius (d. 336)
Cyril of Alexandria (Patriarch 412)
Athanasius (d.373)

Antony (270 hermit)

Tabennisi
Pachomius
(320 organizes monastic community)

RED SEA

This was the period in which the Church defined orthodoxy. At a time of intense theological argument about the natures of the Father, Son and Holy Spirit, a credal formula was approved at the Council of Nicaea (325), expanded later into the Nicene Creed. Arius was excommunicated at this council. Indeed, most of the councils were called primarily to deal with heretical tendencies. However, the Council of Chalcedon in 451 produced what is still the classic 'Definition' of the divine-human person of Christ.

Of the Church Fathers, Basil the Great was an important figure in ending the Arian controversy; his Rule is still the basis of monastic life in the Eastern Church today. Three of the four traditional Doctors of the Western Church lived during this period – Ambrose, a staunch defender of orthodoxy, Jerome, who translated most of the Bible into Latin, and Augustine.

EARLY CHRISTIAN PILGRIMS

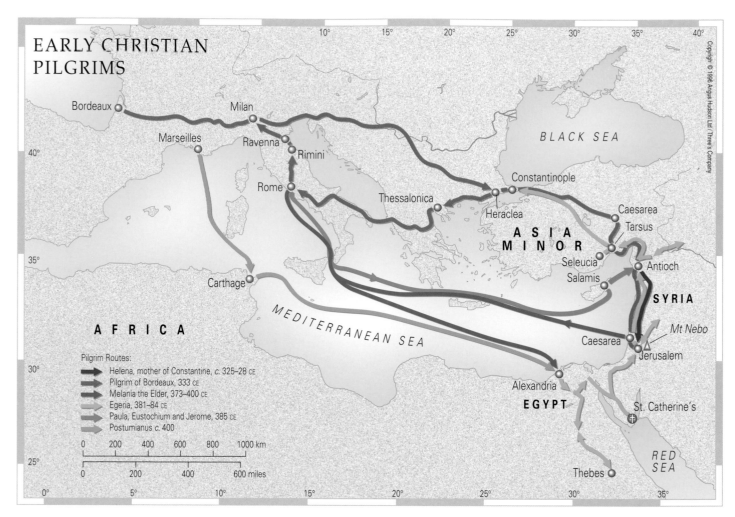

Pilgrim Routes:

➤ Helena, mother of Constantine, c. 325–28 CE
➤ Pilgrim of Bordeaux, 333 CE
➤ Melania the Elder, 373–400 CE
➤ Egeria, 381–84 CE
➤ Paula, Eustochium and Jerome, 385 CE
➤ Postumianus c. 400

```
0    200   400   600   800   1000 km
0         200        400      600 miles
```

THE CHURCH OF ROMAN NORTH AFRICA

By the end of the second century the African Church was a theological force in Catholicism. Tertullian and Cyprian of Carthage laid the groundwork of major Christian doctrines, including the Trinity and Original Sin. Augustine of Hippo developed these doctrines when he expounded his teachings on the church and sacraments, and predestination and grace, during the controversies with the Donatists and the Pelagians.

One of the most bitter controversies of the Early Church was the Donatist schism. Many bishops from Numidia refused to accept Caecilian as the bishop of Carthage because he was consecrated by one who had 'lapsed' during the Great Persecution of Diocletian (303-313). Known from their first great leader as Donatists, they formed the 'true', or pure, church.

Donatism remained the stronger church until the influential ministry of Augustine gave Catholicism the upper hand. However, the Catholic Church suffered a setback when the Vandals, mainly Arian, invaded in 429. Despite a revival under Justinian (534), further expansion of the African Church was halted by the Arab conquest in the seventh century.

The Emperor Diocletian (303-313) initiated the Great Persecution of the church, which affected Africa more severely than elsewhere.

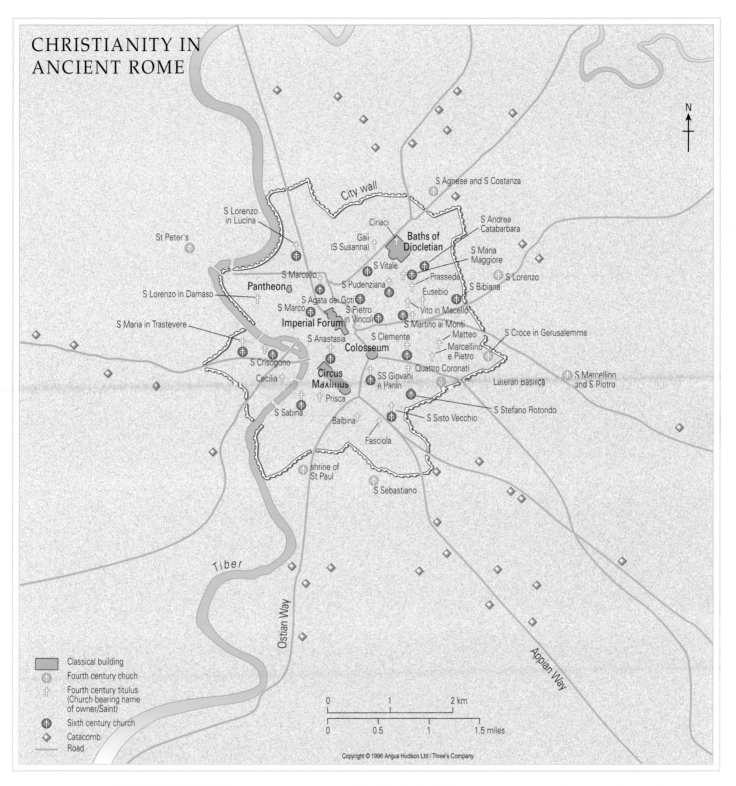

CHRISTIANITY IN ANCIENT ROME

S Agnese and S Costanza

City wall

S Lorenzo
in Lucina

St Peter's

Ciriaci

Gaii
(S Susanna)

Baths of
Diocletian

S Andrea
Catabarbara

S Maria
Maggiore

S Vitale

S Lorenzo

S Marcello

Prassede

Pantheon

S Pudenziana

Eusebio

S Bibiana

S Lorenzo in Damaso

S Agata dei Goti

S Pietro
in Vincoli

Vito in Macello

S Marco

S Martino ai Monti

S Maria in Trastevere

Imperial Forum

S Clemente

Matteo

S Croce in Gerusalemme

S Anastasia

Colosseum

Marcellino
e Pietro

Quattro Coronati

S Crisogono

Circus
Maximus

SS Giovani
e Paolo

Lateran Basilica

S Marcellino
and S Pietro

Cecilia

Prisca

S Sisto Vecchio

S Stefano Rotondo

S Sabina

Balbina

Fasciola

shrine of
St Paul

S Sebastiano

N

Tiber

Ostian Way

Appian Way

▨	Classical building
✛	Fourth century chuch
✝	Fourth century titulus (Church bearing name of owner/Saint)
✛	Sixth century church
◇	Catacomb
—	Road

0   1   2 km

0   0.5   1   1.5 miles

Copyright © 1996 Angus Hudson Ltd / Three's Company

CHRISTIANS IN ANCIENT ROME

The first known Christian community in Rome was that to which Paul addressed his Letter to the Romans, *c.* 58 CE. Both Paul and Peter were martyred, according to tradition, after the fire of Rome (64 CE) during Nero's reign. Christians were often, as then, scapegoats and suffered periodic persecution. During the Decian Persecution (249-51), Fabian, bishop of Rome, was martyred. The Christians built distinctive burial-places, the catacombs, which by Roman law were inviolable but had to be built outside the city wall.

After the toleration of the Edict of Milan (313), the church in Rome grew. The authority of the popes increased and many churches were built under Pope Sylvester I (314-35) and his successors. Christianity appealed to men and women of every class. Marcella (325-410) is famous for using her palace on the Aventine Hill as a Christian centre at which Jerome taught. She, along with many other Christians, died when the Visigoths sacked Rome in 410.

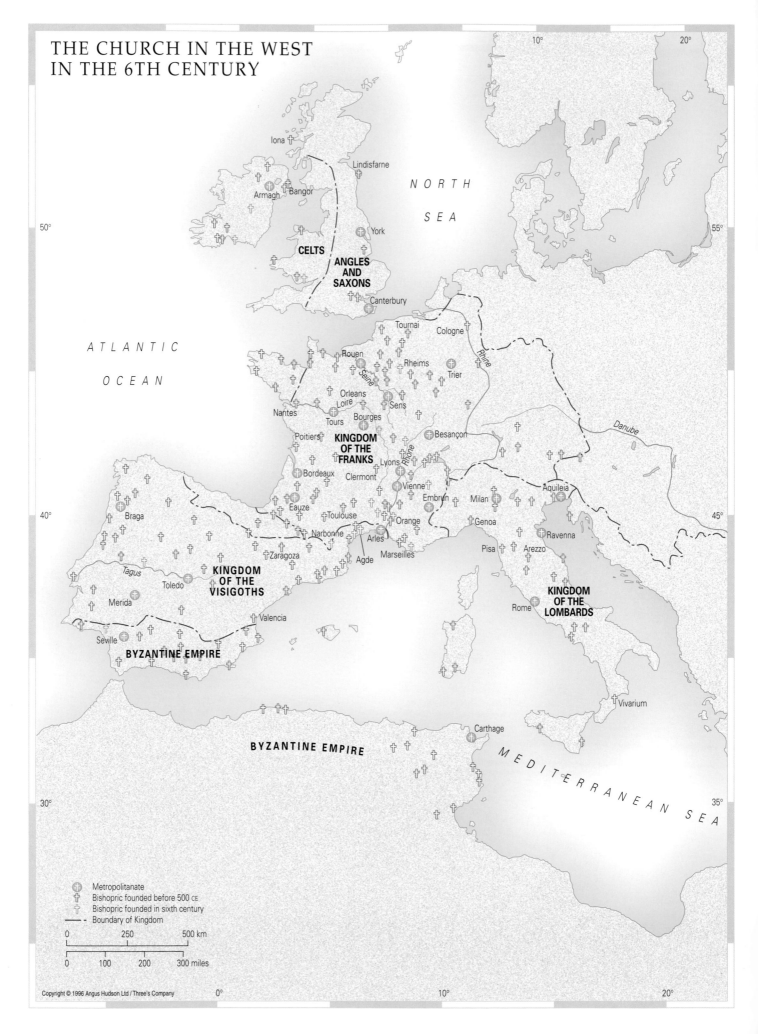

THE CHURCH IN THE WEST
IN THE 6TH CENTURY

NORTH SEA

Iona

Lindisfarne

Armagh · Bangor

York

CELTS

ANGLES AND SAXONS

Canterbury

ATLANTIC OCEAN

Tournai

Cologne

Rouen

Rheims

Trier

Seine

Rhine

Orleans

Loire

Sens

Nantes

Bourges

Besançon

Poitiers

Tours

KINGDOM OF THE FRANKS

Danube

Bordeaux

Clermont

Lyons

Rhône

Vienne

Braga

Eauze

Embrun

Milan

Aquileia

Toulouse

Orange

Narbonne

Arles

Agde

Marseilles

Genoa

Ravenna

Tagus

Zaragoza

Pisa

Arezzo

Toledo

KINGDOM OF THE VISIGOTHS

Merida

Valencia

KINGDOM OF THE LOMBARDS

Rome

Seville

BYZANTINE EMPIRE

Vivarium

Carthage

BYZANTINE EMPIRE

MEDITERRANEAN SEA

Metropolitanate
Bishopric founded before 500 CE
Bishopric founded in sixth century
Boundary of Kingdom

0   250   500 km
0   100   200   300 miles

Copyright © 1996 Angus Hudson Ltd / Three's Company

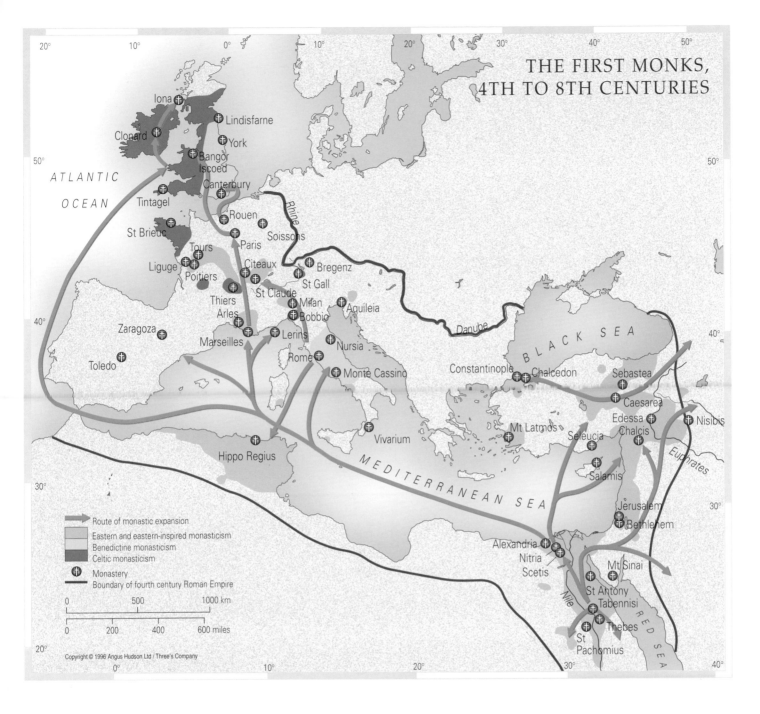

THE CHURCH IN THE WEST IN THE SIXTH CENTURY

The most influential figure in the sixth-century Western Church was Pope Gregory I, 'the Great' (c. 540-604). He set his sights on the northern frontiers of Christendom, and his attempts to gather in the pagan tribes of England and Germany signalled the gradual turning of Christianity from a Mediterranean to a European religion. Church leaders encouraged popular forms of Christian piety which appealed to the pagan mind. Miraculous cures associated with shrines and holy relics, and the protection of patron saints became more prevalent.

As the authority of the papacy grew, so did its estates. Known later as the Patrimony of St Peter, they grew from Constantine's reign, when the churches could own property without restriction. The Ostrogothic Kingdom was supplanted by Lombard invaders from Germany who formed a kingdom in 584.

THE FIRST MONKS

From the middle of the third century Christian hermits led ascetic lives in the Egyptian and Syrian deserts. St Antony (251?-356) attracted a large community of hermits, c. 305; St Pachomius (c. 290-346) initiated the communal style of living with his first monastery at Tabennisi. Monasticism spread out from Egypt and Syria in the fourth century. Basil of Caesarea wrote a less extreme Rule for the Eastern Church, and Benedict of Nursia formulated a Rule which was adopted in the West. Benedictine monasticism was slow to catch on, but from the eighth century until the twelfth became virtually the sole form of religious life.

81

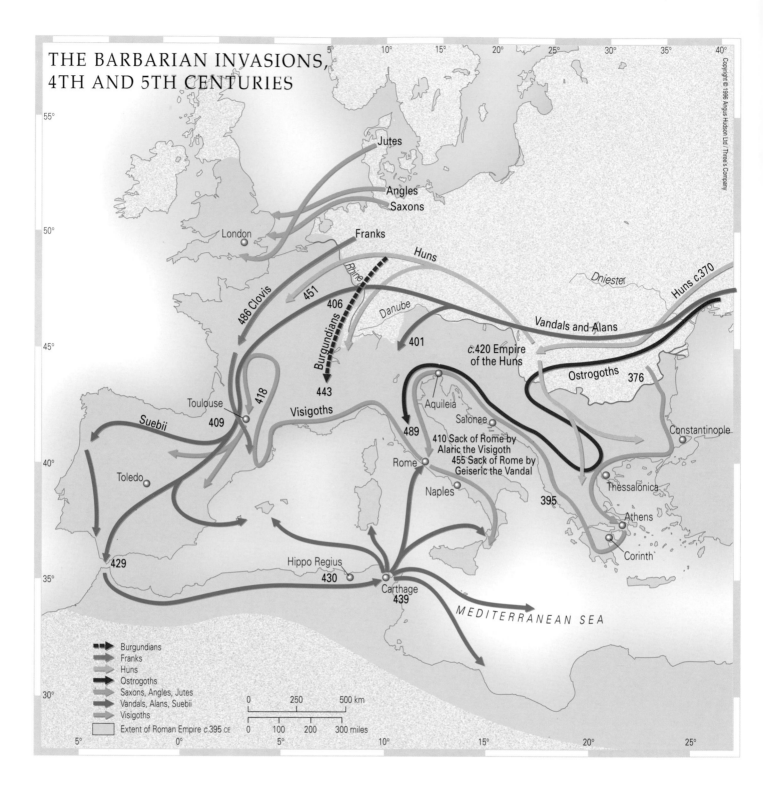

Jutes

Angles
Saxons

Franks

Huns

London

486 Clovis

451

406

Burgundians

443

401

*c.*420 Empire
of the Huns

Dniester

Huns *c.*370

Vandals and Alans

Ostrogoths   376

Toulouse

418

Visigoths

Suebii

409

Aquileia

Salonae

489

410 Sack of Rome by
Alaric the Visigoth
455 Sack of Rome by
Geiseric the Vandal

Constantinople

Toledo

Rome

Naples

395

Thessalonica

Athens

Corinth

Hippo Regius

430

Carthage
439

MEDITERRANEAN SEA

Burgundians
Franks
Huns
Ostrogoths
Saxons, Angles, Jutes
Vandals, Alans, Suebii
Visigoths
Extent of Roman Empire *c.*395 CE

0   250   500 km

0   100   200   300 miles

THE BARBARIAN
INVASIONS

Ever since the third century the Goths
had been making raids on the Danube
frontier of the Roman Empire. In the
fourth century the Goths divided into
the Visigoths (west of the River
Dniester) and the Ostrogoths (east of
the River Dniester), and both were
forced southwards and westwards after
376 by the Huns. The Visigoths were
allowed to settle in the Balkans, but
only under a huge tax burden. Their
rebellion eventually brought about the
sack of Rome in 410.

In the fifth century, massive
population movements threw Western
Europe into political turmoil. When the
menace of the Huns diminished after
the death of Attila in 453, other
Barbarian peoples asserted claims to
territories. The Frankish leader Clovis
took advantage of the disintegrating
Roman Empire and united northern
Gaul under himself in 494. His adoption
of Christianity brought the mass
conversion of Franks to the Catholic
Church. Clovis' successors formed the
successful Merovingian dynasty, who
ruled the Frankish Kingdom until the
Carolingians emerged in the eighth
century. The Visigoths maintained a
strong kingdom in Spain and southern
Gaul. The Vandals established a
kingdom in North Africa.

Wulfila the Goth converted most of
his people to Arian Christianity around
350. In turn, many of the Germanic
tribes who came into contact with the
Goths, such as the Vandals, also
adopted Arianism. The threat to

THE BARBARIAN KINGDOMS, *c.* 530

ATLANTIC OCEAN

CELTS

ANGLES

SAXONS

London

JUTES

JUTES

SAXONS

THURINGIANS

Rhine

Trier

Paris

LOMBARDS

Danube

SLAVS

FRANKS

ALAMANNI

BURGUNDIANS

Geneva

Milan

OSTROGOTHS

Sirmium

Ravenna

ROMAN EMPIRE

Constantinople

SUEBII

BASQUES

Toulouse

Narbonne

CORSICA

Rome

Thessalonica

Toledo

SARDINIA

VISIGOTHS

BALEARICS

Athens

Cordoba

SICILY

CRETE

Carthage

Hippo Regius

MEDITERRANEAN SEA

VANDALS

Catholic orthodoxy was compounded when the Arian Ostrogoths ruled in Italy (493-553).

The Anglo-Saxon invasions of Britain pushed back the Celtic Church and left the field clear for the Roman Christianity of Augustine to take new hold in England after 597.

Canterbury Cathedral, Kent.

83

JUSTINIAN'S EMPIRE

When Justinian I became Byzantine emperor in 527, Italy, western North Africa and southern Spain were in the hands of Germanic tribes. By the end of his reign in 565 he had conquered all these lands and at Ravenna instituted an 'Exarchate' government over Italy. This extension of the Byzantine Empire over lands of the West helped to strengthen Catholicism as the Arian leadership of the Vandals in North Africa and the Ostrogoths in Italy disappeared.

Justinian strove in vain to unite opposing factions in the Church. At the Council of Chalcedon in 451 the Monophysites and Nestorians had been declared heretics. However, the Monophysites remained strong in the Middle East, giving rise to the Coptic Church in Egypt and, in time, the Syrian Orthodox Church. Nestorianism took root in the Persian Empire and gradually expanded eastwards.

Justinian is credited with building a number of churches, including the reconstruction of Hagia Sophia after its burning during riots in Constantinople, and developing St Catherine's Monastery at the foot of Mt Sinai.

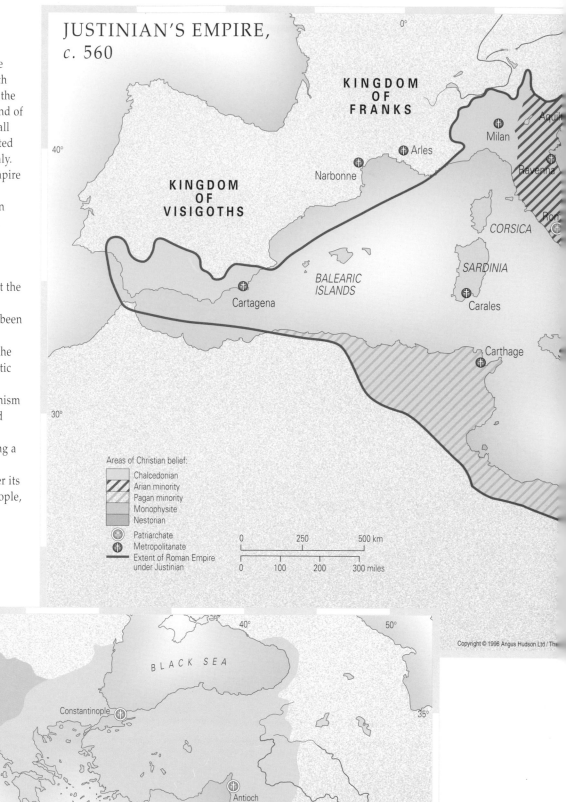

JUSTINIAN'S EMPIRE, *c. 560*

KINGDOM OF FRANKS

KINGDOM OF VISIGOTHS

Arles
Narbonne
Milan
Ravenna
Aqui
Rom
CORSICA
SARDINIA
Carales
Cartagena
BALEARIC ISLANDS
Carthage

Areas of Christian belief:
- Chalcedonian
- Arian minority
- Pagan minority
- Monophysite
- Nestorian
- ⊕ Patriarchate
- ⊕ Metropolitanate
- — Extent of Roman Empire under Justinian

| 0 | 250 | 500 km |
| 0 | 100 | 200 | 300 miles |

BLACK SEA

Rome
Constantinople
Antioch
MEDITERRANEAN SEA
Jerusalem
Alexandria
RED SEA

THE FIVE PATRIARCHATES, 6TH CENTURY

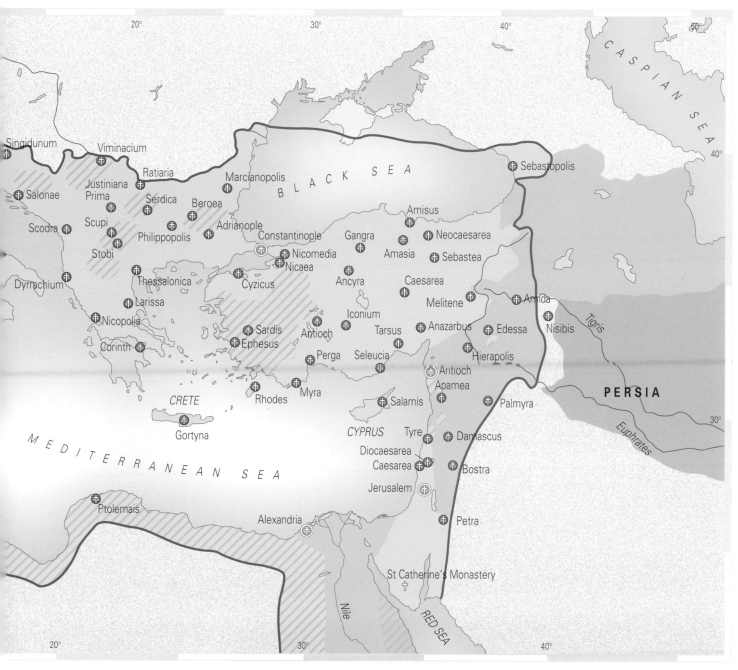

Singidunum
Viminacium
Ratiaria
Salonae
Justiniana Prima
Serdica
Beroea
Scodra
Scupi
Philippopolis
Stobi
Dyrrachium
Thessalonica
Larissa
Nicopolis
Corinth
Sardis
Ephesus
CRETE
Gortyna

MEDITERRANEAN SEA

Ptolemais
Alexandria

BLACK SEA
Marcianopolis
Adrianople
Constantinople
Nicomedia
Nicaea
Cyzicus
Antioch
Perga
Rhodes
Myra

Amisus
Gangra
Neocaesarea
Amasia
Sebastea
Ancyra
Caesarea
Iconium
Melitene
Tarsus
Anazarbus
Seleucia
Antioch
Apamea
Salamis
CYPRUS
Tyre
Diocaesarea
Caesarea
Jerusalem

Sebastopolis
Amida
Edessa
Nisibis
Hierapolis
Palmyra
Damascus
Bostra
Petra

CASPIAN SEA
PERSIA
Tigris
Euphrates

Nile
RED SEA

St Catherine's Monastery

20° 30° 40° 50°
40°
30°
20° 30° 40°

THE PATRIARCHATES

At the beginning of the fourth century, Rome, Alexandria and Antioch were the primary sees of the Church. The later rise in importance of the sees at Constantinople and Jerusalem meant that by the sixth century there were five pre-eminent bishops who were titled 'Patriarchs', with jurisdiction over their associated lands.

St Catherine's Monastery, at the foot of Mount Sinai, was probably developed by Justinian.

85

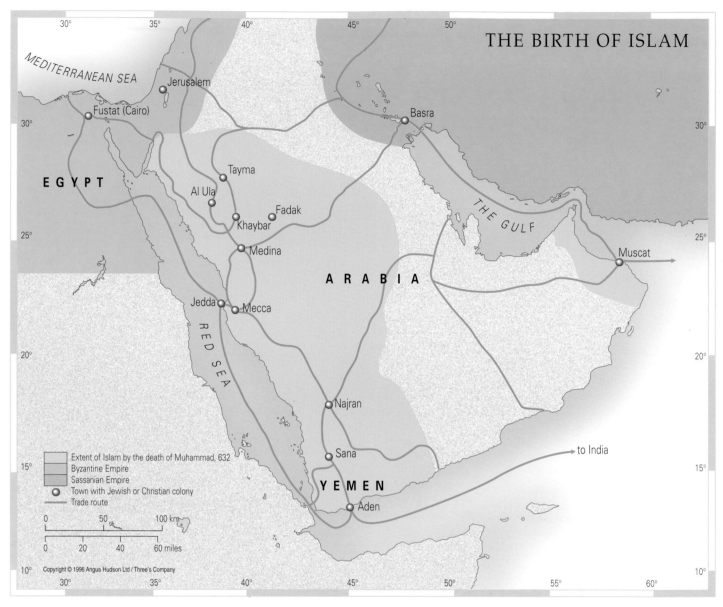

Extent of Islam by the death of Muhammad, 632
Byzantine Empire
Sassanian Empire
Town with Jewish or Christian colony
Trade route

0   50   100 km
0   20   40   60 miles

Copyright © 1996 Angus Hudson Ltd / Three's Company

THE BIRTH OF ISLAM

The *'hijra'* or 'emigration' of the Prophet Muhammad from Mecca to Medina in 622 CE marks the beginning of the Islamic calendar. The people of Medina were sympathetic to his teachings about the oneness of God and the wickedness of materialism. As an outsider, Muhammad was also able to arbitrate in tribal quarrels and soon established an authority as a leader. His successes on the battlefield meant that, by his death in 632, most of western Arabia had turned to follow his new religion, Islam.

Muhammad saw Judaism and Christianity as precursors of Islam. He regarded himself as the 'seal' of a line of prophets which began with Abraham and included Jesus. He was therefore friendly to Jewish and Christian populations of the towns he converted to Islam. The rapidity with which Islam swept through North Africa and the Middle East in the early years is an indicator partly of how tolerant Islam was as a society allowing the practice of other monotheistic religions, and partly of how receptive those 'conquered' peoples were to Islam. In only one or two generations most Christians had converted to Islam, after some six centuries of Roman and Byzantine rule.

The Monophysite and Nestorian churches of Egypt, Ethiopia and the Middle East not only survived Islam but had a common enemy with it: Byzantium. An Arab Christian culture had developed since the fifth century and it came to reside more easily in an Islamic community than in a Byzantine one which was dominated by Chalcedonian orthodoxy. The successor to Muhammad, Abu Bakr (632-34), took Islam to the frontier of Byzantium in Syria and his successor, Umar (634-44), provoked a counter-offensive. The ensuing battle at Yarmuk (*c.* 636) resulted in a Muslim victory and opened the door to further conquests in northern Syria and Iraq.

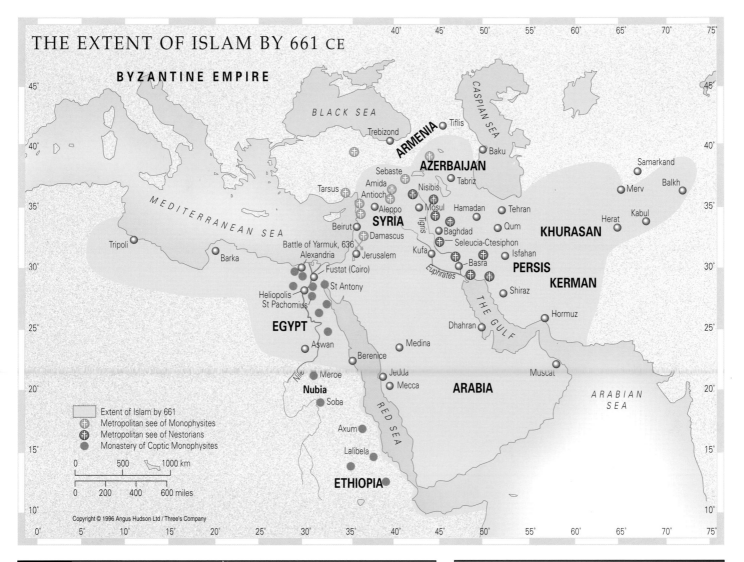

THE EXTENT OF ISLAM BY 661 CE

BYZANTINE EMPIRE

BLACK SEA

MEDITERRANEAN SEA

CASPIAN SEA

Trebizond

Tiflis

ARMENIA

Baku

AZERBAIJAN

Sebaste

Tarsus

Amida

Tabriz

Nisibis

Samarkand

Antioch

Mosul

Merv

Balkh

Aleppo

Hamadan

Tehran

KHURASAN

Herat

Kabul

Beirut

SYRIA

Baghdad

Qum

Damascus

Seleucia-Ctesiphon

Battle of Yarmuk, 636

Kufa

Isfahan

PERSIS

Tripoli

Jerusalem

Basra

Alexandria

Shiraz

KERMAN

Barka

Fustat (Cairo)

St Antony

Heliopolis

St Pachomius

Dhahran

Hormuz

EGYPT

Aswan

Medina

Berenice

Jedda

Muscat

ARABIA

ARABIAN SEA

Meroe

Mecca

Nubia

Soba

Axum

RED SEA

Lalibela

ETHIOPIA

	Extent of Islam by 661
	Metropolitan see of Monophysites
	Metropolitan see of Nestorians
	Monastery of Coptic Monophysites

0   500   1000 km

0   200   400   600 miles

Copyright © 1996 Angus Hudson Ltd / Three's Company

The Dome of the Rock, Jerusalem, is a major Islamic shrine.

Islam spread to Egypt too at this time.

87

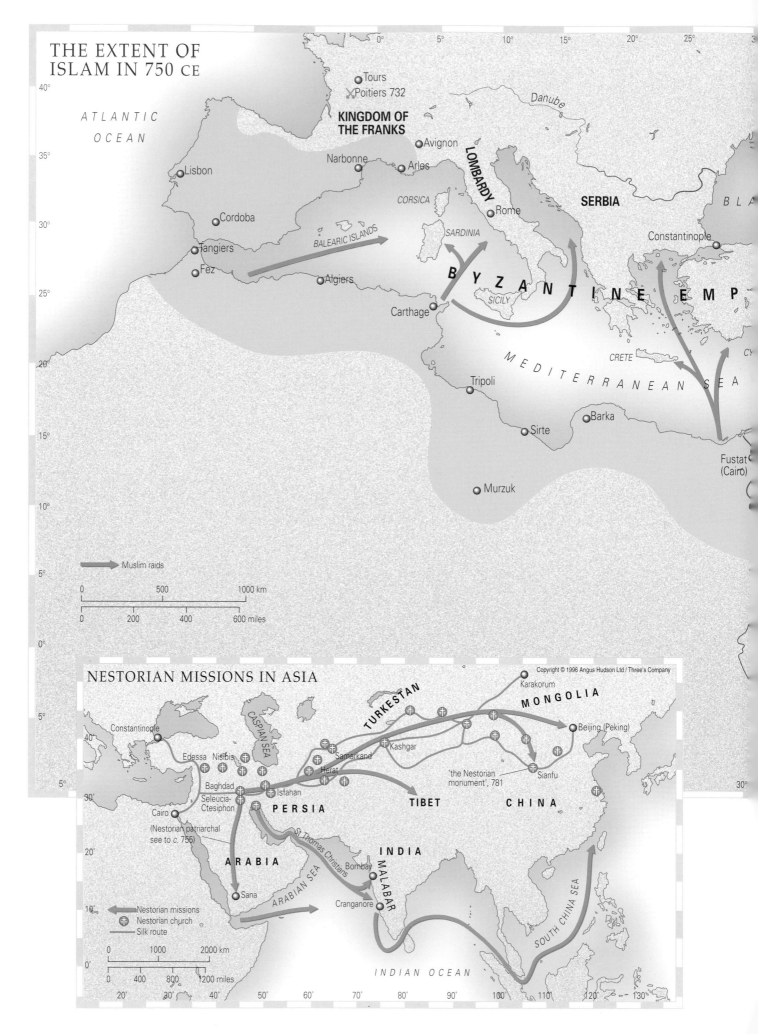

THE EXTENT OF ISLAM IN 750 CE

ATLANTIC OCEAN

Tours
Poitiers 732

KINGDOM OF THE FRANKS

Avignon

Narbonne
Arles

LOMBARDY

Lisbon

Cordoba

CORSICA

Rome

SARDINIA

SERBIA

Constantinople

B Y Z A N T I N E   E M P

BALEARIC ISLANDS

Tangiers
Fez

Algiers

SICILY

Carthage

BLA

CRETE

CY

M E D I T E R R A N E A N   S E A

Tripoli

Barka

Sirte

Fustat (Cairo)

Murzuk

→ Muslim raids

0   500   1000 km

0   200   400   600 miles

NESTORIAN MISSIONS IN ASIA

Copyright © 1996 Angus Hudson Ltd / Three's Company

Karakorum

TURKESTAN

MONGOLIA

Constantinople

CASPIAN SEA

Samarkand

Kashgar

Beijing (Peking)

Edessa Nisibis

Herat

'the Nestorian monument', 781

Sianfu

Baghdad
Seleucia-Ctesiphon

Isfahan

PERSIA

TIBET

CHINA

Cairo

(Nestorian patriarchal see to c. 755)

St Thomas Christians

INDIA

Bombay

MALABAR

ARABIA

ARABIAN SEA

Cranganore

Sana

← Nestorian missions
✠ Nestorian church
— Silk route

SOUTH CHINA SEA

0   1000   2000 km

0   400   800   1200 miles

INDIAN OCEAN

88

HAZAR KHANATE

CASPIAN SEA

Tiflis

Baku

○ Samarkand

○ Bukhara

Tabriz

Kabul

Tehran

Herat

Mosul

Kandahar

Multan

Antioch

Euphrates

Tarsus

Tigris

Damascus

Isfahan

Mansurd

Indus

Jerusalem

Baghdad

Basra

Shiraz

Kufa

THE GULF

U M A Y Y A D   E M P I R E

ARABIAN SEA

Muscat

Medina

Mecca

RED SEA

Talas 751

✕ Battle with date

Aden

ISLAM TO 750 CE

After the death of Ali, the fourth caliph (leader of Islam), the Islamic community became split into the majority orthodox Sunni and the Shiites, who followed the descendants of Ali. The first Sunni caliphate was the Umayyad dynasty, ruling from Damascus, which lasted until 750 CE. It was a dynamic period of expansion.

Within a century of its foundation Islam had overrun more than half of Christendom. The relentless advance was finally halted in the West at Poitiers by the Franks in 732, after which Islam retreated behind the Pyrenees to establish itself in Spain.

To the peoples of the conquered countries, Islamic supremacy meant little more than a change of masters. The embracing nature of Islam allowed native cultures to continue and there

was no attempt at religious conversion. Jews and Christians were allowed to practise their own faiths as long as they paid the *jizya*, or poll tax.

One result of tolerant Islam was the flourishing of Nestorian churches in the east and their proliferation along the Silk Road into China.

THE EMPIRE OF CHARLEMAGNE

North Sea

Atlantic Ocean

Mediterranean Sea

BRITAIN

York

SAXONY

Corvey

THURINGIA

Cologne

Mainz · Fulda

Aachen

Echternach

BOHEMIA

St Wandrille · St Riquier
Corbie · Laon · Rheims
Rouen · Soissons
Prum
Trier
Metz

Paris
Chartres

Lorsch

BAVARIA

BRITTANY

Le Mans · Orleans · Auxerre

Hirsau

Kremsmunster

Angers · Tours · Sens
Noirmoutier

Luxeuil

Strasbourg

Reichenau · Salzburg
St Gallen

Bourges

Besançon

CARINTHIA

AQUITANIA

Poitiers

ALAMANNIA

Ferrières

BURGUNDY

LOMBARDY

Aquileia

Limoges

Lyons
Vienne

Venice

Bordeaux

Tarentaise

Milan · Brescia
Pavia
Bobbio

Embrun

GASCONY

Toulouse

PROVENCE

Arles · Aix-en-Provence

Ravenna

Narbonne

Marseilles

UMAYYAD CALIPHATE

Barcelona

CORSICA

Rome
Monte Cassino

Frankish Empire at accession of Charlemagne, 768
Conquests of Charlemagne to 814
Marches
△ Archbishopric
✠ Important monastery
✠ Notable Carolingian school (and monastery)

Copyright © 1996 Angus Hudson Ltd / Three's Company

CHARLEMAGNE

Charlemagne (Charles the Great, *c.* 742-814) was crowned the first Holy Roman Emperor by Pope Leo III in 800. After his accession to the Frankish throne in 771, Charles extended his realm, mainly eastwards across Saxony and Bavaria, and southwards across Lombardy. He gave military support to the Pope and enlarged the Patrimony of St Peter by granting it conquered lands. The alliance thus forged between church and state added considerable power to the papal institution over the next seven hundred years. In their aim to control the West, the Carolingian kings (750-887), and in particular Charlemagne, dreamed of reviving the Roman Empire. A renaissance of Latin culture saw the building of new schools in which calligraphy was restyled, and renowned ancient works, both religious and

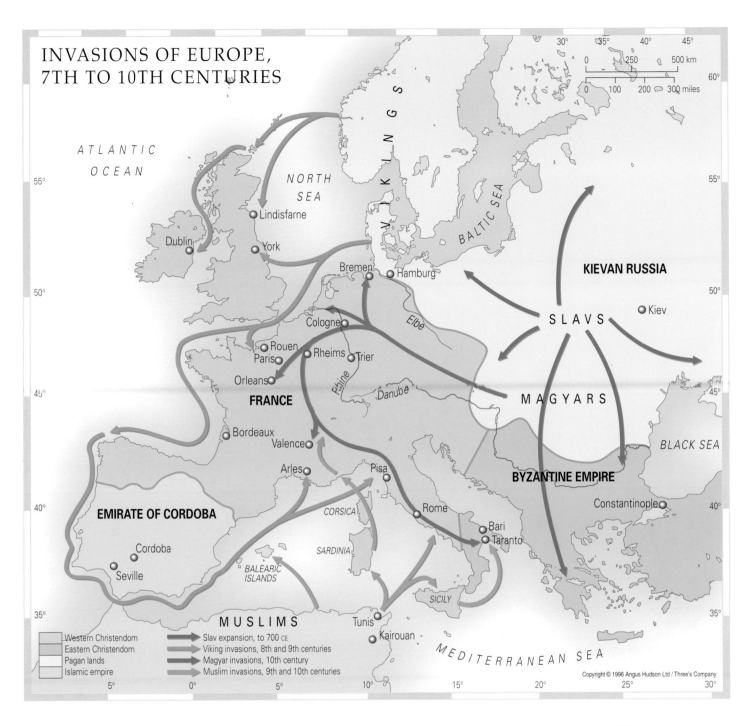

INVASIONS OF EUROPE, 7TH TO 10TH CENTURIES

ATLANTIC OCEAN

NORTH SEA

BALTIC SEA

V I K I N G S

KIEVAN RUSSIA

S L A V S

○ Kiev

○ Lindisfarne

Dublin ○

○ York

Bremen ○

○ Hamburg

Elbe

Cologne ○

○ Rouen

Paris ○   ○ Rheims   ○ Trier

○ Orleans

FRANCE

Rhine

Danube

M A G Y A R S

○ Bordeaux

Valence ○

Arles ○

Pisa ○

BYZANTINE EMPIRE

BLACK SEA

Constantinople ○

EMIRATE OF CORDOBA

Cordoba ○

○ Seville

CORSICA

SARDINIA

BALEARIC ISLANDS

Rome ○

○ Bari
○ Taranto

SICILY

M U S L I M S

Tunis ○

○ Kairouan

MEDITERRANEAN SEA

Legend	
Western Christendom	Slav expansion, to 700 CE
Eastern Christendom	Viking invasions, 8th and 9th centuries
Pagan lands	Magyar invasions, 10th century
Islamic empire	Muslim invasions, 9th and 10th centuries

profane, were copied. *The City of God* by St Augustine, for example, was painstakingly copied by monks. In this way, much of Latin literature was saved from the cultural extinction threatened by the Dark Ages.

INVASIONS OF EUROPE

As the Germanic barbarians migrated westwards, so a power vacuum in eastern Europe was filled by Slavic tribes in the seventh century. Their further migration southwards into the Balkans formed a barrier between Byzantium and the West by 700.

In western Europe during the ninth century, invasions came on all fronts and severely disrupted the political stability gained under Charlemagne. Vikings from Norway and Denmark plundered and colonized eastern parts of Britain and Ireland, and settled into what became the duchy of Normandy in northern France. Magyar penetration through Germanic lands into the heart of France, and Saracen (Muslim) attacks from across the Mediterranean weakened the Frankish Empire.

Ironically the Vikings, who had attacked the northern frontiers, helped in the tenth century to rebuff the growing threat of Islam which had occupied most of Spain since 756.

IRISH/CELTIC AND BRITISH MISSIONS TO EUROPE, 6TH TO 8TH CENTURIES

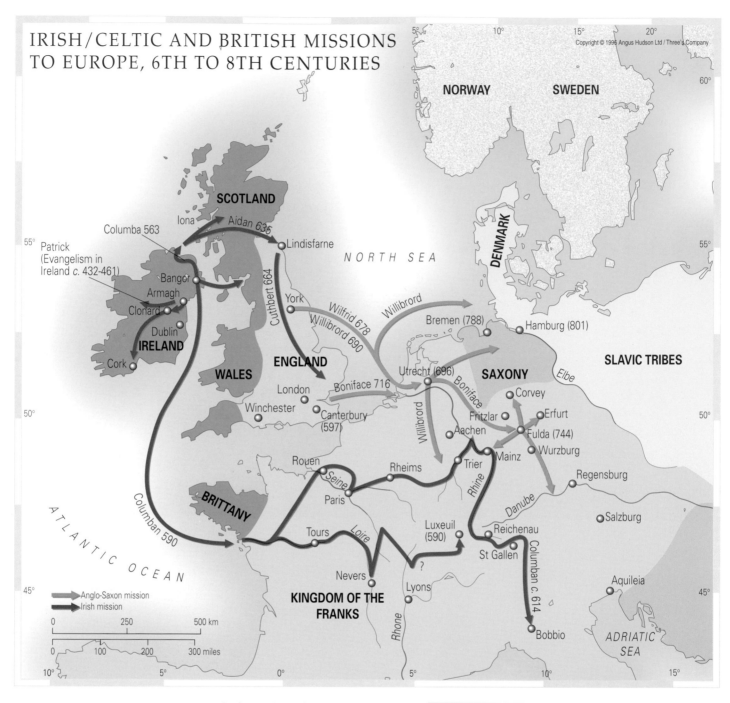

Copyright © 1996 Angus Hudson Ltd / Three's Company

IRISH AND ANGLO-SAXON MISSIONS

The conversion to Christianity of the pagan peoples of northern Europe was the result of two major influences: Pope Gregory the Great's policy of evangelization through the Anglo-Saxons, and the 'peregrinatio' (self-imposed exile in foreign lands) of Irish monks. From the centre founded by Columba on Iona, Aidan moved to Holy Island on Lindisfarne, and Columban took the gospel as far as Bobbio in Lombardy.

After Pope Gregory dispatched Augustine to England in 597 to become the first bishop of Canterbury, the two most successful missionaries to the continent were Willibrord, known as the Apostle to the Frisians, and Boniface, the outstanding Apostle to the Germans. They usually travelled in a group of monks, and established churches, holy days and the cult of saints to replace the shrines and superstitions of the pagan cults of the north, such as Thor, god of thunder.

There was also a political dimension involving the Frankish rulers and the papacy. The conversion and befriending of pagans on the eastern border of the Frankish Empire provided greater security and opened the way for expansion eastwards.

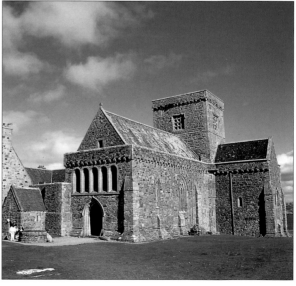

Iona became the focus for the spread of Celtic Christianity.

ROMAN MISSIONS IN WESTERN EUROPE

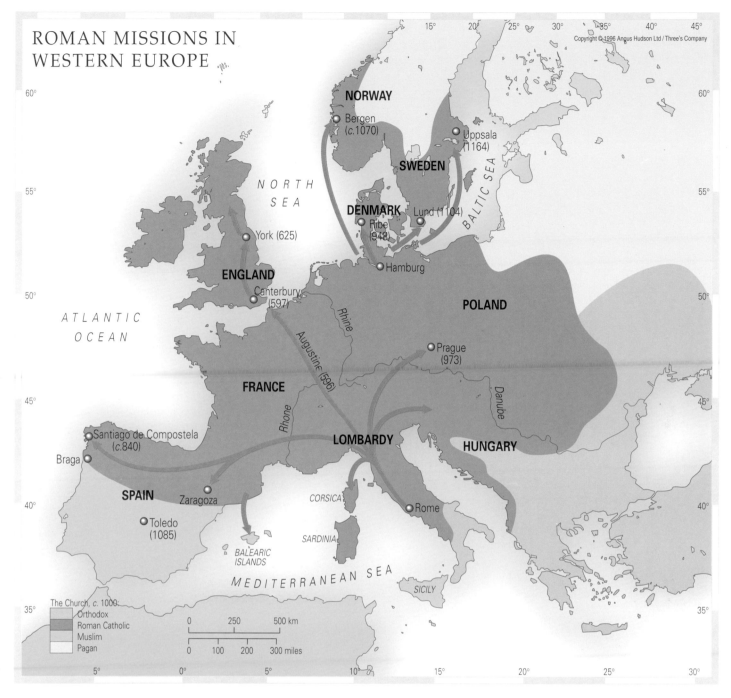

Map labels:
- NORWAY
- Bergen (c.1070)
- Uppsala (1164)
- SWEDEN
- DENMARK
- Lund (1104)
- Ribe (948)
- NORTH SEA
- BALTIC SEA
- York (625)
- Hamburg
- ENGLAND
- Canterbury (597)
- POLAND
- ATLANTIC OCEAN
- Rhine
- Augustine (596)
- Prague (973)
- FRANCE
- Rhone
- Danube
- Santiago de Compostela (c.840)
- Braga
- LOMBARDY
- HUNGARY
- SPAIN
- Zaragoza
- CORSICA
- Rome
- Toledo (1085)
- SARDINIA
- BALEARIC ISLANDS
- MEDITERRANEAN SEA
- SICILY

The Church, c. 1000:
- Orthodox
- Roman Catholic
- Muslim
- Pagan

0 250 500 km
0 100 200 300 miles

Copyright © 1996 Angus Hudson Ltd / Three's Company

Boniface, the 'Apostle to the Germans'.

ROMAN MISSIONS IN WESTERN EUROPE

With the coronation of Charlemagne as the first Holy Roman Emperor in 800, western Europe experienced a period of evangelization. With crusader-like zeal and military might the frontier of Christendom was pushed steadily northwards and eastwards. The title of the emperor reflected the new ideal of a ruler that Charlemagne envisaged. Following the example of the Israelite King David, he conquered and converted, built churches and prayed to God. Missions from Rome fanned out in all directions in the wake of conquest in order to sustain a faith beyond nominal conversion.

To the south, the threat of Islam was upon every north Mediterranean shore. Rome itself was plundered in 846, Sicily was taken by 902 and Muslim strongholds were set up in southern Italy. Steady losses of Christians through conversion to Islam brought new missions to old lands. The important pilgrim centre of Santiago de Compostela was founded during this period.

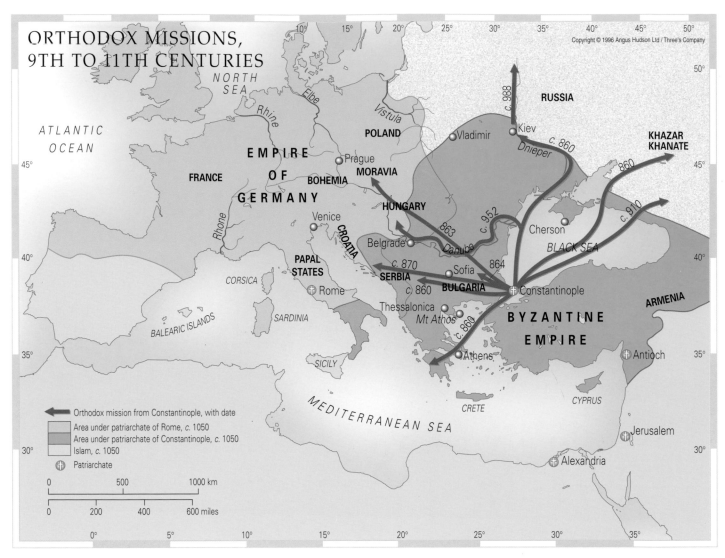

ORTHODOX MISSIONS, 9TH TO 11TH CENTURIES

Copyright © 1996 Angus Hudson Ltd / Three's Company

Legend:
- ← Orthodox mission from Constantinople, with date
- Area under patriarchate of Rome, *c.* 1050
- Area under patriarchate of Constantinople, *c.* 1050
- Islam, *c.* 1050
- ✠ Patriarchate

0   500   1000 km
0   200   400   600 miles

ORTHODOX MISSIONS

In eastern Europe the foundations of the modern Orthodox national churches were laid in the ninth century. Competition between Rome and Constantinople over territory thus far unclaimed continually brought into question the boundary of their Patriarchates. Missionaries from both East and West operated in the Balkans. The main missionary advance from Constantinople was led by Cyril and Methodius. Boris of Bulgaria adopted the eastern rite *c.* 870, whereupon Rastislav, prince of Moravia (now Slovakia), turned also to Byzantium. Byzantine Christianity became the official religion in Serbia by 891.

Unlike the Western church, which was unified by its dependence on a Latin liturgy, the Byzantines allowed each nation or people to foster its own independent church with a liturgy conducted in the local language.

Kariye Camii, built as a Byzantine church in Constantinople in the eleventh century, converted into a mosque, but today functioning as a church again in modern Istanbul.

CHRISTIANITY IN RUSSIA *c.*1050

VOLGA
BULGARS

Lake
Ladoga

BALTIC SEA

Jurev
(Dorpat)

Novgorod

Pskov

Volga

Pereyaslavl

Rostov

Volga

Nizhniy Novgorod

LITHUANIANS

Dvina

Vladimir

Polotsk

Moscow

Ryazan

Smolensk

Minsk

KIEVAN
RUSSIA

POLES

Pinsk

Ugrovsk

Turov

Krakow

Chernigov

Vladimir-Volynsk

Kiev

Przemysl

Belgorod

Pereyaslavl

Don

Galich

Yurev

Dnieper

PECHENEGS

Dniester

MAGYARS

KHAZARS

Danube

Tmutarakan

Extent of Kievan Russia, *c.*1050
Archbishopric
Bishopric

BLACK SEA

0   250   500 km

0   100   200   300 miles

CHRISTIANITY COMES TO RUSSIA

The first recorded Russian convert was Olga, widow of Igor, who ruled from 945 to 964. There was no mass conversion, however, until the later ruler Vladimir, who established the Kievan state of Rus, saw the advantage of having a state religion. While on a trip to Constantinople he was impressed by the splendour of Byzantine worship, architecture and culture, and his advisors are quoted in the Russian Chronicle as saying 'If the Greek faith were evil, it would not have been adopted by your grandmother, Olga, who was wiser than anyone.'

Vladimir returned to Kiev, and a mass baptism of his people followed in 988. Russia imported many features of Byzantine culture, including a literary language, aesthetic styles of masonry and mosaics, music and the liturgy as well as an elaborate theological system. Byzantium, for its part, greatly enlarged the extent of the patriarchate of Constantinople.

An artist's impression of a typical medieval monastery.

MONASTIC REFORM

Since the eighth century nearly all monasteries in the West followed the Benedictine Rule. However, in time reforms became necessary. In the tenth and eleventh centuries a major monastic reform movement spread through Europe following the Order of Cluny, founded in 910. Some houses found that this reform did not go far enough and a more austere model was founded at Cîteaux, near Dijon, in 1098. This gave rise to the new Order of Cistercian monasteries. These reforms returned to a strict observance of the Benedictine Rule.

The Cistercian monasteries were built in remote places to avoid contact with

town dwellers. They cultivated wasteland and ran sheep farms to satisfy the growing demand for wool. Their financial success and growing popularity resulted in the establishment of 694 Cistercian monasteries in Europe by the end of the thirteenth century. There were five 'daughter' houses which together supervised standards among the other houses. One of the first to join the Cistercians was St Bernard who became abbot of Clairvaux.

The reforming monks wished to present to ordinary people a radical alternative way of life to that led by the clergy – a clergy who, in the opinion of many, were dissolute and too affluent. The Cluniac monks joined as young boys and received all their training in the cloister. The Cistercian monks, on the other hand, had already lived part

of their adult lives in society before they rejected its values and joined the monastery. The Cistercians came to be more damning of the mores of contemporary society than were the more moderate Cluniacs. The Cluniac movement in turn had a major influence on reform in the Western Church, especially under Pope Gregory VII.

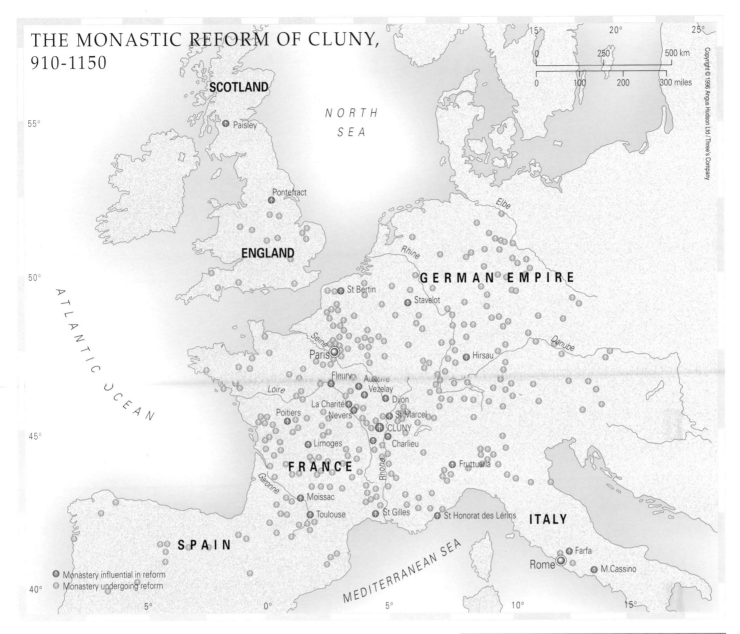

THE MONASTIC REFORM OF CLUNY, 910-1150

500 km
300 miles

SCOTLAND

Paisley

NORTH SEA

Pontefract

ENGLAND

ATLANTIC OCEAN

St Bertin
GERMAN EMPIRE
Stavelot

Rhine

Elbe

Seine
Paris○
Hirsau

Danube

Fleury
Auxerre
Vezelay
Loire
Dijon
La Charité
St Marcel
Poitiers
Nevers
CLUNY
Charlieu

Limoges

Fruttuaria

FRANCE

Rhône

Garonne

Moissac

Toulouse
St Gilles
St Honorat des Lérins

ITALY

Farfa
Rome ○
M.Cassino

⊕ Monastery influential in reform
○ Monastery undergoing reform

MEDITERRANEAN SEA

CISTERCIAN MONASTICISM, 12TH TO 13TH CENTURIES

SWEDEN

SCOTLAND

NORTH SEA

DENMARK

IRELAND

ENGLAND

WALES

GERMAN EMPIRE

ATLANTIC OCEAN

Clairvaux

Pontigny
Fontenay
Morimond

CÎTEAUX

La Ferté

⊙ One of five first daughter monasteries of Cîteaux
• Cistercian monastery

FRANCE

ITALY

SPAIN

MEDITERRANEAN SEA

0   250   500 km
0 100 200 300 miles

The ruins of Tintern Abbey, a Cistercian house in England's Wye Valley.

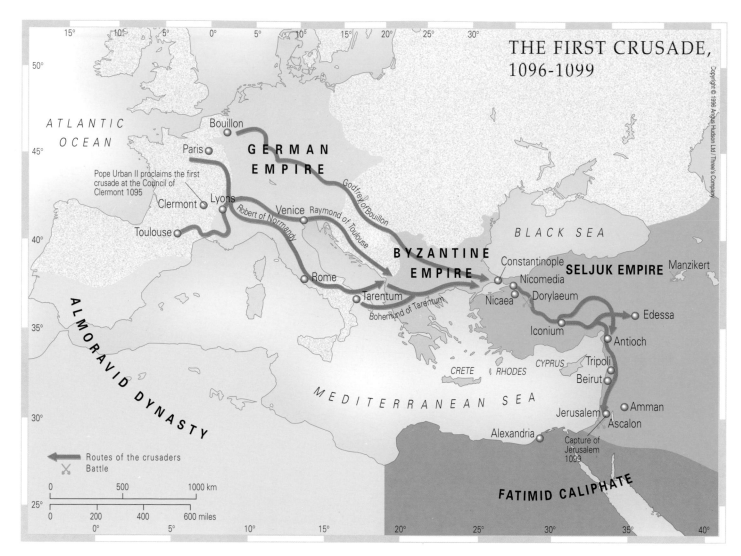

ATLANTIC
OCEAN

GERMAN
EMPIRE

Bouillon

Paris

Pope Urban II proclaims the first
crusade at the Council of
Clermont 1095

Clermont   Lyons

Godfrey of Bouillon

Robert of Normandy   Venice   Raymond of Toulouse

Toulouse

Rome

Tarentum

Bohemund of Tarentum

BLACK SEA

BYZANTINE
EMPIRE

Constantinople   SELJUK EMPIRE   Manzikert

Nicomedia

Nicaea   Dorylaeum

Iconium   Edessa

Antioch

ALMORAVID DYNASTY

CRETE   RHODES   CYPRUS   Tripoli

Beirut

MEDITERRANEAN SEA

Jerusalem   Amman

Ascalon

Alexandria   Capture of
Jerusalem
1099

FATIMID CALIPHATE

Routes of the crusaders
Battle

0   500   1000 km

0   200   400   600 miles

THE CRUSADES

The Crusades were a series of
expeditions first intended to recover the
Holy Land from Muslim occupation and
to secure free access for pilgrims. The
call to the First Crusade by Pope Urban
II at the Council of Clermont in 1095
was prompted by an offensive deep into
Asia Minor by the Seljuk Turks
mounting pressure on Byzantium's
eastern border. Those who joined the
Crusades were granted indulgences
and, in the event of death, were assured
of martyrdom status.

In 1099 Jerusalem was captured. Over
the next twenty years a series of Latin
Crusader states was established in the
Levant. Subsequent crusades were
instigated to defend these kingdoms.
Bernard of Clairvaux preached the
Second Crusade (1147) to recapture
Edessa. However, it was unsuccessful
and the Muslim leader Saladin captured
Jerusalem. As a result, the Third
Crusade (1189-92) was raised, but it
failed to recover the Holy City.

St Anne's Church, Jerusalem, was built by the victorious Crusaders.

The Byzantines, meanwhile, were
ambivalent to all this. On the one hand
they had repeatedly requested help, and
supported the Crusades because they
relieved pressure on their eastern front;
on the other hand, the establishment of
Crusader states was more than they
bargained for. Feuding broke out
between East and West and led to the
diversion of the Fourth Crusade, in
1202, to Constantinople; the capital was

sacked and a Latin emperor enthroned.
A Latin empire of Constantinople then
held power from 1204 until 1261. A
number of Byzantine centres of
resistance were set up in exile, and the
main one, at Nicaea, organized a
campaign with help from Genoa and
reduced the Latin presence to minor
states in southern Greece.

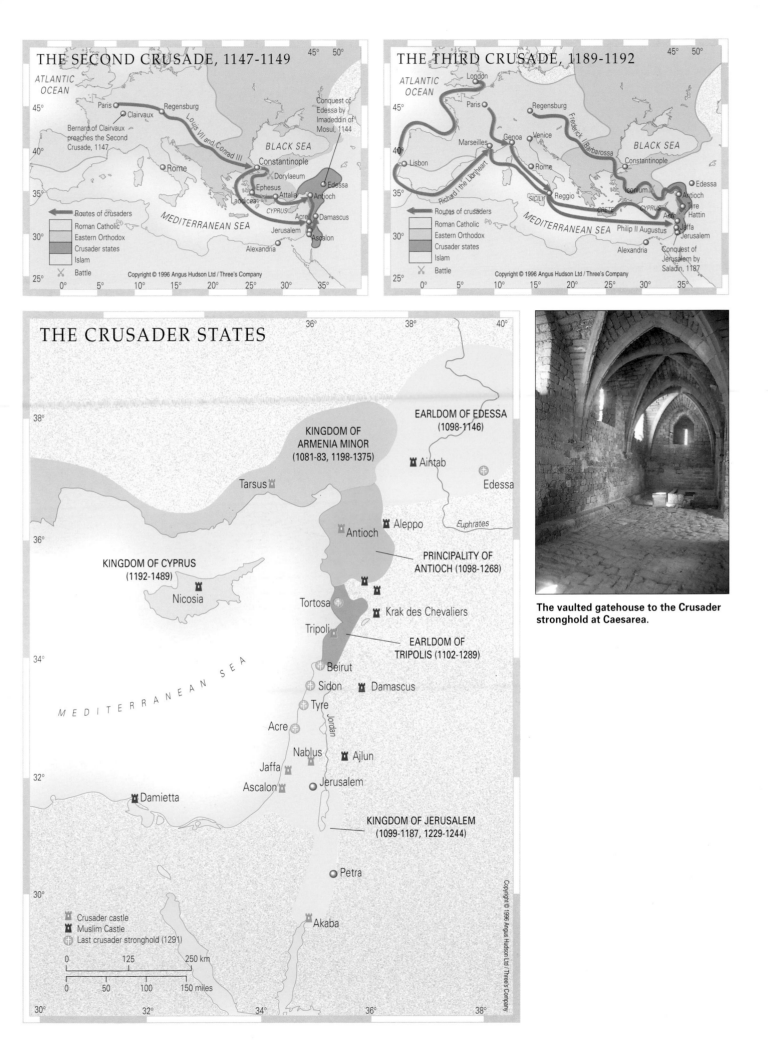

THE SECOND CRUSADE, 1147-1149

ATLANTIC OCEAN

45°
50°

Paris
Clairvaux
Regensburg

Bernard of Clairvaux
preaches the Second
Crusade, 1147

Louis VII and Conrad III

BLACK SEA

Rome

Conquest of
Edessa by
Imadeddin of
Mosul, 1144

Constantinople

Dorylaeum
Edessa
Ephesus
Antioch
Laodicea
Attalia
CYPRUS
Acre
Damascus

MEDITERRANEAN SEA

Jerusalem
Ascalon

Alexandria

→ Routes of crusaders
Roman Catholic
Eastern Orthodox
Crusader states
Islam
✗ Battle

Copyright © 1996 Angus Hudson Ltd / Three's Company

THE THIRD CRUSADE, 1189-1192

ATLANTIC OCEAN

45°
50°

London
Paris
Regensburg
Frederick I Barbarossa

BLACK SEA

Marseilles
Genoa
Venice

Lisbon

Richard I the Lionheart
Rome
Constantinople

Edessa
Iconium
Antioch
SICILY
Reggio
CRETE
CYPRUS
Tyre
Hattin
Acre
Jaffa
Philip II Augustus
Jerusalem

MEDITERRANEAN SEA

Alexandria

Conquest of
Jerusalem by
Saladin, 1187

→ Routes of crusaders
Roman Catholic
Eastern Orthodox
Crusader states
Islam
✗ Battle

Copyright © 1996 Angus Hudson Ltd / Three's Company

THE CRUSADER STATES

36°
38°
40°

EARLDOM OF EDESSA
(1098-1146)

KINGDOM OF
ARMENIA MINOR
(1081-83, 1198-1375)

Aintab

Edessa

Tarsus

Euphrates

Aleppo

Antioch

PRINCIPALITY OF
ANTIOCH (1098-1268)

KINGDOM OF CYPRUS
(1192-1489)

Nicosia

Tortosa

Krak des Chevaliers

Tripoli

EARLDOM OF
TRIPOLIS (1102-1289)

Beirut

MEDITERRANEAN SEA

Sidon
Damascus

Tyre

Acre

Jordan

Nablus
Ajlun

Jaffa

Ascalon
Jerusalem

Damietta

KINGDOM OF JERUSALEM
(1099-1187, 1229-1244)

Petra

Crusader castle
Muslim Castle
Last crusader stronghold (1291)

0   125   250 km
0   50 100 150 miles

Akaba

Copyright © 1996 Angus Hudson Ltd / Three's Company

The vaulted gatehouse to the Crusader
stronghold at Caesarea.

Boundary of communion with Rome, c. 1050
Boundary of communion with Constantinople, c. 1050
Overlapping area of churches with allegiance to Rome or Constantinople
Norman invasions, 1057-85
Northern limit of Islamic rule, c. 1050

THE FINAL RIFT

The final break of Christendom into the Roman Catholic West and Orthodox East was the culmination of centuries of friction that stemmed from the western and eastern divisions of the Roman Empire. Culturally and linguistically diverse, and politically antagonistic, Rome and Constantinople had differences beyond religious questions. Even when under the mutual threat of Norman invasions, a meeting for peace arranged in Constantinople in 1054 ended in bitter recrimination and a papal bull excommunicating the Eastern Church.

Relations over religious questions were rarely harmonious, for example during the iconoclast controversy (726 to 843), over the reverence to be paid to icons. Debate about the nature of the Trinity, whether the Holy Spirit proceeds from the Father *and the Son* (Western standpoint) or from the Father *through the Son* (Eastern standpoint) became critical in the time of Photius (864). The final rift, though, was more political than theological, and concerned the supremacy of Rome. The pope claimed pre-eminence among the patriarchs, whereas Constantinople insisted on Rome as one among equals.

THE CHURCH AND LEARNING, 1100-1700

NORTH SEA

BALTIC SEA

Uppsala

Konigsberg

Aberdeen

St Andrews

Edinburgh

Jarrow

Wearmouth

Rievaulx

York

Dublin

Sempringham

Peterborough

Cambridge

Groningen

Magdeburg

Wittenberg

Oxford

Amsterdam

Leiden

Utrecht

Hildesheim

Corvey

Padorborn

Elbe

Rhine

Canterbury

Marburg

Prague

ATLANTIC OCEAN

Tournai

Mainz

Bamberg

Rouen

Beauvais

Laon

Metz

Worms

Rheims

Speyer

Strasbourg

Fulda

Mont St Michel

Savigny

Paris

Chartres

Seine

Clairvaux

Regensburg

Danube

Loire

Citeaux

St Gall

Salzburg

Fontevrault

Tours

Poitiers

Cluny

Grande Chartreuse

Geneva

Milan

Vicenza

Padua

La Chaise Dieu

Vercelli

Pavia

Ravenna

Rhone

Piacenza

Parma

Bologna

Reggio

Garonne

Toulouse

Montpellier

Aix

Pisa

Florence

Arezzo

Siena

Santiago de Compostela

Oviedo

Palencia

Valladolid

Salamanca

Avila

Alcalá

Tagus

Toledo

Lerida

CORSICA

Rome

Monte Cassino

Naples

Salerno

Lisbon

SARDINIA

BALEARIC ISLANDS

Seville

Granada

Palermo

Messina

Monreale

SICILY

MEDITERRANEAN SEA

Paris Law school

✝ Centre of monastic reform

★ Important cathedral school

★ Important monastic school

University founded

◾ before 1300

◾ 1300–1500

◾ 1500–1700

0   250   500 km

0   100   200   300 miles

THE CHURCH AND LEARNING

In Western Europe during the Middle Ages education was largely in the hands of the Church. Until about the tenth century, the exposition of doctrine was the responsibility of bishops or monks in monasteries. Over the next four centuries, however, they were gradually superseded by the masters who taught in new cathedral schools and universities.

Paris was the main centre of learning, and was adopted by Franciscans and Dominicans as their main training centre. Among the major scholars of this period who studied or taught at Paris were William of Ockham, Anselm of Bec, Peter Abelard, Peter Lombard, Albert the Great, Duns Scotus, Thomas Aquinas and Pope Innocent III. Their main legacy, in a systematic account known as scholasticism, was to harmonize the foundational theology of Augustine with the philosophy of classical Greek thinkers, especially Aristotle. Bringing together the Catholic articles of faith and the method of reasoning by logic was the crowning achievement of Thomas Aquinas in his *Summa Theologica*, which was to form the chief basis of future Catholic theology.

(Above) York Minster, England, at dusk; (right) Cologne Cathedral, Germany; (below) detail from the intricate stone carvings outside Chartres Cathedral, France.

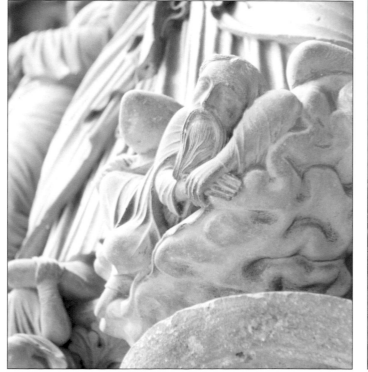

MAJOR GOTHIC CATHEDRALS
OF WESTERN EUROPE

NORWAY

Trondheim

Åbo

Uppsala

Reval

SWEDEN

Linköping

Visby

Riga

DENMARK

Lübeck

Elbe

York

Lincoln

ENGLAND

Magdeburg

Munster

Hereford

Gloucester

Rochester

Rhine

Paderborn

Naumburg

Wells

London

Canterbury

Exeter

Chichester

Utrecht

Cologne

Limburg

Prague

Salisbury

Winchester

Rouen

Amiens

Bamberg

Bayeux

Beauvais

Laon

Trier

HOLY

Lisieux

Seine

Paris

Rheims

ROMAN

ATLANTIC

Chartres

Senlis

Soissons

EMPIRE

Danube

Vienna

OCEAN

Le Mans

Orleans

Sens

Troyes

Strasbourg

Angers

Auxerre

Dijon

Loire

Bourges

Citeaux

Basel

Poitiers

Nevers

Limoges

FRANCE

Milan

Bordeaux

Lyons

Garonne

Genoa

Rhone

Albi

Avignon

Florence

Toulouse

Pisa

Arezzo

Siena

Leon

Burgos

Orvieto

Palencia

Rome

ITALY

Zaragoza

Segovia

Barcelona

Gerona

Naples

Tarragona

Toledo

SPAIN

Valencia

Palma

Palermo

Origin of gothic architecture, 1130 – 1300

Cathedral city with influential gothic style

City with major gothic cathedral

MEDITERRANEAN SEA

| 0 | | 250 | | 500 km |

| 0 | 100 | 200 | 300 miles |

GOTHIC CATHEDRALS

The Gothic style of cathedral building emerged in early twelfth-century France and became the dominant style of the Latin West. The new structural development was the use of external flying buttresses. By taking some of the weight of the main construction, they allowed masons to build to much greater heights and dispose of the massive, and less elegant, structural style typical of earlier cathedrals. At first only a select handful of masons and craftsmen knew this engineering secret, and so the earliest examples of Gothic architecture were confined to a region around Paris. The Gothic influence gradually spread to Germany, Italy, Spain, Sweden and elsewhere, where French architectural styles could be recognized.

103

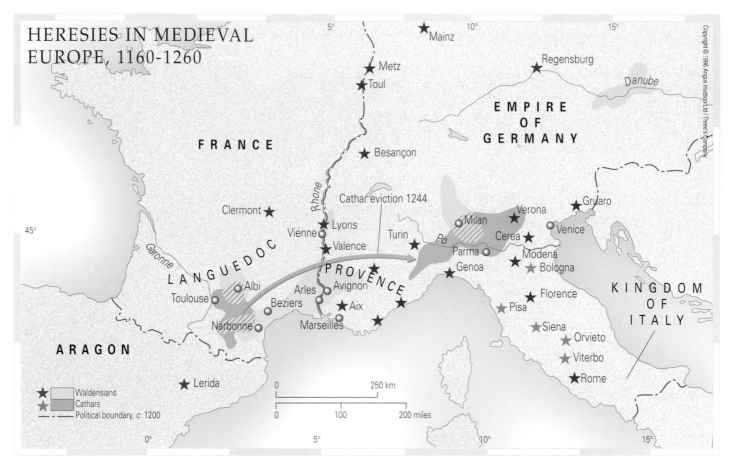

EMPIRE
OF
GERMANY

FRANCE

Mainz

Metz
Toul

Regensburg

Danube

Besançon

Rhone

Cathar eviction 1244

Clermont

Vienne
Valence

Lyons

Turin

Po
Parma

Milan

Cerea

Verona

Gruaro

Venice

Genoa

Modena

Bologna

LANGUEDOC

PROVENCE

Florence

KINGDOM
OF
ITALY

Toulouse

Albi

Arles
Beziers

Avignon

Aix

Pisa

Narbonne

Marseilles

Siena

Orvieto

ARAGON

Viterbo

Rome

Lerida

★ Waldensians
★ Cathars
— · — Political boundary, c. 1200

0   250 km

0   100   200 miles

HERESY AND DISSENT

An increased emphasis on vows of poverty among the reforming monasteries inadvertently opened the door for dissenters to challenge the lifestyle of the more affluent clergy and corrupt monasteries. One proponent of the vow of poverty was a rich merchant from Lyons, named Peter Valdes (Waldo), who decided to sell everything he owned. He translated the New Testament into the local language and preached to ordinary illiterate people, who for the first time could understand the gospel. The group became known as the Waldensians. Their rejection of ecclesiastical authority led to their condemnation as heretics before 1200. However, the movement grew and by the end of the thirteenth century had spread through much of Europe.

A much more menacing sect, called the Cathars or Albigensians (from Albi), whom in fact the Waldensians preached against, appeared early in the eleventh century. They spread rapidly and by the 1160s were established in two main areas: Languedoc in southern France (where they became known as the Albigensians) and Lombardy. They

The fortress-like cathedral of Albi, France.

believed all creation and matter to be evil, and the incarnation and crucifixion both to be false. The path to salvation was the release of the soul from the cage of sinful flesh and its reunification with God.

Innocent III launched a crusade in 1209 to combat the Albigensian and Waldensian heretics by force. It turned into a long struggle, taking on an almost civil-war scale as many southern Catholics supported the Albigensians in

defence of their property. A partial peace was agreed in 1229. Pope Gregory IX instigated a series of inquisitions in 1231 to root out heresy in France, Italy and Germany. This marked the beginning of a more repressive papal regime.

LATIN KINGDOM OF CONSTANTINOPLE, 1205

BLACK SEA

BULGARIAN EMPIRE

EPIRUS

THESSALONICA

Adrianople

Constantinople

Nicomedia

Nicaea

LESBOS

AEGEAN SEA

CHIOS

DUCHY OF ATHENS

ACHAEA

Athens

NICAEAN EMPIRE

MEDITERRANEAN SEA

BYZANTIUM FALLS

After the recapture of Constantinople from Latin possession, various Western leaders pushed for further campaigns to regain it. Byzantine emperors had to appease the West, and particularly the pope of the day, to keep that ambition in check. Meanwhile the Byzantine rulers, who needed military help from the West to halt the Ottoman Turks, had to manoeuvre with great diplomatic skill. The Byzantine emperor John V (1354-91) appealed to the pope for help in 1355 when the Ottomans were poised to invade the Balkans. The popes were concerned for the Christian East, but wary of helping while the Byzantine Church remained in schism from Rome.

In 1371 the Ottomans defeated the Serbs near Adrianople. Serbia, Bulgaria and ultimately Byzantium, were forced to capitulate, becoming vassal states of the Ottoman Empire. Attempts to rebel against the Ottomans resulted in the eventual capture and sack of Constantinople in 1453.

THE DECLINE AND FALL OF BYZANTIUM

KINGDOM OF HUNGARY

GOLDEN HORDE

Belgrade

Cherson

BOSNIA

Danube

BLACK SEA

KINGDOM OF SERBIA

KINGDOM OF BULGARIA

Sophia

BALKANS

Philippopolis

1453 Falls to the Ottomans

Adrianople 1371

Constantinople (Istanbul)

Thessalonica

Gallipoli

Nicomedia

Nicaea

Ankara

TURKS

LEMNOS

Caesarea

AEGEAN SEA

Smyrna

ANATOLIA

Corinth

Athens

Miletus

Edessa

LESSER ARMENIA

RHODES

CYPRUS

Antioch

CRETE

Tripoli

MEDITERRANEAN SEA

Damascus

- - - - Boundary of Byzantine Empire in 1265
Byzantine Empire in 1355
Ottoman Empire in 1355
✗ Battle with date

0 — 250 km

0 — 100 — 200 miles

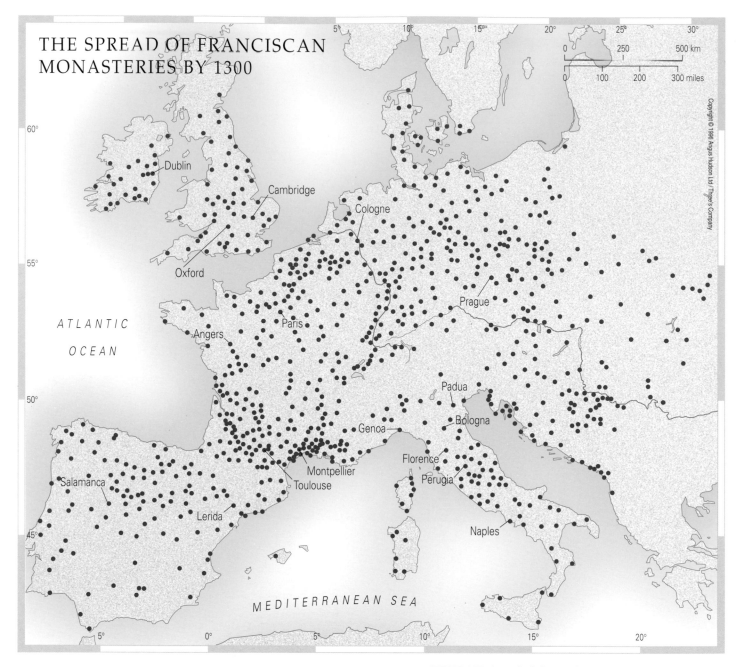

THE SPREAD OF FRANCISCAN MONASTERIES BY 1300

ATLANTIC OCEAN

Dublin

Cambridge

Cologne

Oxford

Prague

Paris

Angers

Padua

Bologna

Genoa

Florence

Montpellier

Perugia

Toulouse

Salamanca

Lerida

Naples

MEDITERRANEAN SEA

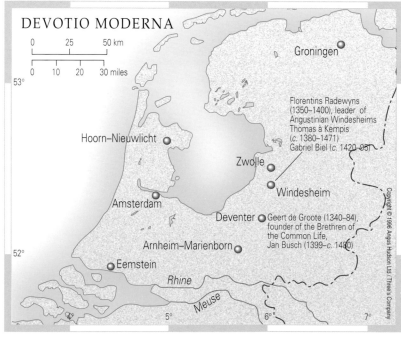

DEVOTIO MODERNA

Groningen

Florentins Radewyns (1350–1400), leader of Angustinian Windesheims
Thomas à Kempis (c. 1380–1471)
Gabriel Biel (c. 1420–95)

Hoorn–Nieuwlicht

Zwolle

Windesheim

Amsterdam

Deventer — Geert de Groote (1340–84), founder of the Brethren of the Common Life, Jan Busch (1399–c. 1480)

Arnheim–Marienborn

Eemstein

Rhine

Meuse

THE FRANCISCANS

As towns and cities developed in medieval Europe, the cloistered monastery began to decline in importance. Some of the clergy felt the need for a way of working in the world while still living under a spiritual rule. Early in the thirteenth century new groups of ascetic preaching monks, known as friars, arose. One group, the Franciscans, sprang from the example and teaching of Francis of Assisi (1182-1226), who renounced his inheritance to live a life of prayer and poverty. Despite these ascetic beginnings, it was not long before the order began to own property and take on the trappings of an organisation.

THE SPREAD OF DOMINICAN MONASTERIES BY 1300

THE DOMINICANS

Dominic de Guzman (1170-1221), a priest from Castile, recognized that clergymen needed better teaching in order to pass on the faith to the people. He founded the Dominican order, another order of friars, officially known as the Order of Preachers, to fulfil this need. The Dominicans went on to found colleges and seminaries to train the clergy, and produced such medieval thinkers as Albertus Magnus and Thomas Aquinas. The friars achieved a great deal in pastoral work, education and mission.

The basilica of S. Francesco, Assisi.

107

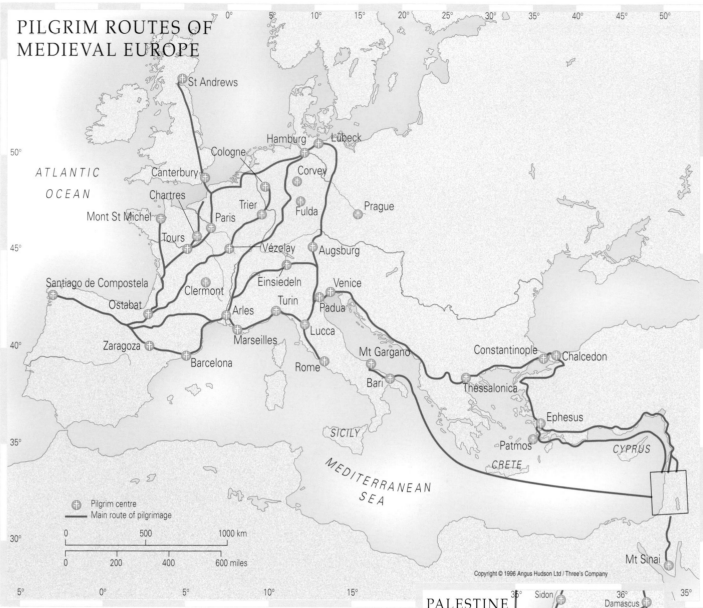

PILGRIM ROUTES OF MEDIEVAL EUROPE

ATLANTIC OCEAN

St Andrews

Hamburg
Lübeck
Cologne
Corvey
Canterbury
Chartres
Trier
Fulda
Prague
Paris
Mont St Michel
Vézelay
Augsburg
Tours
Einsiedeln
Santiago de Compostela
Clermont
Venice
Ostabat
Turin
Padua
Arles
Lucca
Zaragoza
Marseilles
Mt Gargano
Constantinople
Chalcedon
Barcelona
Rome
Bari
Thessalonica
SICILY
Ephesus
MEDITERRANEAN SEA
Patmos
CYPRUS
CRETE
Mt Sinai

⊕ Pilgrim centre
— Main route of pilgrimage

0   500   1000 km
0   200   400   600 miles

Copyright © 1996 Angus Hudson Ltd / Three's Company

PILGRIMAGES

Pilgrimages to holy sites had been made since the fourth century, but became more common in the medieval period, when they carried the specific aims of winning God's grace through penance, or even of gaining eternal life. Irish monks regarded the Christian life itself as a pilgrimage to heaven, ideally to be lived in exile. The self-denial of a long, arduous journey was symbolic of this personal quest. Pilgrimage could replace public penance as an act of absolving sin, and journeys to holy sites were organized on a large scale from the eleventh century.

Three main places were visited: Rome, with the traditional tombs of Saints Peter and Paul; Jerusalem, together with other sites in the Holy

Land associated with Jesus; and Santiago de Compostela, where St James' tomb was believed to have been discovered around 830. The Holy Land became especially popular once the recapture of Jerusalem during the First Crusade (1099) and the instituting of the Orders of knights made travel there more secure. However, with the Muslim reconquest of Jerusalem in 1187, the number of pilgrimages to Rome and Santiago de Compostela greatly increased.

The routes through France via Tours and Vézelay were the most thronged, owing chiefly to Cluniac influence. The idea of the holiness of saints' relics and of their supernatural power developed, with the result that relics proliferated along these routes. A certain tourism was exploited. Local shrines, hospices and the owners of relics recovered from

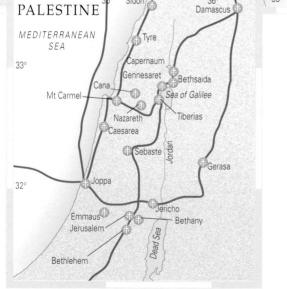

PALESTINE

MEDITERRANEAN SEA

Sidon
Damascus
Tyre
Capernaum
Bethsaida
Gennesaret
Cana
Sea of Galilee
Mt Carmel
Tiberias
Nazareth
Caesarea
Sebaste
Jordan
Gerasa
Joppa
Jericho
Emmaus
Bethany
Jerusalem
Dead Sea
Bethlehem

the Holy Land would grow affluent on the expenditure of people undertaking organized pilgrimage packages.

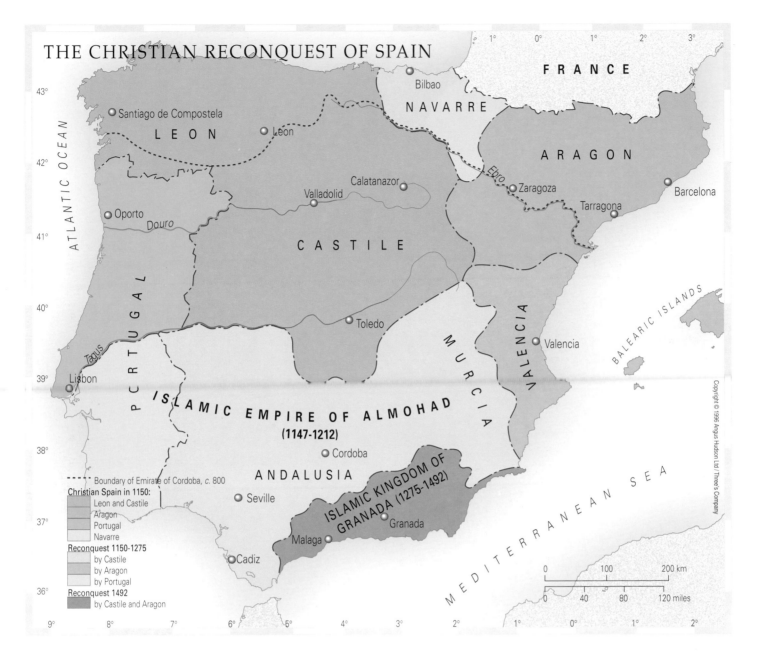

THE CHRISTIAN RECONQUEST OF SPAIN

FRANCE

Bilbao

NAVARRE

ATLANTIC OCEAN

Santiago de Compostela

LEON

Leon

ARAGON

Calatanazor

Valladolid

Zaragoza

Barcelona

Oporto

Douro

Tarragona

CASTILE

PORTUGAL

Toledo

VALENCIA

MURCIA

Valencia

BALEARIC ISLANDS

Tagus

Lisbon

ISLAMIC EMPIRE OF ALMOHAD

(1147-1212)

Cordoba

ANDALUSIA

ISLAMIC KINGDOM OF GRANADA (1275-1492)

MEDITERRANEAN SEA

Seville

Granada

Malaga

Cadiz

Boundary of Emirate of Cordoba, c. 800

Christian Spain in 1150:
Leon and Castile
Aragon
Portugal
Navarre
Reconquest 1150-1275
by Castile
by Aragon
by Portugal
Reconquest 1492
by Castile and Aragon

0 100 200 km

0 40 80 120 miles

Copyright © 1996 Angus Hudson Ltd / Three's Company

The Alhambra Palace, Granada, a peak of Moorish cultural achievement.

THE RECONQUEST OF SPAIN

The Christian reconquest of Spain began with victory at the Battle of Calatanazor in 1002, at a time when the ruling Umayyad Caliphate was embroiled in civil war. A long period of Christian assaults on successive Islamic dynasties resulted in the capitulation of Islamic power in 1236 at Cordoba. The Arabic state of Granada became a vassal to Castile for the next 250 years, during which the great Alhambra Palace in the city of Granada was built, the peak of Moorish cultural achievement. The reconquest of Spain was completed in 1492.

With the gradual recovery of Spain came monastic influence from France.

Many religious houses of the Cistercian and Cluniac orders were established and cathedrals in the Gothic style were built, for example at Léon and Toledo.

Many Muslims continued to live in Spain after 1492, until their final expulsion by edict in 1614. It was the end of a civilization which had brought great thinkers, such as Averroës, who lived as a judge in Cordoba, and had reintroduced to the West the lost classical philosophy of Aristotle.

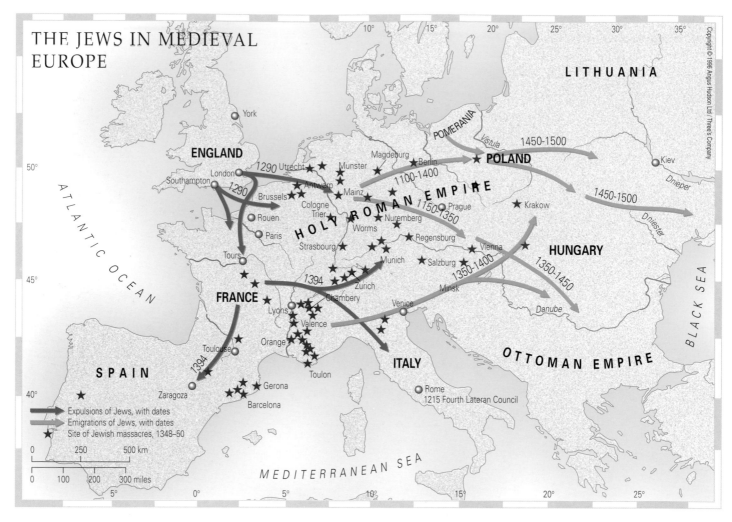

THE JEWS IN MEDIEVAL EUROPE

During the Roman Empire Jews were already widespread throughout Mediterranean Europe. After the Jewish War of 66-73 in Palestine many fled the Holy Land to find new homes. The Frankish Emperor Charlemagne (724-814) actively encouraged Jewish immigration. Jewish merchants were treated favourably, because of their trade connections with the Mediterranean and the East, and they soon developed good business relations, especially as money lenders, with the kings and nobles of western Europe. The Jews were 'useful', since usury was forbidden to Christians. Jewish settlements spread out from north-eastern France along the valleys of the Rhine, the Elbe and the Danube, and across the English Channel to London.

The Jews of northern Europe were known as the Ashkenazim. There was also an equally large Jewish colonization in Spain and Portugal, known as the Sephardim. By 1100 the Ashkenazim and Sephardim together far outnumbered the ancient Jewish communities of the Middle East.

Resentment of their increasing numbers and their economic rise in society grew steadily among the townsfolk, and Jews were frequently scapegoated. The advent of the Crusades provided the excuse for intensified discrimination against Jews, and two centuries of persecutions and expulsions followed. Jews were attacked by mobs in the Rhineland during the First Crusade. They were expelled from England in 1290 and from France from the thirteenth century, culminating in a major expulsion in 1394. Pope Innocent III passed restrictive measures in the Fourth Lateran Council of 1215, requiring Jews to wear distinctive dress. They were also forced to live in separate districts, or ghettos.

The result was a steady migration of Jews eastwards across central Europe to Poland, Hungary, Lithuania and Russia.

The Rhine valley.

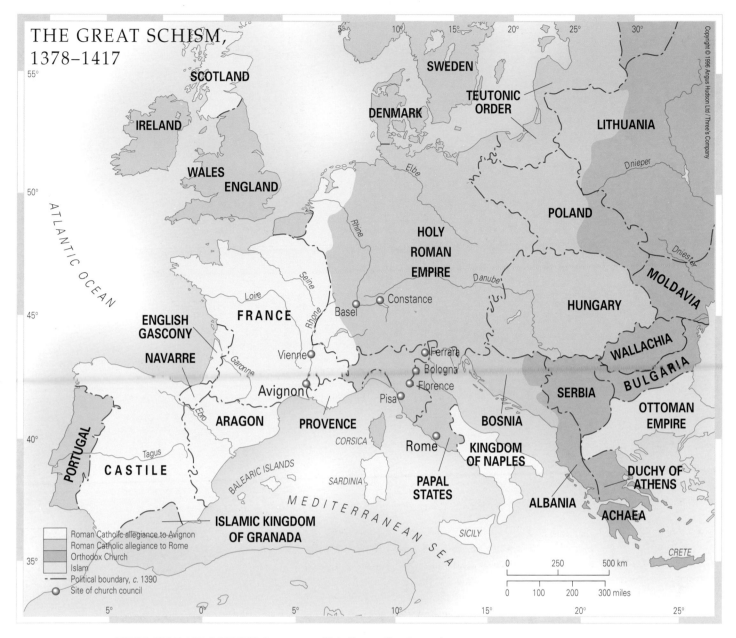

THE GREAT SCHISM, 1378–1417

SCOTLAND

IRELAND

WALES
ENGLAND

ATLANTIC OCEAN

SWEDEN

DENMARK

TEUTONIC
ORDER

LITHUANIA

Dnieper

POLAND

Elbe

Rhine

HOLY
ROMAN
EMPIRE

Danube

Dniester

MOLDAVIA

Seine

Loire

FRANCE

Constance

Basel

Vienne

HUNGARY

Rhône

WALLACHIA

ENGLISH
GASCONY

NAVARRE

Garonne

Ferrara

Bologna

Florence

Avignon

Pisa

BULGARIA

SERBIA

OTTOMAN
EMPIRE

Ebro

ARAGON

PROVENCE

CORSICA

Rome

BOSNIA

KINGDOM
OF NAPLES

DUCHY OF
ATHENS

PORTUGAL

Tagus

CASTILE

BALEARIC ISLANDS

SARDINIA

PAPAL
STATES

ALBANIA

ACHAEA

MEDITERRANEAN SEA

SICILY

CRETE

ISLAMIC KINGDOM
OF GRANADA

Roman Catholic allegiance to Avignon
Roman Catholic allegiance to Rome
Orthodox Church
Islam
Political boundary, c. 1390
Site of church council

0   250   500 km

0   100   200   300 miles

THE GREAT SCHISM

The Great Schism was a division of Western Christendom into two camps, following the exile of the papacy at Avignon, known as the 'Babylonian Captivity'. In 1302 Pope Boniface VIII issued the bull 'Unam Sanctam', in which he declared the pope to have authority over any king. The next year he excommunicated Philip IV of France. Philip promptly ordered the arrest of Boniface, who died shortly afterwards.

Political instability in Italy and the Papal States, together with the need of protection from the French king, rendered the papal seat in Rome untenable. The papacy was moved to Avignon, where a succession of French Popes presided, under French control, in effect, from 1309 to 1377. These popes were resented in England and in the

Holy Roman Empire, and pressure began to build from devout Christians who revered the See of St Peter as the true centre of the Roman church. Eventually, the Avignon Pope Gregory XI returned to Rome, where he died soon after. A fraught period of electing his successor was followed by the withdrawal of support from French cardinals, and soon rival popes divided the allegiance of Europe between them.

At one point there were three competing popes. A series of councils, led by conciliarists who sought to make council superior to pope, tried to heal the divide. It was not until the Council of Constance (1414-17) that the split was effectively healed. Martin V was acknowledged by nearly all as the sole and rightful pope, but antipopes did not die out until mid-century.

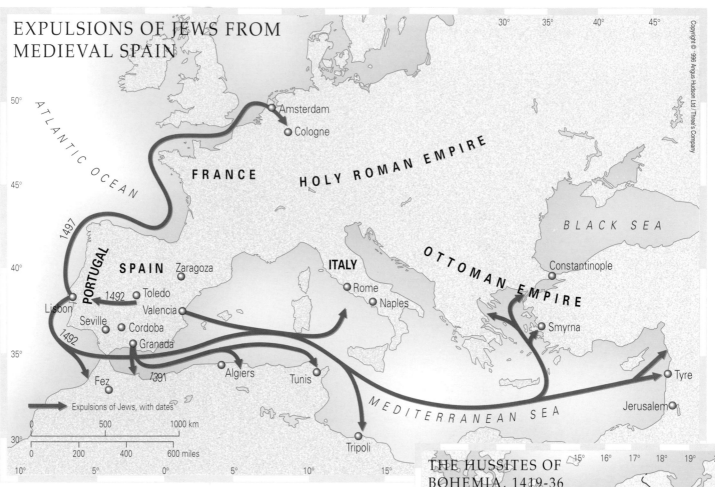

EXPULSIONS OF JEWS FROM MEDIEVAL SPAIN

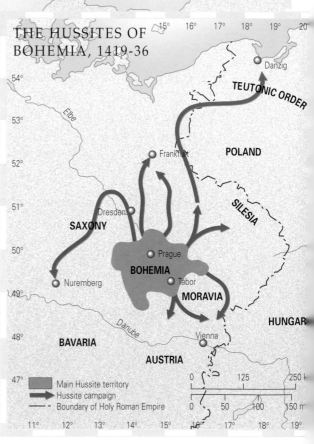

THE EXPULSION OF THE JEWS FROM SPAIN

Until the second half of the fourteenth century the Jews of Spain, or the Sephardim, had been spared the persecutions which the Ashkenazi Jews of northern Europe had suffered. Most were unaffected by the Christian reconquest of Spain and lived in established communities. However, growing political instability, and the sermons of church leaders, turned the populace against them. In 1391 anti-Jewish violence in Seville spread through Castile and Aragon.

Instead of martyrdom, tens of thousands of Jews opted to convert to Christianity and became labelled by their enemies as *marranos* ('swine'). They reconstructed their communities, but by the middle of the fifteenth century had aroused hostility again. The genuineness of their new 'Christian' faith was tried by councils of the Spanish Inquisition, often with barbaric methods, and secret Jews were rooted out. With the capture of the Alhambra of Granada, the last bastion of Islam, in 1492, a decree was issued by

Ferdinand and Isabella banishing all Jews from Spain.

Between 100,000 and 150,000 Jews departed. Some went across the border to Portugal, but most set sail for North Africa and Ottoman Turkey.

THE HUSSITES

As well as ending the Great Schism, the Council of Constance was called to combat heresy. One of those condemned to death was Jan Hus (John Huss) (*c.* 1372-1415). Hus was a reformer from Bohemia whose preaching against the morals of the clergy angered the church authorities but won him wide support among the townsfolk.

He became a national hero on his death and the Czech people established the Hussite church. This church formed a national focus for rebellion against both the papacy and the Holy Roman Empire. It was also known as the Bohemian Brethren. It survived until the Hapsburgs restored the Roman

Catholic church in 1620. Remnants regrouped and became influential in Moravia.

ATLAS of the Bible and Christianity

THE MODERN CHURCH

VOYAGES OF DISCOVERY

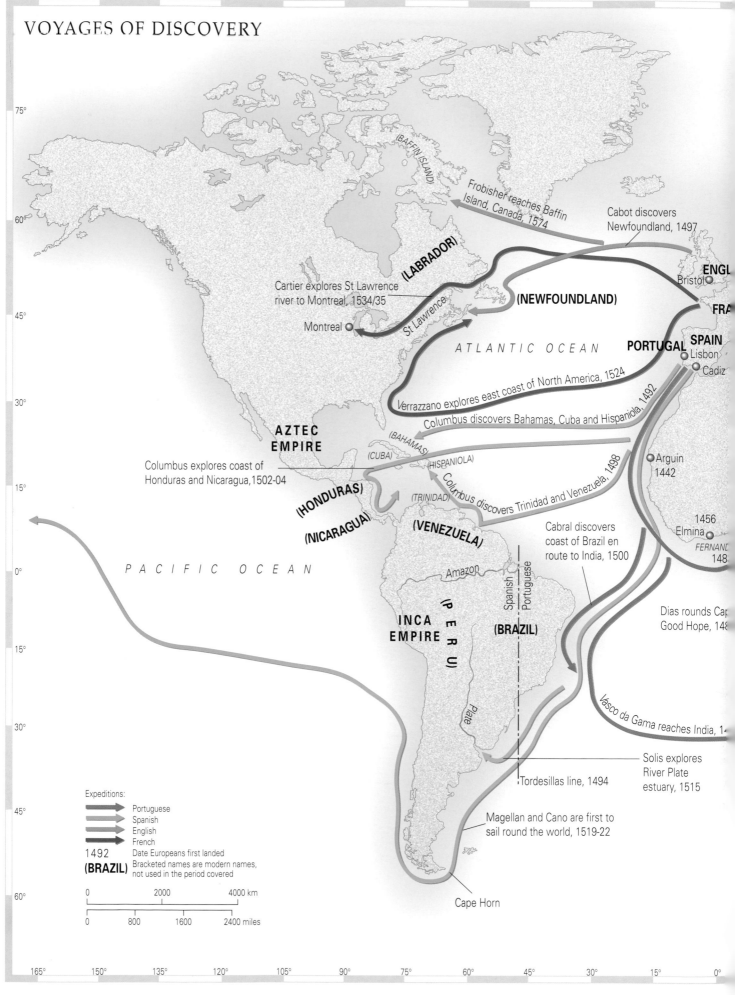

(BAFFIN ISLAND)

Frobisher reaches Baffin Island, Canada, 1574

Cabot discovers Newfoundland, 1497

(LABRADOR)

ENGL

Bristol

Cartier explores St Lawrence river to Montreal, 1534/35

(NEWFOUNDLAND)

FRA

Montreal

St Lawrence

ATLANTIC OCEAN

PORTUGAL **SPAIN**

Lisbon

Cadiz

Verrazzano explores east coast of North America, 1524

Columbus discovers Bahamas, Cuba and Hispaniola, 1492

AZTEC EMPIRE

(BAHAMAS)

(CUBA)

(HISPANIOLA)

Arguin 1442

Columbus explores coast of Honduras and Nicaragua, 1502-04

Columbus discovers Trinidad and Venezuela, 1498

1456
Elmina

FERNAND
148

(HONDURAS)

(TRINIDAD)

(NICARAGUA)

(VENEZUELA)

Cabral discovers coast of Brazil en route to India, 1500

PACIFIC OCEAN

Amazon

Spanish

Portuguese

Dias rounds Cap Good Hope, 148

INCA EMPIRE

(P E R U)

(BRAZIL)

Vasco da Gama reaches India, 1

Plate

Solis explores River Plate estuary, 1515

Tordesillas line, 1494

Magellan and Cano are first to sail round the world, 1519-22

Expeditions:

Portuguese
Spanish
English
French

1492   Date Europeans first landed
(BRAZIL)   Bracketed names are modern names, not used in the period covered

0   2000   4000 km

0   800   1600   2400 miles

Cape Horn

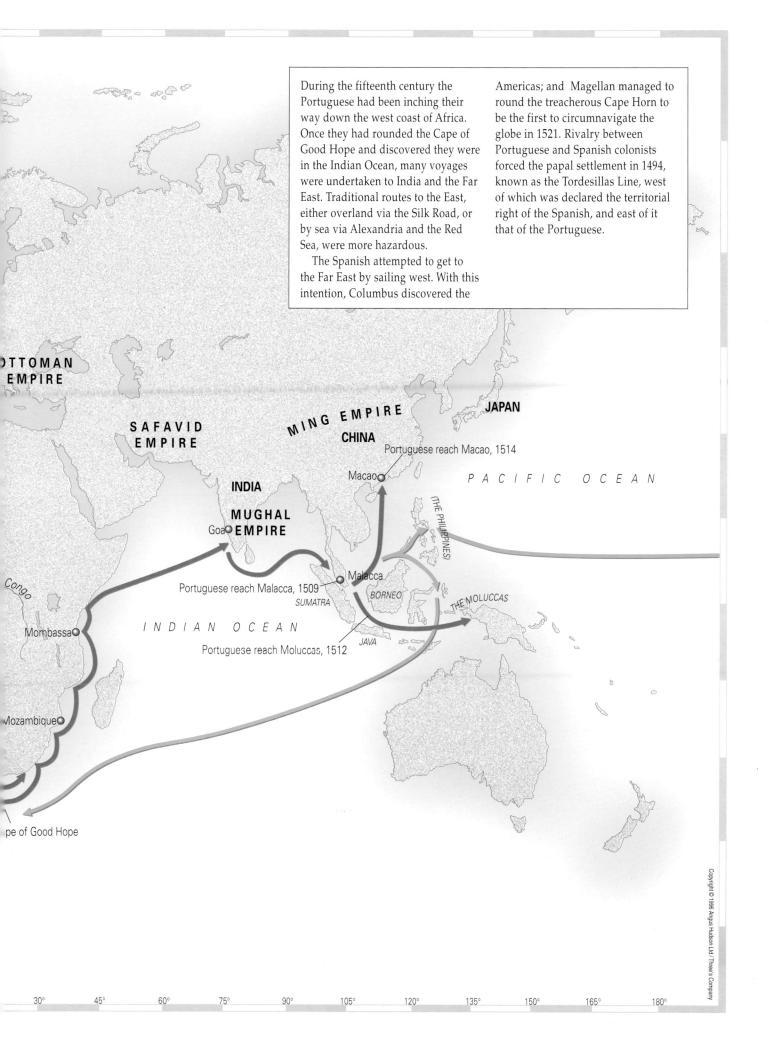

During the fifteenth century the Portuguese had been inching their way down the west coast of Africa. Once they had rounded the Cape of Good Hope and discovered they were in the Indian Ocean, many voyages were undertaken to India and the Far East. Traditional routes to the East, either overland via the Silk Road, or by sea via Alexandria and the Red Sea, were more hazardous.

The Spanish attempted to get to the Far East by sailing west. With this intention, Columbus discovered the Americas; and Magellan managed to round the treacherous Cape Horn to be the first to circumnavigate the globe in 1521. Rivalry between Portuguese and Spanish colonists forced the papal settlement in 1494, known as the Tordesillas Line, west of which was declared the territorial right of the Spanish, and east of it that of the Portuguese.

OTTOMAN EMPIRE

SAFAVID EMPIRE

MING EMPIRE

CHINA

JAPAN

Portuguese reach Macao, 1514

Macao

PACIFIC OCEAN

INDIA

MUGHAL EMPIRE

Goa

(THE PHILIPPINES)

Malacca

Portuguese reach Malacca, 1509

SUMATRA

BORNEO

THE MOLUCCAS

Congo

Mombassa

INDIAN OCEAN

Portuguese reach Moluccas, 1512

JAVA

Mozambique

Cape of Good Hope

30°   45°   60°   75°   90°   105°   120°   135°   150°   165°   180°

REFORMATION EUROPE

In 1517, Martin Luther posted his 95 Theses on the church door at Wittenberg. In 1520, Huldreich Zwingli of Zurich revolted against Rome, and John Calvin, in 1533, had a vision that he should lead a mission to restore the Church to its original purity, an objective he held in common with most of the Protestant reformers.

However, as much of the Reformation was motivated by politics as by religion. The opportunity was there for kings and leaders in Europe to take advantage of the Church's unpopularity and seize some of its wealth and power. Henry VIII declared himself absolute head of the Church of England in 1534. Many German princes supported Luther. After the condemnation of his teachings at the Diet of Worms by Emperor Charles V in 1521, the princes forced the Peace of Augsburg (1555), in which a prince was allowed to adopt either Catholicism or Lutheranism for his subjects. Luther was obliged to turn against the more radical dissenters in Germany, such as the Anabaptists, who precipitated the Peasants' Revolt in 1525. Calvinism took root in France, Poland, Hungary and Scotland; the Calvinist Church of Scotland being formed in 1560.

St Giles' Cathedral, Edinburgh, from which John Knox led the Scottish Reformation.

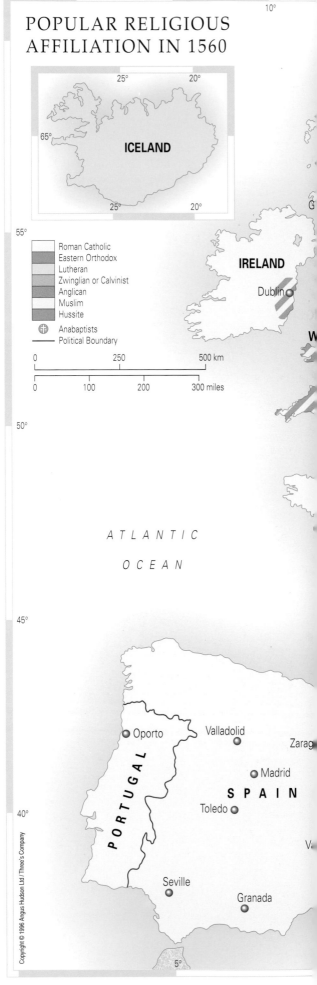

POPULAR RELIGIOUS AFFILIATION IN 1560

- Roman Catholic
- Eastern Orthodox
- Lutheran
- Zwinglian or Calvinist
- Anglican
- Muslim
- Hussite
- ✠ Anabaptists
- — Political Boundary

0   250   500 km
0   100   200   300 miles

ICELAND

IRELAND

Dublin

ATLANTIC

OCEAN

Oporto

Valladolid

Zarag

PORTUGAL

Madrid

SPAIN

Toledo

Seville

Granada

NORWAY

SWEDEN

FINLAND

ESTONIA

RUSSIA

LIVONIA

COURLAND

•Stockholm

York
ENGLAND

NORTH
SEA

BALTIC
SEA

DENMARK

•Copenhagen

Konigsberg

LITHUANIA

PRUSSIA

Danzig

Groningen

Bremen Hamburg

Amsterdam

Munster

Antwerp

Magdeburg

Warsaw

POLAND

London

Canterbury

HOLY ROMAN

Wittenberg

EMPIRE

Zwickau

Frankfurt

Rouen   Rheims

Edict of Worms, 1521,
condemns Lutheranism

•Prague

BOHEMIA

Paris

Worms

Regensburg

MORAVIA

Brno

Augsburg

Tours

Zurich

Munich

Vienna

Budapest

Salzburg

Poitiers

Nevers

Peace of Augsburg, 1555,
recognizes existence of Lutheranism

FRANCE

HUNGARY

Lyons

Geneva

Milan

Venice

deaux

Toulouse   Avignon

Modena   Ferrara

ADRIATIC
SEA

Bucharest

Marseilles

Florence

OTTOMAN EMPIRE

CORSICA

PAPAL
STATES

Barcelona

•Rome

KINGDOM
OF NAPLES

BALEARIC ISLANDS

SARDINIA

•Naples

MEDITERRANEAN   SEA

SICILY

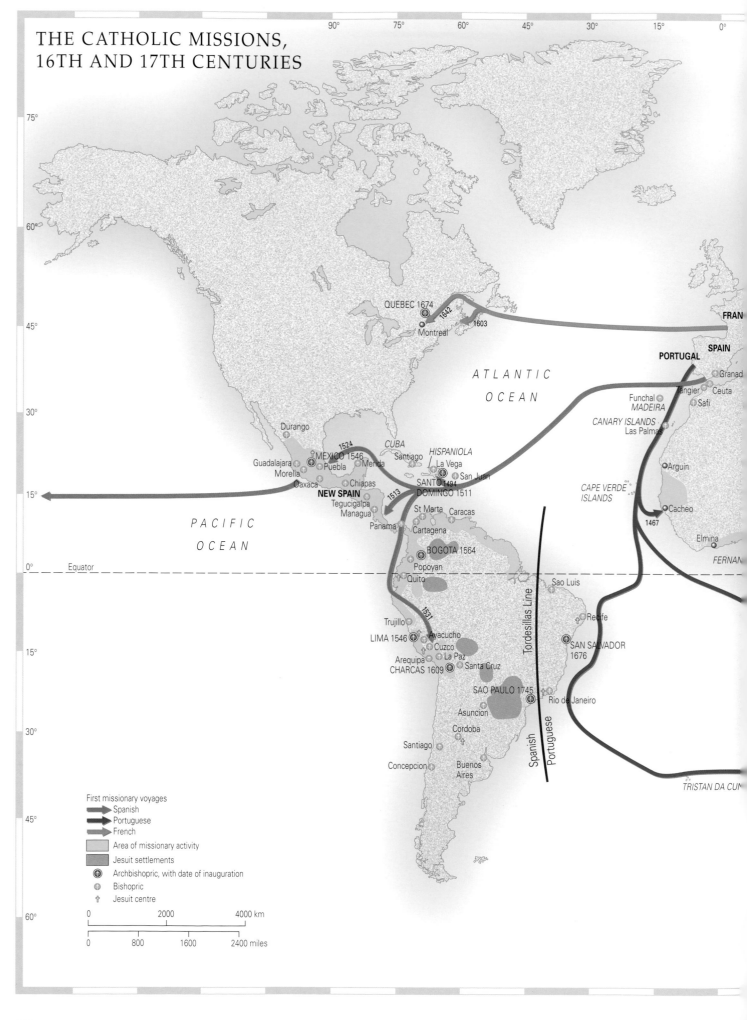

THE CATHOLIC MISSIONS,
16TH AND 17TH CENTURIES

90°   75°   60°   45°   30°   15°   0°

75°

60°

45°

ATLANTIC

OCEAN

QUEBEC 1674
Montreal
1642
1603

FRAN

SPAIN

PORTUGAL

Granad
Funchal
MADEIRA
Tangier
Ceuta
Safi
CANARY ISLANDS
Las Palmas

30°

Durango

1524
CUBA
MEXICO 1546
Guadalajara   Puebla   Santiago
Morelia   Merida
Oaxaca   Chiapas
NEW SPAIN
SANTO 1494
DOMINGO 1511
HISPANIOLA
La Vega
San Juan

Arguin

CAPE VERDE
ISLANDS

Cacheo
1467

Elmina

FERNAN

15°

Tegucigalpa
Managua
Panama
1513
St Marta   Caracas
Cartagena

BOGOTA 1564
Popoyan
Quito

PACIFIC

OCEAN

0°   Equator

Sao Luis

Tordesillas Line

Recife

SAN SALVADOR
1676

1531
Trujillo
LIMA 1546   Ayacucho
Cuzco
Arequipa   La Paz
CHARCAS 1609   Santa Cruz

15°

SAO PAULO 1745
Rio de Janeiro
Asuncion
Cordoba
Santiago
Concepcion   Buenos
Aires

Spanish
Portuguese

30°

TRISTAN DA CUN

45°

First missionary voyages
Spanish
Portuguese
French
Area of missionary activity
Jesuit settlements
Archbishopric, with date of inauguration
Bishopric
Jesuit centre

60°

0   2000   4000 km
0   800   1600   2400 miles

30° 45° 60° 75° 90° 105° 120° 135° 150° 165° 180°

PACIFIC OCEAN

Beijing

1601

JAPAN

Nanjing Nagasaki Funai
Kagoshima

CHINA

Macao

Francis Xavier 1549

INDIA
GOA 1557

Francis Xavier 1542 St Tome
Mylapore
CRANGANORE 1605 Cochin

Matteo Ricci 1582

Vigan
MANILA 1595 1565

PHILIPPINES
Cebu

Matteo Ricci 1578

Malacca MORO
ISLANDS Equator
SUMATRA BORNEO

Mombasa

INDIAN OCEAN

Francis Xavier 1547

JAVA

Mozambique

Interior of the Gesù, Rome, mother church of the Jesuit order.

CATHOLIC MISSIONS

Part of the justification for the conquest of unknown lands by European powers was the opportunity it presented of extending the frontier of Christianity. The Pope instructed these powers to take missionaries with them, and to found bishoprics in a diocesan network.

One of the aims of the Jesuit Order was to evangelize the 'heathen'; and Jesuits, along with Dominicans, Franciscans, Augustinians and Capuchins, were the main missionary bodies in the Americas during the sixteenth and seventeenth centuries. One of the first Jesuit missionaries to the East was Francis Xavier, who reached Goa in India in 1542, and Japan in 1549. Matteo Ricci worked in China from 1582. However, in the Far East, some rulers became suspicious of the power of the Pope, and the Church was unable to lay any permanent foundations, especially in China, until future waves of missionaries arrived in the nineteenth century.

Likewise, in Africa, only a superficial impact was made in this earlier period, namely in the Congo and Mozambique.

Not till the time of the later explorer-missionaries of the nineteenth century was any lasting influence established. In South and Central America, wholesale conversions of indigenous communities were organized by missionary teams. The Jesuits invented a social order, known as a *'reduction'*, in which the indigenous population would live isolated from the outside world under the paternalist direction of European Jesuit priests.

The dome of St Peter's Rome.

THE CATHOLIC REFORMATION

The Catholic Reformation was the revival of the Roman Catholic Church in the face of growing support for Protestantism. Internal reform of the religious orders had begun in the 1520s. The Jesuit Society was founded in 1534 by Ignatius Loyola (1491-1556) to spearhead the revival, and was largely responsible for consolidating the Catholic faith in southern Europe. The Council of Trent (1545-63) was called to re-establish doctrines of the Catholicism which had been called into question as a result of Protestantism, and to renew disciplines of the spiritual life. The supremacy of the pope was confirmed. The Thirty Years War (1618-1648) was the final phase of the struggle between Catholics and Protestants. It was fought out in the Holy Roman Empire (Germany), with the Danes, English, Dutch and Swedes supporting German Protestant princes against the Catholic rulers. The main outcome was the recovery for Rome of southern Germany and Poland.

THE CATHOLIC RECOVERY, *c.* 1650

RUSSIA

SWEDEN

BALTIC SEA

BALTIC STATES

DENMARK–NORWAY

Copenhagen

EAST PRUSSIA

Danzig Konigsberg

Vilnius

SCOTLAND

NORTH SEA

Hamburg

Elbe

Vistula

IRELAND

WALES

ENGLAND

UNITED PROVINCES

HOLY ROMAN EMPIRE

Munster

Warsaw

POLAND

London

Antwerp

Mons

Liege

Rhine

Prague

Krakow

Douai

Rouen

Mainz

Wurzburg

Rheims

Trier

ATLANTIC OCEAN

Seine

Paris

Verdun

Molsheim

Danube

HUNGARY

Nancy

Dillingen

Ingolstadt

Vienna

La Flèche

Pont-à-Mousson

Zurich

Budapest

OTTOMAN EMPIRE

Loire

Tours

Bourges

Dôle

SWISS CONFEDERATION

MILAN

Graz

REPUBLIC OF VENICE

FRANCE

Geneva

Lyons

SAVOY

Milan

Venice

Bordeaux

Garonne

Rhone

Avignon

Genoa

Ravenna

Florence

Colonies of Venice

Santiago de Compostela

Toulouse

PARMA

GENOA

MODENA

PAPAL STATES

CORSICA

TUSCANY

Rome

PORTUGAL

Valladolid

Salamanca

Madrid

Ebro

Tagus

Toledo

Sassari

Naples

KINGDOM OF TWO SICILIES

Lisbon

SPAIN

Valencia

BALEARIC ISLANDS

SARDINIA

Cagliari

Seville

Palermo

Messina

MEDITERRANEAN SEA

Catholic

Protestant

Eastern Orthodox

Muslim

Important Jesuit centre

Political Boundary

0   250   500 km

0   100   200   300 miles

GERMAN PROTESTANTISM IN 1618

NORTH SEA

DENMARK

BALTIC SEA

MECKLENBURG

Elbe

BREMEN

POLAND

Berlin

BRANDENBURG

UNITED PROVINCES

Rhine

MUNSTER

Wittenberg

SPANISH NETHERLANDS

Cologne

SAXONY

HESSE

GERMAN (HOLY ROMAN) EMPIRE

Dresden

SILESIA

Frankfurt

Worms

PALATINATE

BOHEMIA

Nuremberg

MORAVIA

WURTTEMBERG

Strasbourg

BAVARIA

Augsburg

AUGSBURG

Munich

Danube

AUSTRIA

Vienna

HUNGARY

FRANCE

FRANCHE–COMTE

Basel

Lake Constance

Salzburg

STYRIA

SWISS CONFEDERATION

Zurich

SALZBURG

TYROL

Lake Geneva

CARINTHIA

OTTOMAN EMPIRE

Geneva

CARNIOLA

VENICE

Majority denomination:
- Catholic
- Lutheran
- Calvinist and Zwinglian
- Muslim area
- Political Boundary

0   125   250 km
0   50   100   150 miles

ADRIATIC SEA

PAPAL STATES

MEDITERRANEAN SEA

GERMAN PROTESTANTISM

Protestantism reached its greatest extent in Germany under Emperor Maximilian II (1564-76), who was confessionally neutral. Many of the north German bishoprics converted to Protestantism during this time.

After the compromising formula of the Concordat of 1577, most Lutherans adopted a less politically aggressive stance than had been held earlier in the century. In Saxony, the heartland of Lutheran orthodoxy, Lutheranism became a quietistic faith of the common people. Calvinists, on the other hand, hardened their position. They won support from the princes of the Electoral Palatinate, which became common ground for German, French, Dutch and Bohemian Protestantism.

Archduke Ferdinand II led a brutal Catholic reaction in Styria, Carinthia and Carniola, with first the expulsion of, and then the execution of, many Protestants after 1596. Bohemia suffered badly in the Thirty Years War (1618-1648) in which many Protestant nobles either had their property confiscated, or were executed. This laid the foundation for Czech hatred of German domination.

FRENCH PROTESTANTISM

The Huguenot Wars were fought between 1562 and 1598. Peace came when Henry IV of Bourbon converted to Catholicism. The Edict of Nantes (1598) granted the Huguenots freedom of worship and political equality and France accepted a Protestant minority. The Huguenots established themselves in the south and around Poitou in the west.

However, the rise of Absolutism in France, with its ruling maxim of 'one king, one faith, one law', led to a renewed persecution of the Huguenots. Their last stronghold (Rochelle) was taken in 1628. The Revocation of the Edict of Nantes in 1685 prompted about half a million Huguenots to flee the country. Most went to Brandenburg in Germany, Holland and England.

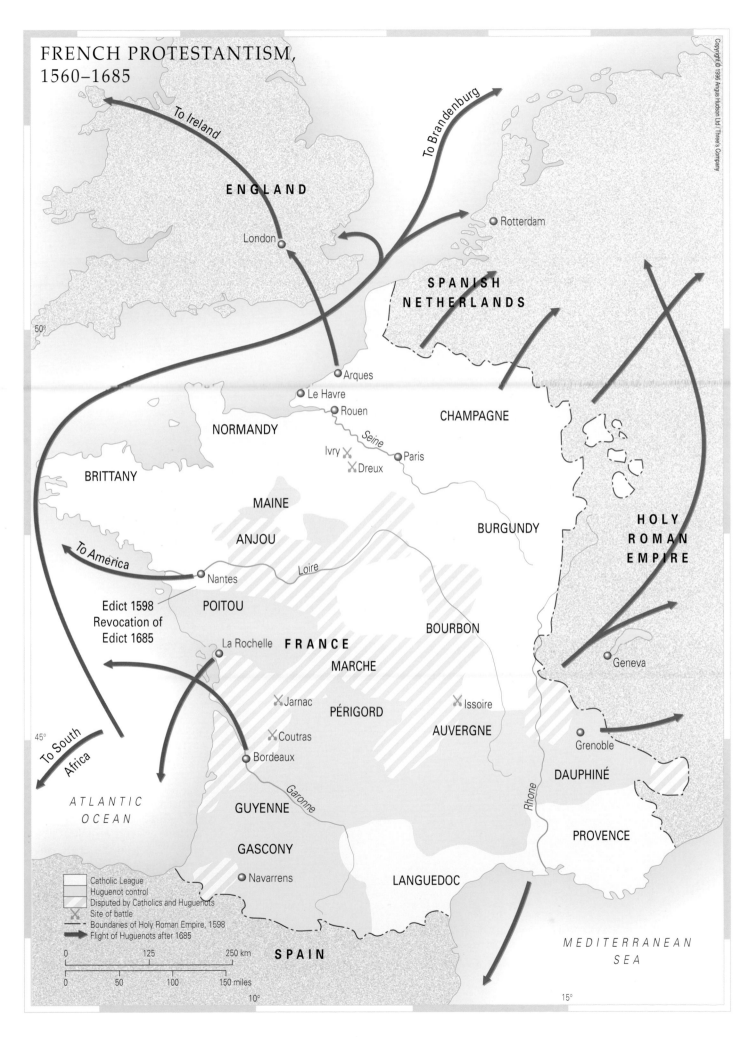

FRENCH PROTESTANTISM, 1560–1685

To Ireland

ENGLAND

To Brandenburg

London

Rotterdam

SPANISH NETHERLANDS

Arques

Le Havre

Rouen

CHAMPAGNE

Seine

NORMANDY

Ivry

Dreux

Paris

BRITTANY

MAINE

BURGUNDY

ANJOU

HOLY ROMAN EMPIRE

To America

Loire

Nantes

Edict 1598
Revocation of
Edict 1685

POITOU

BOURBON

La Rochelle

FRANCE

MARCHE

Geneva

Jarnac

Issoire

PÉRIGORD

To South Africa

Coutras

AUVERGNE

Grenoble

Bordeaux

Garonne

DAUPHINÉ

ATLANTIC OCEAN

GUYENNE

Rhone

PROVENCE

GASCONY

Navarrens

LANGUEDOC

Catholic League
Huguenot control
Disputed by Catholics and Huguenots
Site of battle
Boundaries of Holy Roman Empire, 1598
Flight of Huguenots after 1685

0   125   250 km

0   50   100   150 miles

SPAIN

MEDITERRANEAN SEA

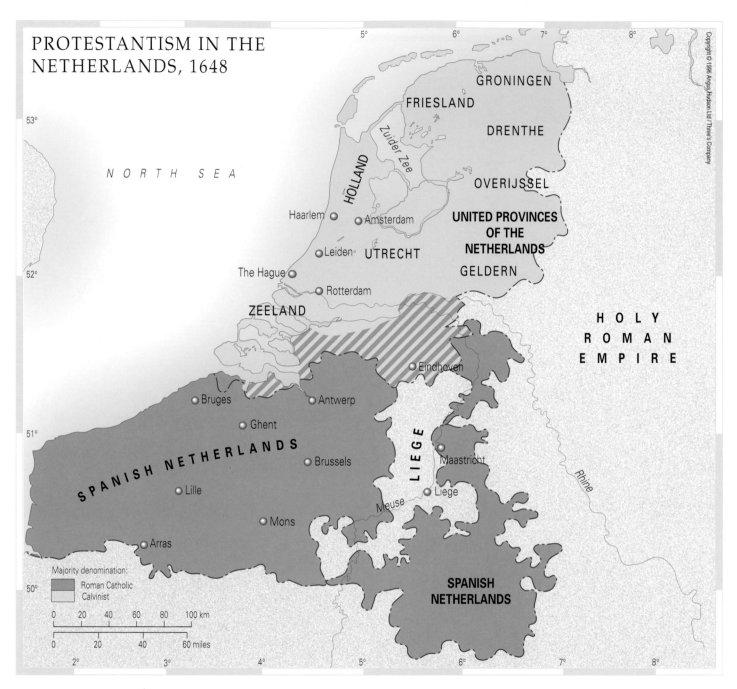

PROTESTANTISM IN THE NETHERLANDS, 1648

5°   6°   7°   8°

GRONINGEN

FRIESLAND

DRENTHE

Zuider Zee

OVERIJSSEL

HOLLAND

53°

N O R T H   S E A

UNITED PROVINCES
OF THE
NETHERLANDS

Haarlem ○   ○ Amsterdam

○ Leiden   UTRECHT

52°

The Hague ○

GELDERN

○ Rotterdam

ZEELAND

H O L Y
R O M A N
E M P I R E

○ Eindhoven

○ Bruges   ○ Antwerp

LIEGE

○ Ghent

Maastricht

51°

S P A N I S H   N E T H E R L A N D S

○ Brussels

Rhine

○ Lille

○ Liege

Meuse

○ Mons

○ Arras

Majority denomination:
Roman Catholic
Calvinist

SPANISH
NETHERLANDS

50°

0   20   40   60   80   100 km

0   20   40   60 miles

2°   3°   4°   5°   6°   7°   8°

PROTESTANTISM IN THE NETHERLANDS

The Netherlands were divided into the Spanish south, which was
Catholic, and the United Provinces of the north, which were Protestant.
Early on the United Provinces followed Luther, but some Dutch
Protestants became Anabaptists. The Melchiorites, named after Melchior
Hoffmann, found supporters in Haarlem and Leiden. They turned from
being a radical millenarian sect to a more quietistic group after the
influence of the Frisian preacher Menno Simons (d. 1559). They became
known as Mennonites, and spread from the Netherlands to Russia and
North America.

From the 1560s, Calvinism became the focus for rebelling against
Spanish rule, which had extended to the north. Strict Calvinism became
the official creed in the United Provinces after the Council of Dort
(1618-19).

PIETISM AND EVANGELICAL AWAKENING

Pietism was a movement within Lutheranism that modified Luther's
doctrine of 'justification' by placing new emphasis on 'sanctification',
believing that the in-dwelling Christ brings the believer to a life of
holiness. Spener formed his 'assembly of piety' in 1669 and proposed
prayer and Bible meetings. No distinct church formed, however, until
Count Zinzendorf founded a colony, in 1722, on his estates in Saxony,
whose inhabitants became known as the Moravian Brethren.

The Moravian Brethren were active missionaries in Europe and across
the Atlantic. Through Moravian influence John Wesley, founder of the
Methodists, had an evangelical experience of assurance of salvation in
1738 at Aldersgate Street in London; Wesley subsequently maintained
links with the Brethren. One notable Pietist, August Francke (1663-
1727), influenced devotion as far east as Moscow, and he educated
Swedish students.

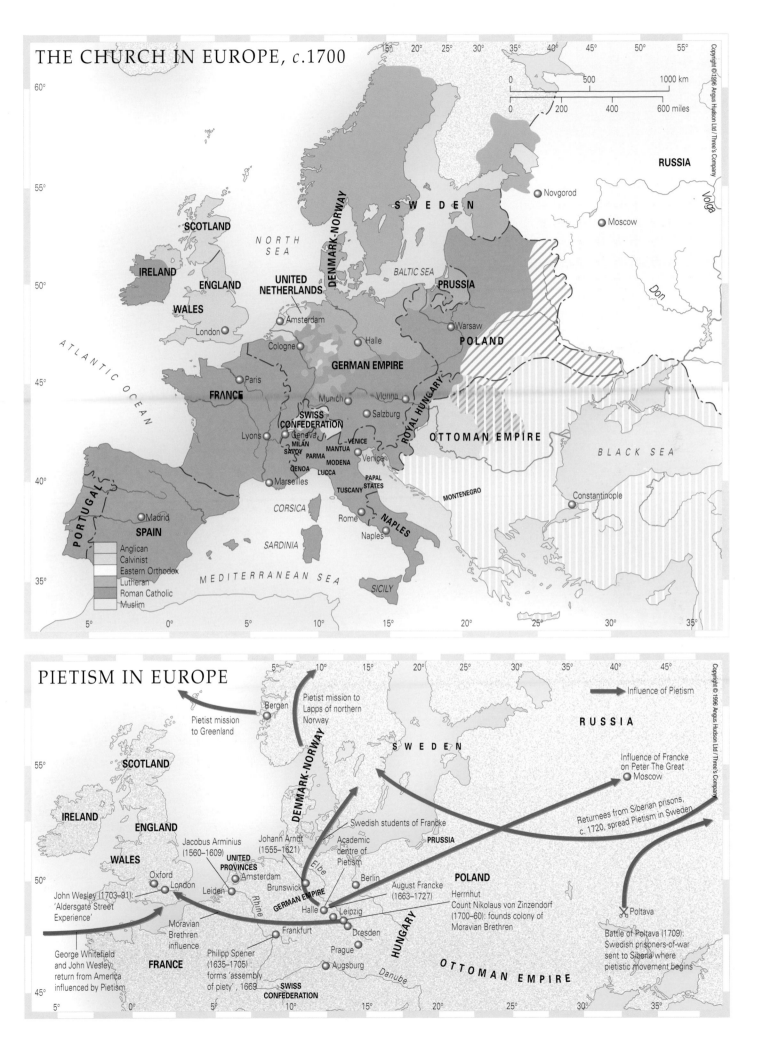

THE CHURCH IN EUROPE, *c.*1700

RUSSIA

Novgorod

Moscow

Volga

SWEDEN

SCOTLAND

NORTH SEA

BALTIC SEA

IRELAND

ENGLAND

WALES

London

UNITED NETHERLANDS

DENMARK-NORWAY

PRUSSIA

Warsaw

POLAND

Don

Amsterdam

Cologne

Halle

ATLANTIC OCEAN

GERMAN EMPIRE

Paris

FRANCE

Munich

Vienna

ROYAL HUNGARY

Salzburg

SWISS CONFEDERATION

Geneva

Lyons

MILAN

SAVOY

PARMA

MANTUA

VENICE

OTTOMAN EMPIRE

BLACK SEA

Venice

MODENA

GENOA

LUCCA

PAPAL STATES

Marseilles

TUSCANY

MONTENEGRO

Constantinople

PORTUGAL

Madrid

SPAIN

CORSICA

Rome

NAPLES

Naples

SARDINIA

MEDITERRANEAN SEA

SICILY

Anglican
Calvinist
Eastern Orthodox
Lutheran
Roman Catholic
Muslim

PIETISM IN EUROPE

→ Influence of Pietism

Bergen

Pietist mission to Greenland

Pietist mission to Lapps of northern Norway

DENMARK-NORWAY

SWEDEN

RUSSIA

Influence of Francke on Peter The Great

Moscow

SCOTLAND

IRELAND

ENGLAND

WALES

Jacobus Arminius (1560–1609)

Johann Arndt (1555–1621)

Swedish students of Francke

Academic centre of Pietism

PRUSSIA

Returnees from Siberian prisons, c. 1720, spread Pietism in Sweden

Oxford

London

UNITED PROVINCES

Amsterdam

Leiden

Elbe

Berlin

POLAND

August Francke (1663–1727)

John Wesley (1703–91) 'Aldersgate Street Experience'

Brunswick

GERMAN EMPIRE

Halle

Leipzig

Herrnhut
Count Nikolaus von Zinzendorf (1700–60): founds colony of Moravian Brethren

Poltava

Moravian Brethren influence

Rhine

Frankfurt

Dresden

HUNGARY

Battle of Poltava (1709): Swedish prisoners-of-war sent to Siberia where pietistic movement begins

George Whitefield and John Wesley return from America influenced by Pietism

FRANCE

Philipp Spener (1635–1705): forms 'assembly of piety', 1669

Prague

Augsburg

SWISS CONFEDERATION

Danube

OTTOMAN EMPIRE

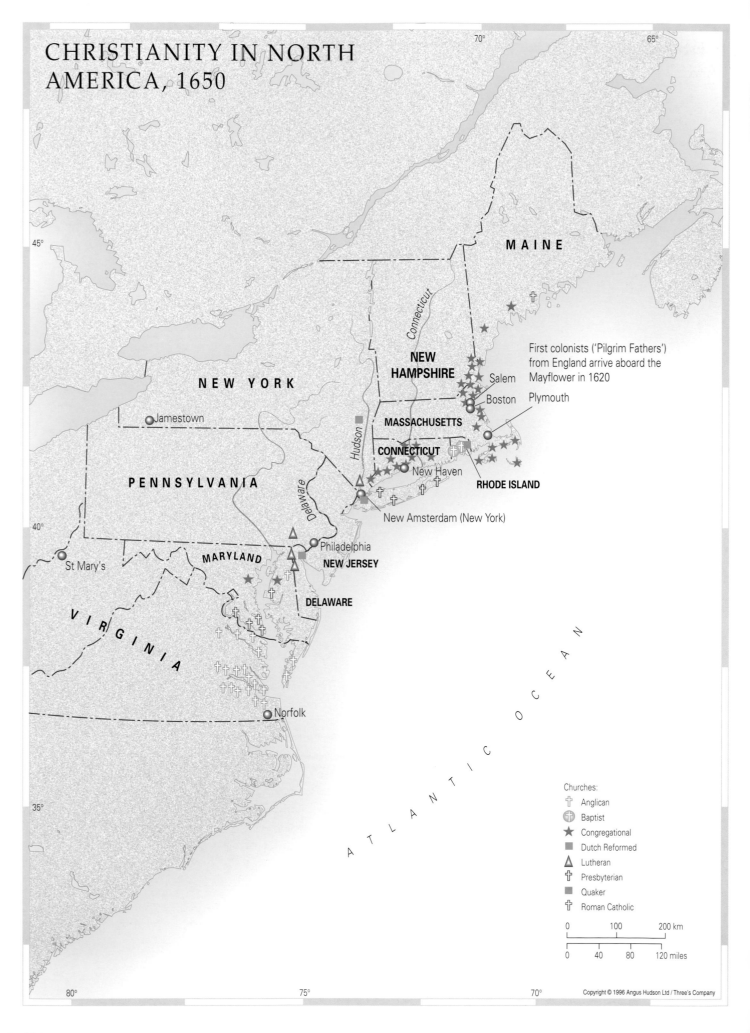

CHRISTIANITY IN NORTH AMERICA, 1650

MAINE

NEW HAMPSHIRE

NEW YORK

Connecticut

First colonists ('Pilgrim Fathers') from England arrive aboard the Mayflower in 1620

Salem

Boston

Plymouth

Jamestown

MASSACHUSETTS

Hudson

CONNECTICUT

New Haven

RHODE ISLAND

PENNSYLVANIA

Delaware

New Amsterdam (New York)

Philadelphia

St Mary's

MARYLAND

NEW JERSEY

DELAWARE

VIRGINIA

Norfolk

ATLANTIC OCEAN

Churches:

✝ Anglican

✪ Baptist

★ Congregational

◼ Dutch Reformed

△ Lutheran

✝ Presbyterian

◼ Quaker

✝ Roman Catholic

| 0 | | 100 | | 200 km |
| 0 | 40 | 80 | | 120 miles |

Copyright © 1996 Angus Hudson Ltd / Three's Company

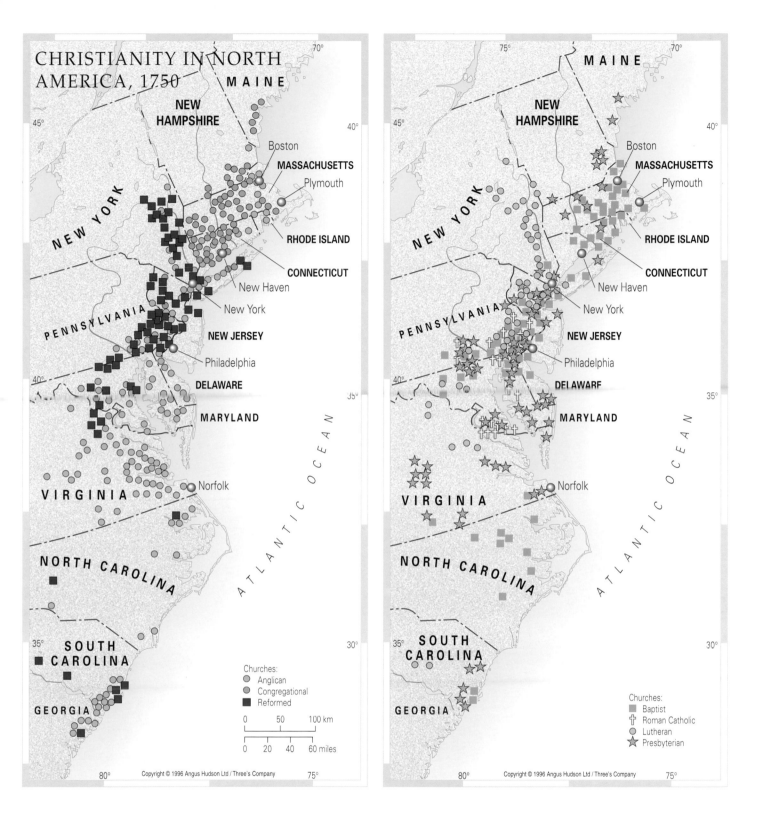

CHRISTIANITY IN NORTH AMERICA, 1750

MAINE
NEW HAMPSHIRE
Boston
MASSACHUSETTS
Plymouth
RHODE ISLAND
NEW YORK
CONNECTICUT
New Haven
New York
PENNSYLVANIA
NEW JERSEY
Philadelphia
DELAWARE
MARYLAND
ATLANTIC OCEAN
VIRGINIA
Norfolk
NORTH CAROLINA
SOUTH CAROLINA
GEORGIA

Churches:
○ Anglican
● Congregational
■ Reformed

0   50   100 km
0 20 40 60 miles

Copyright © 1996 Angus Hudson Ltd / Three's Company

MAINE
NEW HAMPSHIRE
Boston
MASSACHUSETTS
Plymouth
RHODE ISLAND
NEW YORK
CONNECTICUT
New Haven
New York
PENNSYLVANIA
NEW JERSEY
Philadelphia
DELAWARF
MARYLAND
ATLANTIC OCEAN
VIRGINIA
Norfolk
NORTH CAROLINA
SOUTH CAROLINA
GEORGIA

Churches:
■ Baptist
✝ Roman Catholic
○ Lutheran
★ Presbyterian

Copyright © 1996 Angus Hudson Ltd / Three's Company

CHRISTIANITY IN NORTH AMERICA

Persecution of non-conformist churches in Europe resulted in flights to North America. The Pilgrim Fathers established a colony of Calvinists at Plymouth in 1620. After 1630 Puritans founded a colony at Massachusetts Bay. Rhode Island became a colony of religious toleration, and William Penn established Pennsylvania as a refuge for

Quakers. Roman Catholics settled in Maryland from 1634.

A more pluralistic pattern emerged in the eighteenth century with the immigration of new groups, such as the Baptists, Methodists, Presbyterians, Lutherans and the Dutch Reformed. The First Great Awakening (c. 1726-70) was an evangelical revival that swept across the colonies, begun by the Dutch Reformed Church and taken up by the Presbyterians and Congregationalists. After the Independence of the USA in

1776, the state churches of the Church of England in the South, and Congregationalism in the North, were disestablished, and all the American churches became free and voluntary bodies.

Issues of social reform came to the fore after 1800, and denominations such as the Presbyterians, Methodists and Baptists became more politically active.

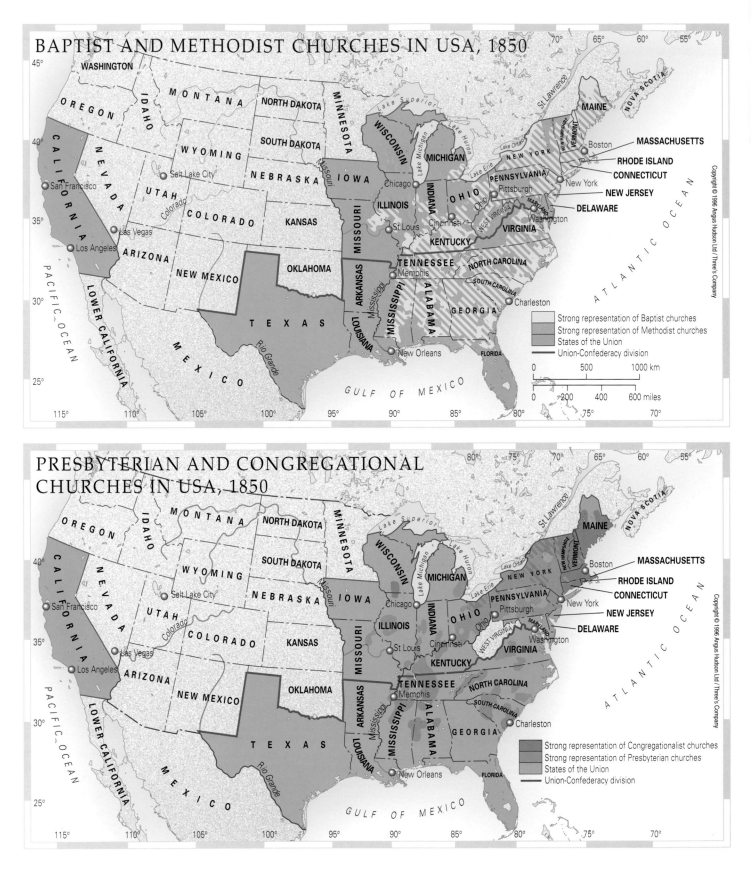

BAPTIST AND METHODIST CHURCHES IN USA, 1850

Strong representation of Baptist churches
Strong representation of Methodist churches
States of the Union
Union-Confederacy division

0 500 1000 km
0 200 400 600 miles

PRESBYTERIAN AND CONGREGATIONAL CHURCHES IN USA, 1850

Strong representation of Congregationalist churches
Strong representation of Presbyterian churches
States of the Union
Union-Confederacy division

MISSIONS TO CHINA

In 1865, James Hudson Taylor set up what became the largest mission in the world, the China Inland Mission. Thousands of volunteer missionaries offered their service, and by 1882

missionaries were resident in all but three of the provinces.

The Roman Catholics had continued to operate even in times of persecution. With official toleration concluded in the Convention of 1860 between China and France, Catholicism was able to expand faster than Protestantism. There were rapid advances after the setback of the

Boxer rebellion in 1900, with the greatest growth in the Hubei and Guang-Dong provinces.

MISSIONS TO CHINA BY 1920

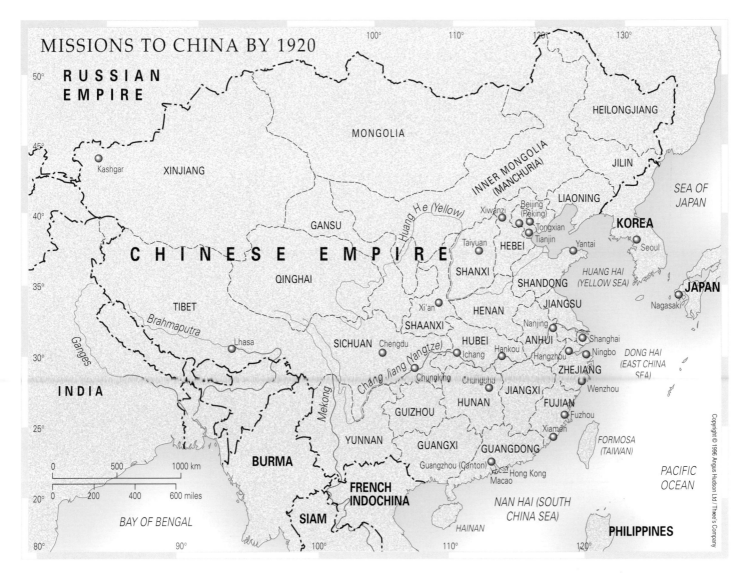

PROTESTANT MISSIONS

Shanghai	Hudson Taylor, founder of China Inland Mission, lands 1854
Yantai	Timothy Richard of Baptist Missionary Society (English) lands 1870
Mecao	Baptist missionaries (US) arrive 1835
Canton, Ningbo, Shanghai	Presbyterians (US)
Canton, Hong Kong, Xiamen, Shanghai	London Missionary Society by1856
Canton, Fuzhou, Shanghai, Xiamen	American Board of Commissioners for Foreign Missions mission stations by 1857
Ningbo	Base of China Inland Mission 1865
Guangdong	Basel Mission, Rhenish Missionary Society expand from Hong Kong, 1895
Tianjin	Methodist New Missionary Society and evangelizes north
Yantai	Society for the Propagation of the Gospel in Foreign Parts from 1874
Ningbo, Wenzhou	English Methodist Free Church Mission 1864 (Ningbo), 1878 (Wenzhou)
Hangzhou	Mission of Presbyterian church (US), 1867
Yingkou, Mukden	Irish and Scottish Presbyterian missions, 1870s
Ichang	Church of Scotland mission, 1878
Taiwan	Canadian Presyterians, 1871
Sichuan	English Quakers, 1884
Nanjing	Ohio Yearly Meeting of Friends, 1887
Nanjing	Disciples of Christ, 1880s
Chengdu	Canadian Methodists, 1894
Fuzhou	Christian Endeavour movement (US), 1895
Guangzhou	United Brethren in Christ (US), 1889
Shandong, Jiangxi	Christian Brethren,1895
Guangzhou	American Swedish Free Mission Society, 1888
Shanxi, Shaanxi, Henan	Swedish Mission in China,1895
Valley of Han	Norwegian Lutheran China Mission Association
Wuchang, Ichang, Kashgar	Swedish Missionary Society, 1890s

ROMAN CATHOLIC MISSIONS

Chang Jiang lower reaches	Jesuits develop missions in 1850s
Hsien Hsien in Hebei	Northern centre of Jesuits from 1854
Xiwanzi	Lazarists found retreats in 1830s, Scheutveld Fathers (Belgian) establish HQ in 1866
Hong Kong	Seminary of Foreign Missions of Milan arrive in 1858
Southern Shandong	Society of the Divine Word 1882
Fujian, Taiwan	Dominicans dominant RC order
Chekiang, Kiangsi	Lazarists main missionary order in 1944
Guangdong, Guangxi, Guizhou, Yunnan, Sichuan, Manchuria, Tibet, Korea	Paris Societé des Missions Etrangéres main mission in 1914
Shandong, Shanxi, Shaanxi, Hubei, Henan	Franciscans dominant RC order
Most widespread women's mission	Franciscan Missionaries of Mary

TABLE OF ESTIMATED NUMBER OF CHRISTIANS IN CHINA
(Western and Chinese)

[Statistics taken from Latourette]

Protestant:	1853 :	350
	1865 :	2,000
	1876 :	13,035
	1886 :	28,000
	1893 :	55,093
Roman Catholic:	1844 :	240,000
	1870 :	383,000
	1901 :	720,540
	1912 :	1,431,258

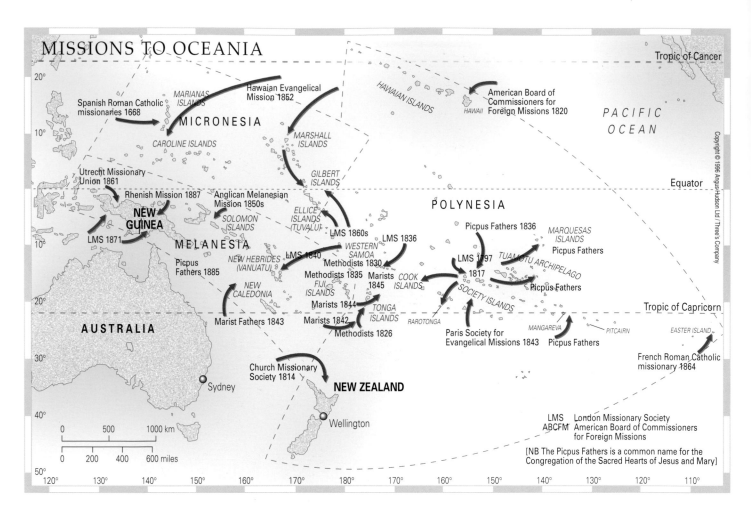

Map labels:

Tropic of Cancer
20°
Spanish Roman Catholic missionaries 1668
MARIANAS ISLANDS
Hawaiian Evangelical Mission 1852
HAWAIIAN ISLANDS
American Board of Commissioners for Foreign Missions 1820
PACIFIC OCEAN
MICRONESIA
10°
CAROLINE ISLANDS
HAWAII
MARSHALL ISLANDS
Equator
Utrecht Missionary Union 1861
Rhenish Mission 1887
Anglican Melanesian Mission 1850s
GILBERT ISLANDS
POLYNESIA
NEW GUINEA
SOLOMON ISLANDS
ELLICE ISLANDS (TUVALU)
LMS 1860s
LMS 1836
Picpus Fathers 1836
MARQUESAS ISLANDS
Picpus Fathers
10°
LMS 1871
MELANESIA
NEW HEBRIDES (VANUATU)
WESTERN SAMOA
LMS 1840
Methodists 1830
LMS 1797 1817
TUAMOTU ARCHIPELAGO
Picpus Fathers 1885
NEW CALEDONIA
Methodists 1835
FIJI ISLANDS
Marists 1845
COOK ISLANDS
SOCIETY ISLANDS
Picpus Fathers
Marists 1844
TONGA ISLANDS
20°
Tropic of Capricorn
AUSTRALIA
Marist Fathers 1843
Marists 1842
Methodists 1826
RAROTONGA
Paris Society for Evangelical Missions 1843
Picpus Fathers
MANGAREVA
PITCAIRN
EASTER ISLAND
French Roman Catholic missionary 1864
Sydney
30°
Church Missionary Society 1814
NEW ZEALAND
40°
Wellington
LMS London Missionary Society
ABCFM American Board of Commissioners for Foreign Missions
[NB The Picpus Fathers is a common name for the Congregation of the Sacred Hearts of Jesus and Mary]
50°
120° 130° 140° 150° 160° 170° 180° 170° 160° 150° 140° 130° 120° 110°
0 500 1000 km
0 200 400 600 miles

MISSIONS TO OCEANIA

The progression of missionary activity in the South Seas was generally from east to west. Favourable early reports of Tahiti meant that missionaries went there first, progressing eventually to the more hostile Melanesian Islands in the west. After the Society Islands, first encountered by the London Missionary Society (LMS), came the western islands of Polynesia – Tonga, Western Samoa and Fiji – first evangelized by the Methodists.

Spanish Roman Catholics had crossed from the Philippines to western Micronesia in the seventeenth century and converted the Marianas Islands, but no further Catholic evangelization occurred until late in the nineteenth century.

The main Catholic missionary bodies were French: in Melanesia, the Congregation of the Sacred Hearts of Jesus and Mary, known as the Picpus Fathers; and in Polynesia, the Marist Fathers. On many islands their arrival caused tension and sometimes conflict with the Protestant converts. In New Guinea, the island was divided by agreement into mission fields to avoid such confrontation.

French Catholics established themselves in New Caledonia and southern New Guinea, and also in the far eastern islands: Tahiti, the Marquesas Islands, Mangareva and Easter Island.

After the American Board converted the Hawaiians, a huge enterprise crossing the Pacific was undertaken in 1852 to the Marshall Islands, and the Caroline and Gilbert Islands.

MISSIONS TO ASIA

William Carey of the Baptist Missionary Society led the way to evangelizing north India in 1793, when he landed at Calcutta. A major Christian centre was set up at nearby Serampore, from where missions spread along the Ganges Valley. By 1855, the Church Missionary Society had reached Peshawar. Large numbers of missions from Europe and North America landed in south India during the first half of the nineteenth century, where they encountered the Catholic Church founded by Francis Xavier and the Malabar Christian communities of Travancore, believed to date from about the sixth century.

The Cross tended to follow the flag. Where the European powers colonized, the missionary societies preached. The Netherlands Missionary Society was active in the Dutch East Indies. In China, the earliest missionary of this period was the Scot Robert Morrison, who arrived in Canton in 1807. However, China did not 'open' itself to the foreigner in any practical sense until the signing of the Treaty of Nanking in 1842, after the Opium Wars.

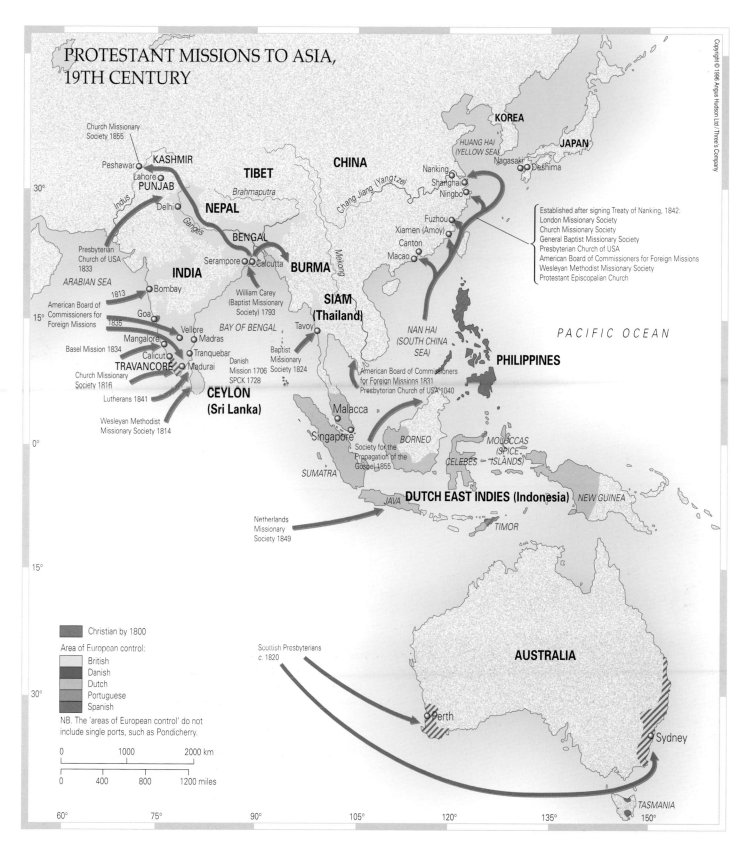

PROTESTANT MISSIONS TO ASIA, 19TH CENTURY

KOREA

JAPAN

CHINA

TIBET

KASHMIR

Church Missionary
Society 1855

Peshawar

Lahore

PUNJAB

Delhi

NEPAL

BENGAL

Brahmaputra

Ganges

Indus

30°

Presbyterian
Church of USA
1833

ARABIAN SEA

INDIA

Serampore

Calcutta

BURMA

William Carey
(Baptist Missionary
Society) 1793

SIAM
(Thailand)

Mekong

Chang Jiang (Yangtze)

Nanking

Shanghai

Ningbo

Fuzhou

Xiamen (Amoy)

Canton

Macao

Nagasaki

Deshima

HUANG HAI
(YELLOW SEA)

Established after signing Treaty of Nanking, 1842:
London Missionary Society
Church Missionary Society
General Baptist Missionary Society
Presbyterian Church of USA
American Board of Commissioners for Foreign Missions
Wesleyan Methodist Missionary Society
Protestant Episcopalian Church

1813

Bombay

15°

American Board of
Commissioners for
Foreign Missions

1835

Goa

Mangalore

Basel Mission 1834

Calicut

TRAVANCORE

Church Missionary
Society 1816

Lutherans 1841

Wesleyan Methodist
Missionary Society 1814

Vellore

Madras

Tranquebar

Madurai

Danish
Mission 1706
SPCK 1728

BAY OF BENGAL

Tavoy

Baptist
Missionary
Society 1824

American Board of Commissioners
for Foreign Missions 1831
Presbyterian Church of USA 1040

NAN HAI
(SOUTH CHINA
SEA)

PACIFIC OCEAN

PHILIPPINES

CEYLON
(Sri Lanka)

Malacca

Singapore

Society for the
Propagation of the
Gospel 1855

SUMATRA

BORNEO

0°

JAVA

DUTCH EAST INDIES (Indonesia)

MOLUCCAS
(SPICE
ISLANDS)

CELEBES

NEW GUINEA

TIMOR

Netherlands
Missionary
Society 1849

15°

Scottish Presbyterians
c. 1820

AUSTRALIA

Christian by 1800

Area of European control:

British
Danish
Dutch
Portuguese
Spanish

NB. The 'areas of European control' do not
include single ports, such as Pondicherry.

30°

Perth

0   1000   2000 km

0   400   800   1200 miles

Sydney

TASMANIA

60°   75°   90°   105°   120°   135°   150°

Five 'treaty ports' – Canton, Xiamen (Amoy), Fuzhou, Ningbo and Shanghai – were designated cities for foreign settlement. British and American missions made inroads into China from there.

Japan remained steadfastly hostile to the Westerner, and South Korea only received its first missionary in 1865. The Philippines had been colonized by the Spanish in the seventeenth century and most Filipinos had become Roman Catholic.

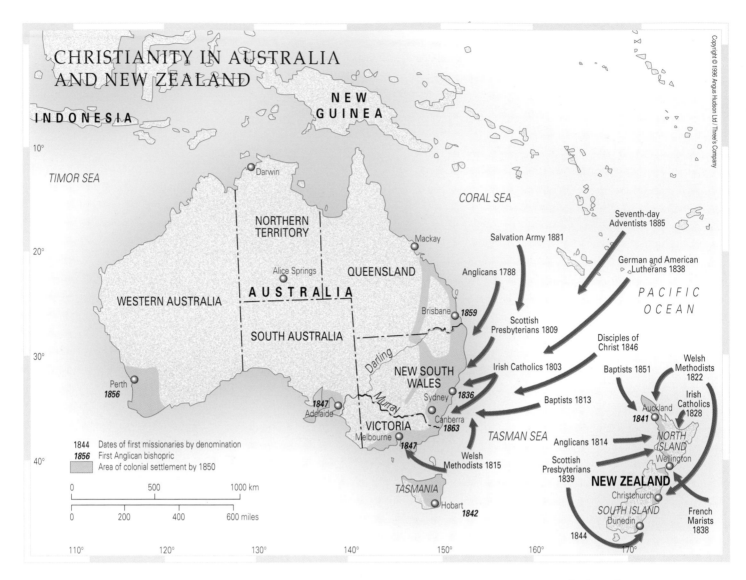

CHRISTIANITY IN AUSTRALIA AND NEW ZEALAND

INDONESIA

NEW GUINEA

TIMOR SEA

Darwin

NORTHERN TERRITORY

CORAL SEA

Seventh-day Adventists 1885

Salvation Army 1881

Anglicans 1788

QUEENSLAND

Alice Springs

AUSTRALIA

WESTERN AUSTRALIA

Mackay

German and American Lutherans 1838

PACIFIC OCEAN

SOUTH AUSTRALIA

Brisbane *1859*

Scottish Presbyterians 1809

Disciples of Christ 1846

Welsh Methodists 1822

Darling

Perth *1856*

Irish Catholics 1803

Baptists 1851

Irish Catholics 1828

NEW SOUTH WALES

Baptists 1813

Auckland *1841*

Murray

Sydney *1836*

1847 Adelaide

Canberra *1863*

NORTH ISLAND

VICTORIA

Wellington

Melbourne *1847*

TASMAN SEA

Anglicans 1814

NEW ZEALAND

1844 Dates of first missionaries by denomination
1856 First Anglican bishopric
Area of colonial settlement by 1850

Welsh Methodists 1815

Scottish Presbyterians 1839

Christchurch

0   500   1000 km

TASMANIA

SOUTH ISLAND

Dunedin

0   200   400   600 miles

Hobart *1842*

1844

French Marists 1838

CHRISTIANITY IN AUSTRALIA AND NEW ZEALAND

James Cook charted the coasts of Australia and New Zealand in 1770. A Church of England chaplain sailed with the first convict ship for Australia in 1788. Wesleyan ministries began in 1815, and Presbyterians in 1823. The Church of England received special government grants of land to build churches and schools in New South Wales, though after 1836 grants were undenominational. By 1820, Roman Catholic priests were serving the predominantly Irish Catholic population.

The first European settlements in New Zealand were made in 1805, and the first missionaries arrived in 1814. Anglicans form the majority of the population, with large minorities of Scottish Presbyterians, Roman Catholics and Methodists.

MISSIONS TO AFRICA

Very little remained of the early Roman Catholic missions to Africa. The first wave of missionary activity to make deep inroads was in the 1830s and 1840s, especially in West Africa. Christianity was seen by many West African tribal rulers as a means to prosperity through trade with European countries. Missionaries set up stations and schools. Islam held sway over northern Africa. The ancient churches of the Copts in Egypt and the Ethiopian Church were exceptions.

The earliest missions to southern Africa in this period were naturally launched from the Cape of Good Hope, where there had long been European settlement. David Livingstone blazed trails from here which many other missions would follow. Roman Catholic missions were as active as Protestant

ones in this period, especially the Holy Ghost Fathers (1848) and the White Fathers (1868).

Inter-denominational rivalry over mission fields intensified at the time of the European 'Scramble' for Africa, after 1880.

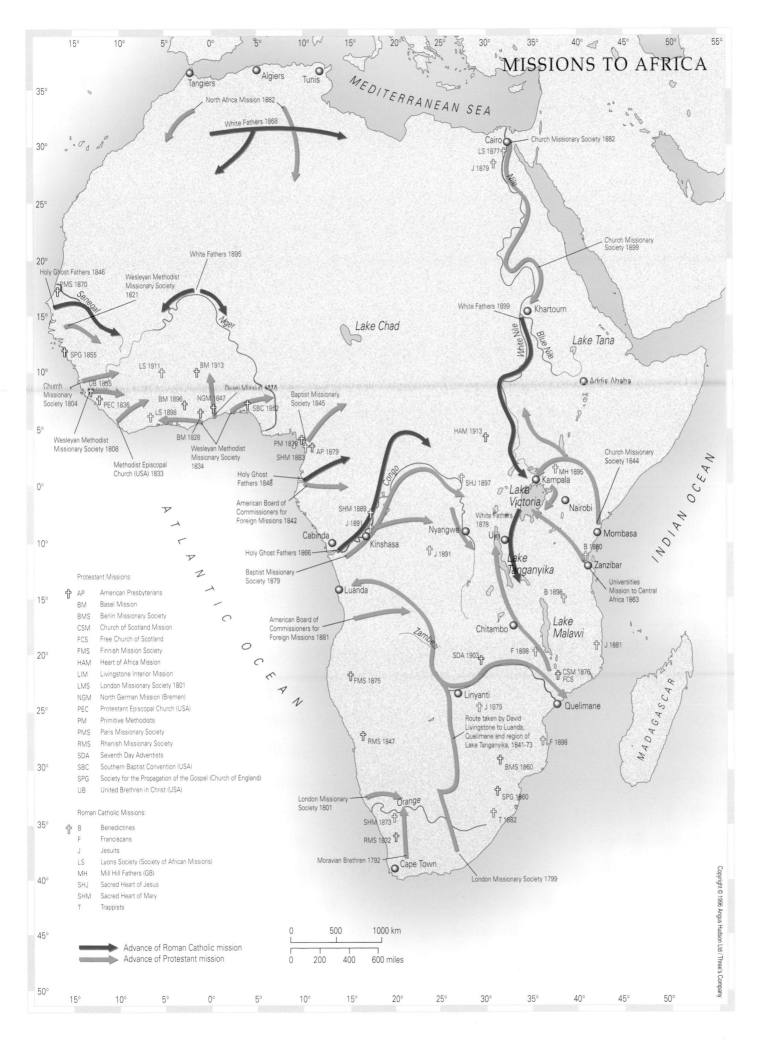

MISSIONS TO AFRICA

MEDITERRANEAN SEA

Tangiers
Algiers
Tunis

North Africa Mission 1882

White Fathers 1868

Cairo
Church Missionary Society 1882
LS 1877
J 1879

Nile

Church Missionary Society 1899

White Fathers 1895

Holy Ghost Fathers 1846
PMS 1870

Senegal

Wesleyan Methodist Missionary Society 1821

Niger

White Fathers 1899
Khartoum

Lake Chad

Lake Tana

SPG 1855

LS 1911
BM 1913

White Nile
Blue Nile

Church Missionary Society 1804

UB 1855
BM 1896
NGM 1847
Basel Mission 1828
SBC 1852

Addis Ababa

PEC 1836
LS 1898

Baptist Missionary Society 1845

Wesleyan Methodist Missionary Society 1808

BM 1828

PM 1879
SHM 1883
AP 1879

HAM 1913

Church Missionary Society 1844

Methodist Episcopal Church (USA) 1833

Wesleyan Methodist Missionary Society 1834

Holy Ghost Fathers 1848

Congo

SHJ 1897

MH 1895
Kampala

American Board of Commissioners for Foreign Missions 1842

SHM 1889
J 1891

Nyangwe

Lake Victoria
Nairobi

White Fathers 1878

Cabinda

Holy Ghost Fathers 1866

Kinshasa

J 1891

Ujiji

Mombasa

B 1880
Zanzibar

Baptist Missionary Society 1879

Lake Tanganyika

Universities Mission to Central Africa 1863

Luanda

ATLANTIC OCEAN

INDIAN OCEAN

American Board of Commissioners for Foreign Missions 1881

B 1898

Chitambo

Lake Malawi

J 1881

Protestant Missions:

AP	American Presbyterians	
BM	Basel Mission	
BMS	Berlin Missionary Society	
CSM	Church of Scotland Mission	
FCS	Free Church of Scotland	
FMS	Finnish Mission Society	
HAM	Heart of Africa Mission	
LIM	Livingstone Interior Mission	
LMS	London Missionary Society 1801	
NGM	North German Mission (Bremen)	
PEC	Protestant Episcopal Church (USA)	
PM	Primitive Methodists	
PMS	Paris Missionary Society	
RMS	Rhenish Missionary Society	
SDA	Seventh Day Adventists	
SBC	Southern Baptist Convention (USA)	
SPG	Society for the Propagation of the Gospel (Church of England)	
UB	United Brethren in Christ (USA)	

SDA 1903
F 1898

CSM 1876
FCS

FMS 1875

Zambezi

Linyanti
J 1879

Quelimane

Route taken by David Livingstone to Luanda, Quelimane and region of Lake Tanganyika, 1841–73

F 1898

Roman Catholic Missions:

B	Benedictines	
F	Franciscans	
J	Jesuits	
LS	Lyons Society (Society of African Missions)	
MH	Mill Hill Fathers (GB)	
SHJ	Sacred Heart of Jesus	
SHM	Sacred Heart of Mary	
T	Trappists	

RMS 1847

BMS 1860

SPG 1860

T 1882

London Missionary Society 1801

Orange

SHM 1873

RMS 1832

Moravian Brethren 1792
Cape Town

London Missionary Society 1799

MADAGASCAR

0   500   1000 km
0 200 400 600 miles

→ Advance of Roman Catholic mission
→ Advance of Protestant mission

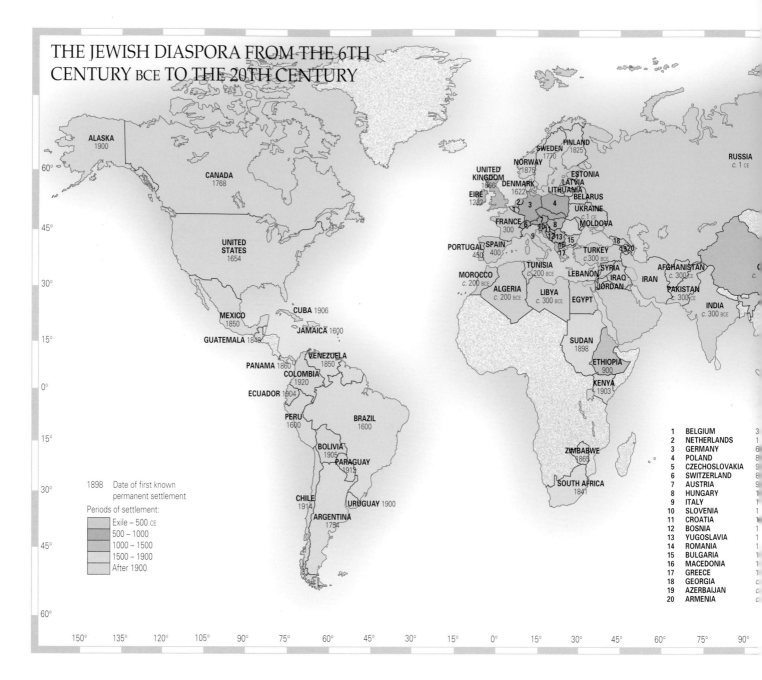

ALASKA
1900

CANADA
1768

UNITED
STATES
1654

MEXICO
1850

CUBA 1906

JAMAICA 1600

GUATEMALA 1848

VENEZUELA
1850

PANAMA 1860

COLOMBIA
1920

ECUADOR 1904

PERU
1600

BRAZIL
1600

BOLIVIA
1905

PARAGUAY
1915

CHILE
1914

URUGUAY 1900

ARGENTINA
1784

SWEDEN
1770

FINLAND
1825

NORWAY
1875

UNITED
KINGDOM
1066

DENMARK
1622

ESTONIA

LATVIA

LITHUANIA

BELARUS

RUSSIA
c. 1

EIRE
1232

FRANCE
300

UKRAINE
c. 1 CE

MOLDOVA

PORTUGAL
450

SPAIN
400

TURKEY
c. 300 BCE

GEORGIA

AFGHANISTAN
c. 300 CE

MOROCCO
c. 200 BCE

TUNISIA
c. 200 BCE

LEBANON

SYRIA
c. 300 BCE

IRAQ

IRAN

PAKISTAN
300 BCE

ALGERIA
c. 200 BCE

LIBYA
c. 300 BCE

EGYPT

JORDAN

INDIA
c. 300 BCE

SUDAN
1898

ETHIOPIA
900

KENYA
1903

ZIMBABWE
1865

SOUTH AFRICA
1841

1898 Date of first known
permanent settlement

Periods of settlement:

Exile – 500 CE
500 – 1000
1000 – 1500
1500 – 1900
After 1900

1	BELGIUM
2	NETHERLANDS
3	GERMANY
4	POLAND
5	CZECHOSLOVAKIA
6	SWITZERLAND
7	AUSTRIA
8	HUNGARY
9	ITALY
10	SLOVENIA
11	CROATIA
12	BOSNIA
13	YUGOSLAVIA
14	ROMANIA
15	BULGARIA
16	MACEDONIA
17	GREECE
18	GEORGIA
19	AZERBAIJAN
20	ARMENIA

THE JEWISH DIASPORA

In the period of the biblical Exile (after the fall of Jerusalem in 587 BCE), Jews were to be found in many cities of the Ancient Near East. Up to the beginning of the Christian Era, Jewish Greek traders were moving around the Mediterranean and Black Sea areas, settling as merchants and farmers in what we know as Georgia, southern Ukraine and Russia. Jews of the Parthian Empire settled in Armenia and Azerbaijan. Jewish communities also flourished throughout the Carthaginian Empire in North Africa. By 1 CE Jews were beginning to spread to the Latin-speaking West of the Roman Empire. Alexandria was the centre of Greco-Jewish culture at this time.

Jewish settlement was widespread in Western Europe between 800 and 1200. Persecutions and expulsions forced migrations to Central and Eastern Europe after 1290. Sephardic Jews were finally expelled from Spain in 1492. They fled Europe for the newly discovered Americas. The Inquisition threatened the existence of many Jewish communities, and by 1640 the only safe refuges were those under Dutch rule. Under legal emancipation, Jewish culture was able to flourish in the Netherlands from the seventeenth century onwards.

The Chmielnicki massacres (1648-51) in Poland/Lithuania sent many Jews back westwards and southwards. However, a strong Jewish culture remained in central Europe until the Nazi holocaust.

Over-population and social tension in Europe led to the Great Migration to the Americas from 1881 to 1914. Over 2 million crossed the Atlantic, 85 per cent of them settling in the USA. Many more had emigrated from Europe by the outbreak of World War II.

Since the creation of the State of Israel in 1948, Jews from many parts of the world, and especially from Russia, have emigrated to Israel. Jews came from the Displaced Persons camps in Europe, detention camps in Cyprus, eastern Europe and northern Africa; and the entire Jewish populations of Yemen and Iraq migrated. The Jewish population of Israel increased from 650,000 in 1948 to 4,448,000 in 1995.

Tensions continued between Israel and the Arab nations, especially after

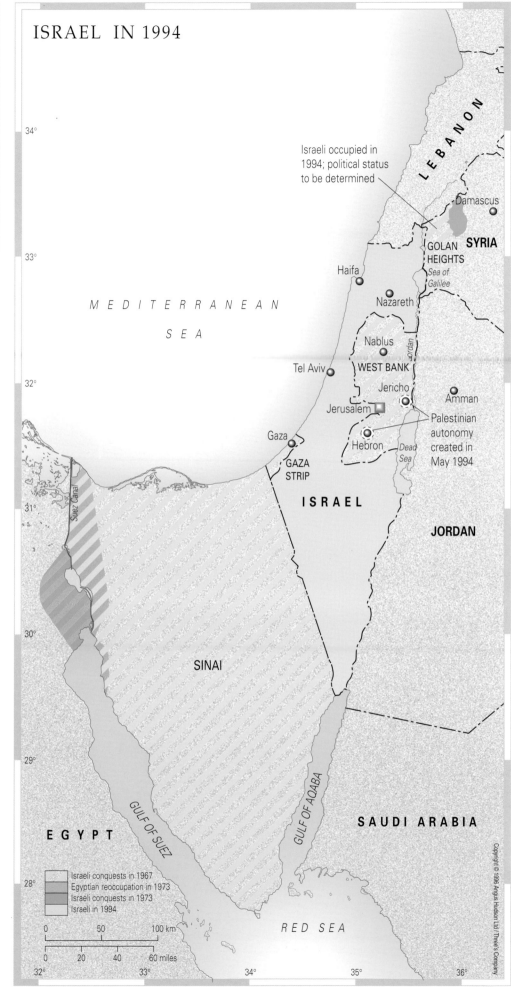

ISRAEL IN 1994

JAPAN
1889

AUSTRALIA
1817

NEW
ZEALAND
1840

LEBANON

Israeli occupied in
1994; political status
to be determined

Damascus

SYRIA

GOLAN
HEIGHTS

Sea of
Galilee

Haifa

Nazareth

M E D I T E R R A N E A N

S E A

Nablus

WEST BANK

Tel Aviv

Jericho

Amman

Jerusalem

Palestinian
autonomy
created in
May 1994

Gaza

Hebron

Dead
Sea

GAZA
STRIP

ISRAEL

JORDAN

Suez Canal

SINAI

GULF OF SUEZ

GULF OF AQABA

SAUDI ARABIA

EGYPT

Israeli conquests in 1967
Egyptian reoccupation in 1973
Israeli conquests in 1973
Israeli in 1994

RED SEA

0   50   100 km

0   20   40   60 miles

the Sinai Campaign of 1956. The Six-Day War of 1967 between Israel and Egypt resulted in large territorial gains for Israel: the Sinai Peninsula, the Gaza Strip, eastern Palestine and the Golan Heights. Egypt and Syria attempted to recover lands in the Yom Kippur War of 1973, but without success.

The Camp David Accords of 1978 between Israel and Egypt, under the aegis of the USA, resulted in peace and the return to Egypt of the Sinai Peninsula. It was also agreed in principle that the Palestinians of the West Bank and Gaza Strip should be granted self-government. Only in May of 1994 did the Palestinians of the Gaza Strip, and the cities of Hebron and Jericho, achieve autonomy.

THE RISE OF PENTECOSTALISM

CANADA

USA

MEXICO

ATLANTIC

OCEAN

CUBA
DOMINICAN REPUBLIC
JAMAICA
BELIZE
HONDURAS
HAITI
PUERTO RICO
GUATEMALA
EL SALVADOR
NICARAGUA
COSTA RICA
TRINIDAD & TOBAGO
PANAMA
VENEZUELA
GUYANA
COLOMBIA
ECUADOR

PACIFIC OCEAN

BRAZIL

PERU

BOLIVIA

CHILE

PARAGUAY

ARGENTINA

URUGUAY

NORW

NETHERLANDS

UNITED KINGDOM

GERMANY
FRAN

BURKINA FASO

Country with significant Pentecostal minority,
with date of first Pentecostal church.

- pre-1900
- 1900-1919
- 1920-1939
- 1940-

| 0 | 2000 | 4000 km |
| 0 | 800 | 1600 | 2400 miles |

THE RISE OF PENTECOSTALISM

The modern Pentecostal movement is often reckoned to have begun in 1901 in Topeka, Kansas, USA, under the leadership of a former Methodist minister. Most early Pentecostals were active in the Methodist Church. They believed in the holiness of Christian life after conversion, maintaining that Christians should experience the same signs of spiritual power as did the Apostles on the Day of Pentecost.

The first Pentecostal denominations were in the southern USA: the Pentecostal Holiness Church, the Church of God and the predominantly black Church of God in Christ. In 1914 the Assemblies of God formed, and soon became the largest Pentecostal group in the USA.

The Pentecostal movement spread rapidly worldwide, being established in Europe and South America by 1920. It is the fastest growing Christian movement, both within its own specific Pentecostal churches and within the traditional denominations. In Roman Catholicism it is better known as 'Charismatic Renewal'. It is particularly popular in the Third World, notably in Latin America and among the African Independent churches.

SWEDEN

FINLAND

ROMANIA

ITALY

CENTRAL AFRICAN REPUBLIC

KENYA

RWANDA

BURUNDI

TANZANIA

MOZAMBIQUE

SOUTH KOREA

PHILIPPINES

PACIFIC OCEAN

INDIAN OCEAN

INDONESIA

PAPUA NEW GUINEA

30° 45° 60° 75° 90° 105° 120° 135° 150° 165° 180°

WORLDWIDE GROWTH RATE OF CHRISTIANITY *c.* 1995

GREENLAND

ICELAND

NORW

UNITED
KINGDOM

DENMAR
AUS
NETHERLANDS
BELGIUM
LUXEMBOURG

IRELAND

GERMANY
FRAN
SWITZERLAND
PORTUGAL SPAIN AND
ITA
MOROCCO TUNISIA

CANADA

U S A

ATLANTIC

OCEAN

ALGERI

WESTERN
SAHARA

MEXICO

CUBA DOMINICAN
REPUBLIC
JAMAICA
BELIZE PUERTO
HONDURAS HAITI RICO
GUATEMALA
EL SALVADOR NICARAGUA
COSTA RICA
TRINIDAD &
TOBAGO
VENEZUELA GUYANA
PANAMA SURINAM
FRENCH GUIANA
COLOMBIA

MAURITANIA

MALI

SENEGAL
GAMBIA
GUINEA-BISSAU GUINEA
SIERRA LEONE
LIBERIA

BURKINA
FASO
IVORY GHANA
COAST TOGO
BENIN

P
A
C
I
F
I
C

O
C
E
A
N

ECUADOR

PERU

B R A Z I L

BOLIVIA

CHILE

PARAGUAY

A
R
G
E
N
T
I
N
A

URUGUAY

CAMEROON

EQUATORIAL
GUINEA

GABON

ANGOLA

NAMIBIA

Percentage annual Church growth, *c.* 1990
Very rapid (over 5%)
Rapid (3-5%)
Moderate (1-3%)
Little or nil (0-1%)
Decline (less than 0%)

0   2000   4000 km

0   800   1600   2400 miles

75°
60°
45°
30°
15°
0°
15°
30°
45°
60°

150°   135°   120°   105°   90°   75°   60°   45°   30°   15°   0°

SWEDEN

FINLAND

ESTONIA
LATVIA
LITHUANIA
RUSSIA

BELORUS
CZECH
REP.
VAKIA
UKRAINE
MOLDOVA
AND
HUNGARY
ROMANIA
YUGOSLAVIA
GEORGIA
BULGARIA
AZERBAIJAN
MACEDONIA
ALBANIA
GREECE
ARMENIA
TURKEY
CYPRUS
CROATIA
SYRIA
VENIA
LEBANON
ISRAEL
IRAQ
IRAN
JORDAN
KUWAIT
YA
EGYPT
QATAR

R U S S I A

K A Z A K H S T A N

UZBEKISTAN
KYRGYZSTAN
TURKMENISTAN
TAJIKISTAN

M O N G O L I A

C H I N A

NORTH
KOREA

SOUTH
KOREA

JAPAN

SAUDI
ARABIA
ERITREA
OMAN
UNITED
ARAB
EMIRATES
YEMEN

AFGHANISTAN
PAKISTAN
NEPAL
BHUTAN
BURMA
(MYANMAR)

I N D I A

BANGLADESH

TAIWAN
HONG KONG

LAOS

AD

SUDAN
CENTRAL
AFRICAN
REPUBLIC

ETHIOPIA

SOMALIA

THAILAND
VIETNAM

PHILIPPINES

CAMBODIA

SRI
LANKA

MALAYSIA

P A C I F I C   O C E A N

CONGO
UGANDA
KENYA
AIRE
RWANDA
BURUNDI

BRUNEI

TANZANIA
MALAWI

I N D I A N

O C E A N

SINGAPORE

I N D O N E S I A

PAPUA
NEW
GUINEA

SOLOMON
ISLANDS

ZAMBIA

MOZAMBIQUE

MADAGASCAR

ZIMBABWE
BOTSWANA

VANUATU

FIJI

NEW CALEDONIA

SOUTH AFRICA
SWAZILAND
LESOTHO

A U S T R A L I A

NEW
ZEALAND

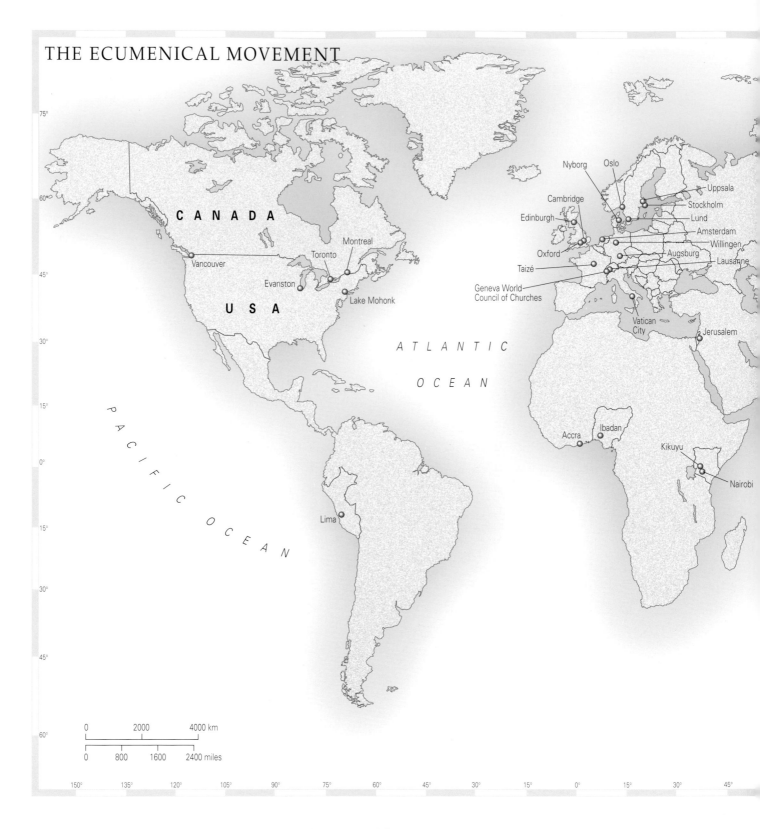

THE ECUMENICAL MOVEMENT

The ecumenical movement grew mainly out of Western Protestantism, for example among the Student Christian Movement and the YMCA, with the aim of promoting closer co-operation and understanding between the different branches of Protestantism. The World Missionary Conference of 1910 held at Edinburgh started the movement in earnest. By 1937 the Eastern Orthodox Church took an active part, as did churches of Africa and Asia. In 1948 the World Council of Churches was formed to lead the ecumenical movement, though without involvement from the Roman Catholics. At the Second Vatican Council (1962-65) the Roman Catholic standpoint shifted somewhat. Other communions became 'separated brethren' rather than being seen as outside the Church.

In some parts of the world successful unifications have been made. One notable example is South India in 1947, where Episcopal, Presbyterian and Congregational churches united. Sometimes denominational differences based on historical circumstances have ceased to be relevant today. In North

RUSSIA

New Delhi

PACIFIC OCEAN

DIAN
CEAN

90°   105°   120°   135°   150°   165°   180°

Cambridge 1893: Founding of Student Christian Movement (SCM) as the Inter-University Christian Union

Edinburgh 1910: World Conference of Protestant Missionaries

1913: Kikuyu conference, Kenya; federation of Anglican, Presbyterian and other Protestant churches proposed

Lake Mohonk 1921: Formation of International Missionary Council (NY, USA)

Oxford 1923: Second Conference of International Missionary Council

Oxford 1923: Second Meeting of International Missionary Council

Stockholm 1925: Universal Christian Conference on Life and Work, relating Christian faith to society, politics and economics

1925: Formation of United Church of Canada (union of Methodists, Presbyterians and Congregationalists)

Lausanne 1927: World Conference on Faith and Order, founding the Faith and Order Movement

Jerusalem 1928: Third Conference of International Missionary Council

Edinburgh 1937: Second World Conference on Faith and Order

Oxford 1937: Second World Christian Conference on Life and Work

Tambaram 1938: Fourth Conference of International Missionary Council

Amsterdam 1939: First World Conference of Christian Youth

1940: Foundation of Taizé (an ecumenical religious community) by Roger Schutz

1947: Foundation of the church of South India (union of Anglican, Methodist, Presbyterian, Congregationalist and Dutch Reformed churches)

Toronto 1947: Fifth meeting of International Missionary Council

Oslo 1947: Second World Conference of Christian Youth

Amsterdam 1948: Foundation of World Council of Churches, union of 'Life and Work' and Faith and Order movements

1948: Formation of National Council of Churches, (USA)

Travancore 1952: Third World Conference of Christian Youth, (India)

Willingen 1952: Sixth Meeting of International Missionary Council, (Germany)

Lund 1952: Third World Conference on Faith and Order, (Sweden)

Evanston 1954: Second Assembly of World Council of Churches, (USA)

Accra 1958: Final Assembly of International Missionary Council, (Ghana)

Ibadan 1958: First All African Christian Conference, (Nigeria)

Nyborg 1959: First Assembly of Conference of European Churches, (Denmark)

New Delhi 1961: Third Assembly of World Council of Churches; integration of International Missionary Council within WCC

1961: Russian Orthodox Church joins WCC

Montreal 1963: Fourth World Conference on Faith and Order

Vatican City 1965: Second Vatican Council Decree withdraws mutual excommunications of 1054 between Eastern and Western Churches

Geneva 1966: World conference on Church and Society

Uppsala 1968: Fourth Assembly of World Council of Churches

1970: Foundation of Church of North India (union of Anglicans, Congregationalists, Presbyterians, some Methodists, Baptists and Disciples of Christ)

1970: Foundation of Church of Pakistan (union of Anglicans, Methodists, Presbyterians and Lutherans)

Augsburg 1971: First Ecumenical Pentecost Meeting for Protestants and Catholics (Germany)

Lima 1971: Third Assembly of World Council of Christian Education

Nairobi 1975: Fifth Assembly of World Council of Churches

Vancouver 1983: Sixth Assembly of World Council of Churches

Canberra 1991: Seventh Assembly of World Council of Churches

America, non-denominational churches have been set up, and co-operative church ventures aimed at counselling in society, such as in prisons and hospitals, can break down denominational barriers.

The Student Christian Movement was founded in Cambridge.

BIBLE SOCIETIES WORLDWIDE

CANADA
1805, 1904

USA
1808, 1816

MEXICO
1878, 1963

GUATEMALA
1988

EL SALVADOR
1807

HONDURAS *1807*

COSTA RICA
1967

NICARAGUA
1807, 1974

PANAMA
1807, 1974

CUBA *1820*

JAMAICA
1834, 1969

HAITI
1807

DOMINICAN *1807, 1968*
REPUBLIC

PUERTO *1807*
RICO

BARBADOS *1979*

VENEZUELA
1958, 1969

COLOMBIA
1834, 1966

ECUADOR
1964

PERU
1821, 1969

BOLIVIA
1905, 1966

CHILE
1864, 1969

BRAZIL
1862, 1948

PARAGUAY
1947, 1969

ARGENTINA
1825, 1963

URUGUAY
1958

SURINAM *1907*

ATLANTIC

OCEAN

PACIFIC OCEAN

NORWAY
1816, 1816

ICELAND
1815, 1915

SCOTLAND
1805, 1861

NORTHERN
IRELAND
1807, 1808

ENGLAND
AND WALES
1804, 1804

DENMA
1814, 18

1806, 1806 IRELAND

NETHERL
1814, 1

1836, 1946 BELGIUM

1710, 1948 GERMANY
1818, 1946

FRAN

1804, 1955 SWITZERLAND

1850, 1970 AUSTRIA

SPAIN
1806, 1975,

PORTUGAL
1868, 1966

MOROCCO
1993

ALGE
1832, 1

1807, 1966 SIERRA LEONE

IVORY
COAST

GHANA

1827, 1966 LIBERIA

1902, 1966

1807, 1966

1807, 1975

CAMEROON
1870, 1965

Dates in *italic*: Beginning of organized work
Dates in plain type: Bible Society formed or office opened

⊕ United Bible Societies Regional Service Centre

⊕ World service centre

0	2000	4000 km
0	800	1600	2400 miles

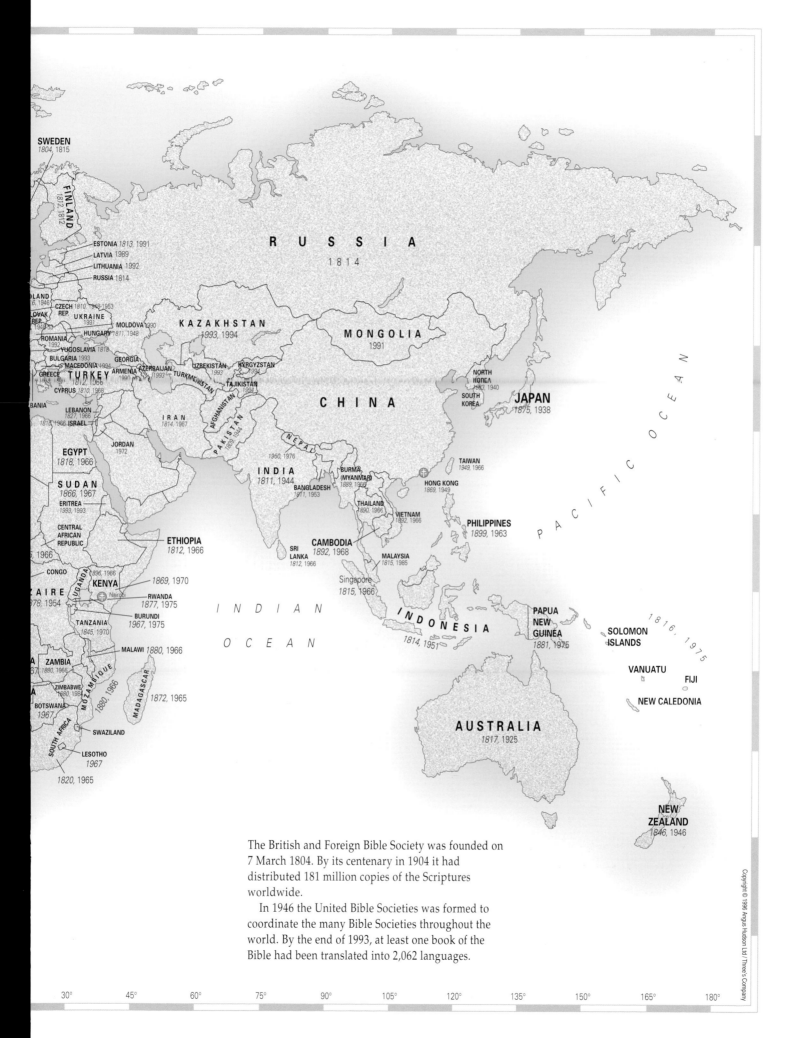

SWEDEN
1804, 1815

FINLAND
1812, 1812

R U S S I A
1814

ESTONIA *1813*, 1991
LATVIA 1989
LITHUANIA 1992
RUSSIA 1814

POLAND
6, 1946
CZECH *1810*, *1948*-1953
REP.
UKRAINE
OVAK 1991
REP.
MOLDOVA 1990
HUNGARY *1811*, 1948
ROMANIA
1992
BULGARIA 1993
YUGOSLAVIA *1818*
MACEDONIA 1994
GREECE
GEORGIA
ARMENIA AZERBAIJAN
1990 *1993*
TURKEY
CYPRUS *1810*, 1966
ALBANIA
LEBANON
1827, 1966
1818, 1966 ISRAEL

KAZAKHSTAN
1993, 1994

MONGOLIA
1991

NORTH
KOREA
1883, 1940

SOUTH
KOREA

JAPAN
1875, 1938

UZBEKISTAN
1993
KYRGYZSTAN
1994
TURKMENISTAN
TAJIKISTAN
1994

C H I N A

I R A N
1814-1967

AFGHANISTAN

PAKISTAN
1819, 1944

NEPAL

EGYPT
1818, 1966

JORDAN
1972

1950, 1976

INDIA
1811, 1944

BURMA,
(MYANMAR)
1889, 1966

TAIWAN
1949, 1966

HONG KONG
1869, 1949

SUDAN
1866, 1967
ERITREA
1993, 1993

BANGLADESH
1811, 1953

THAILAND
1890, 1966

VIETNAM
1892, 1966

PHILIPPINES
1899, 1963

CENTRAL
AFRICAN
REPUBLIC

CAMBODIA
1892, 1968

ETHIOPIA
1812, 1966

SRI
LANKA
1812, 1966

MALAYSIA
1815, 1985

1966

CONGO
UGANDA
1896, 1966
KENYA
1869, 1970
Nairobi

Singapore
1815, 1966

I N D O N E S I A

PAPUA
NEW
GUINEA
1881, 1975

SOLOMON
ISLANDS

1816, *1975*

ZAIRE
78, 1954

RWANDA
1877, 1975
BURUNDI
1967, 1975

I N D I A N

1814, 1951

VANUATU

FIJI

TANZANIA
1845, 1970

O C E A N

NEW CALEDONIA

MALAWI *1880*, 1966

ZAMBIA
67 *1880*, 1966
A

MOZAMBIQUE

AUSTRALIA
1817, 1925

ZIMBABWE
1880, 1964
BOTSWANA
1967

MADAGASCAR
1872, 1965

1880, 1966

SWAZILAND

SOUTH AFRICA

LESOTHO
1967

1820, 1965

NEW
ZEALAND
1846, 1946

P A C I F I C   O C E A N

The British and Foreign Bible Society was founded on
7 March 1804. By its centenary in 1904 it had
distributed 181 million copies of the Scriptures
worldwide.

In 1946 the United Bible Societies was formed to
coordinate the many Bible Societies throughout the
world. By the end of 1993, at least one book of the
Bible had been translated into 2,062 languages.

30°   45°   60°   75°   90°   105°   120°   135°   150°   165°   180°

Strong representation of the following churches:
Anglican
Baptist
Lutheran
Methodist
Mormon
Presbyterian
Roman Catholic

144

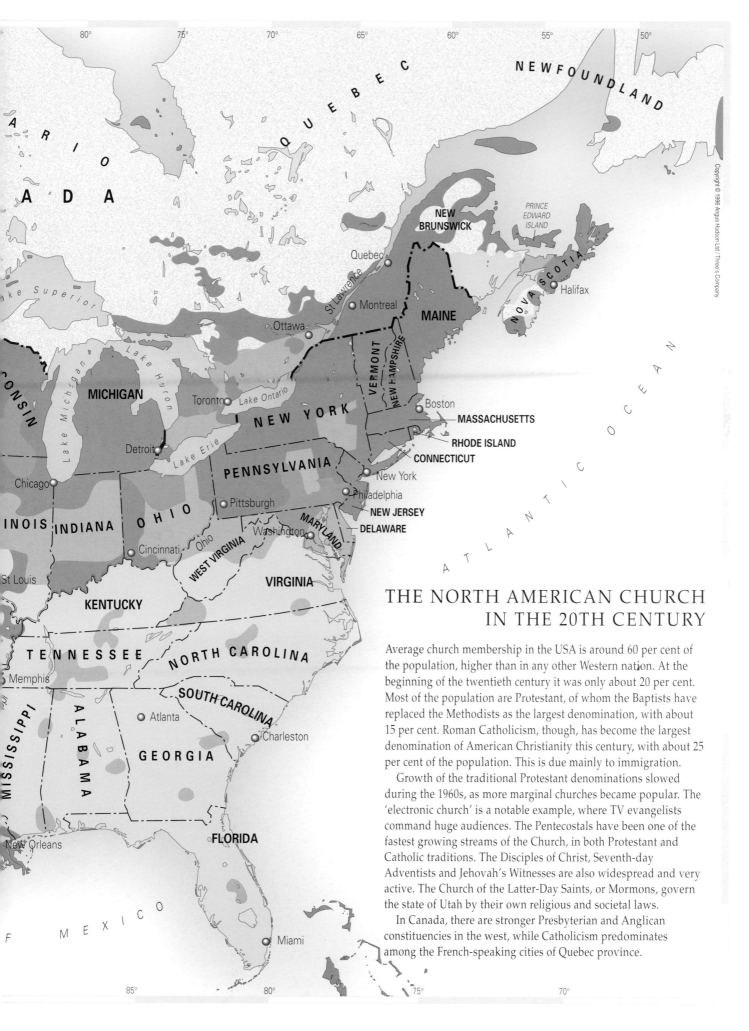

THE NORTH AMERICAN CHURCH IN THE 20TH CENTURY

Average church membership in the USA is around 60 per cent of the population, higher than in any other Western nation. At the beginning of the twentieth century it was only about 20 per cent. Most of the population are Protestant, of whom the Baptists have replaced the Methodists as the largest denomination, with about 15 per cent. Roman Catholicism, though, has become the largest denomination of American Christianity this century, with about 25 per cent of the population. This is due mainly to immigration.

Growth of the traditional Protestant denominations slowed during the 1960s, as more marginal churches became popular. The 'electronic church' is a notable example, where TV evangelists command huge audiences. The Pentecostals have been one of the fastest growing streams of the Church, in both Protestant and Catholic traditions. The Disciples of Christ, Seventh-day Adventists and Jehovah's Witnesses are also widespread and very active. The Church of the Latter-Day Saints, or Mormons, govern the state of Utah by their own religious and societal laws.

In Canada, there are stronger Presbyterian and Anglican constituencies in the west, while Catholicism predominates among the French-speaking cities of Quebec province.

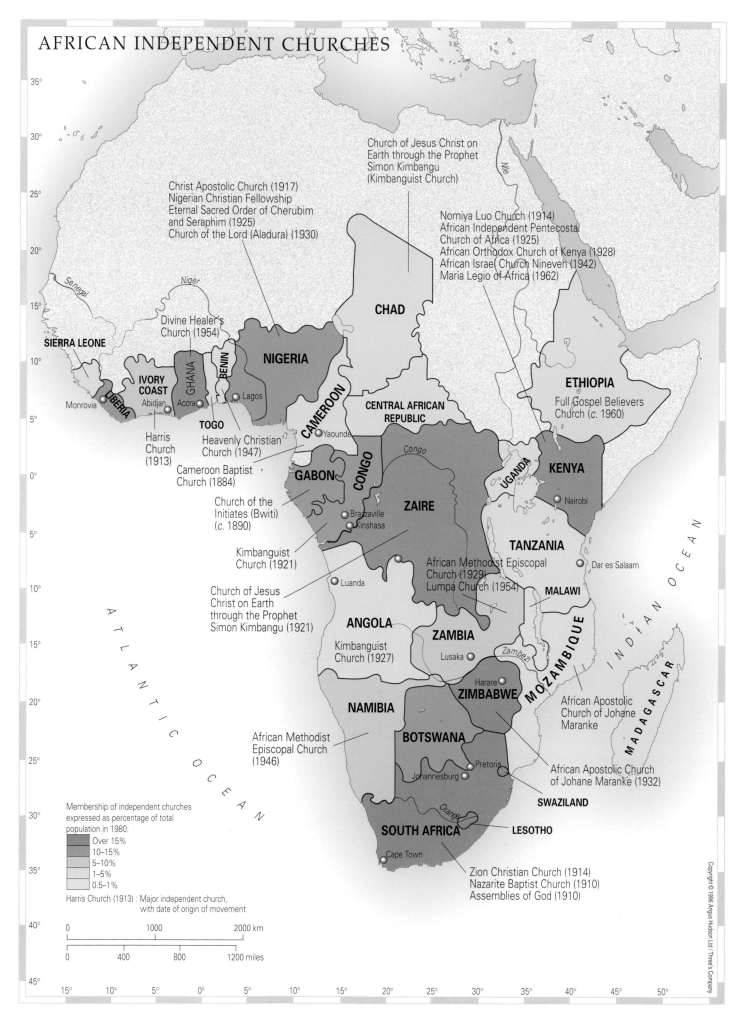

AFRICAN INDEPENDENT CHURCHES

Church of Jesus Christ on
Earth through the Prophet
Simon Kimbangu
(Kimbanguist Church)

Christ Apostolic Church (1917)
Nigerian Christian Fellowship
Eternal Sacred Order of Cherubim
and Seraphim (1925)
Church of the Lord (Aladura) (1930)

Nomiya Luo Church (1914)
African Independent Pentecostal
Church of Africa (1925)
African Orthodox Church of Kenya (1928)
African Israel Church Nineveh (1942)
Maria Legio of Africa (1962)

Divine Healer's
Church (1954)

SIERRA LEONE

IVORY
COAST

GHANA

BENIN

NIGERIA

CHAD

ETHIOPIA

Full Gospel Believers
Church (c. 1960)

Monrovia

LIBERIA

Abidjan

Accra

TOGO

Lagos

CENTRAL AFRICAN
REPUBLIC

CAMEROON

Harris
Church
(1913)

Heavenly Christian
Church (1947)

Yaounde

Congo

KENYA

Cameroon Baptist
Church (1884)

GABON

CONGO

Nairobi

Church of the
Initiates (Bwiti)
(c. 1890)

ZAIRE

Brazzaville

Kinshasa

UGANDA

Kimbanguist
Church (1921)

TANZANIA

Dar es Salaam

African Methodist Episcopal
Church (1929)
Lumpa Church (1954)

Church of Jesus
Christ on Earth
through the Prophet
Simon Kimbangu (1921)

Luanda

MALAWI

ANGOLA

ZAMBIA

Kimbanguist
Church (1927)

Lusaka

Zambezi

MOZAMBIQUE

MADAGASCAR

African Apostolic
Church of Johane
Maranke

Harare

ZIMBABWE

NAMIBIA

BOTSWANA

African Methodist
Episcopal Church
(1946)

African Apostolic Church
of Johane Maranke (1932)

Pretoria

Johannesburg

SWAZILAND

Orange

SOUTH AFRICA

LESOTHO

Cape Town

Zion Christian Church (1914)
Nazarite Baptist Church (1910)
Assemblies of God (1910)

ATLANTIC OCEAN

INDIAN OCEAN

Senegal

Niger

Nile

Membership of independent churches
expressed as percentage of total
population in 1980:

Over 15%
10–15%
5–10%
1–5%
0.5–1%

Harris Church (1913) : Major independent church,
with date of origin of movement

0   1000   2000 km

0   400   800   1200 miles

CHRISTIANITY IN AFRICA

Some 44 per cent of the African Christian population is Roman Catholic. Protestants represent the mainstream colonial churches: Anglican, Baptist, Congregational, Lutheran, Methodist and Reformed. Many churches are growing rapidly, including some of the African Independent churches (see below and opposite).

Roman Catholicism is strongest in the Central African republics that were ruled by Catholic colonial regimes, such as Congo under the French, Zaire under the Belgians, and Angola under the Portuguese. Likewise, the country with the largest Protestant population is Namibia, a former German and South African colony. Denominational strength also reflects colonial legacy: for example, the Lutheran church in Namibia; the Dutch Reformed in South Africa; the Anglican church in East Africa.

The complexity, though, of African Christianity defies neat pigeon-holing. Whilst origins may be useful starting points, African religion is so multifarious and changeable that the depiction of any pattern is of limited value. Christians are still a minority in Africa, and animism is a major religious force. In some churches formal organization can be virtually absent, and Christian doctrine may be wedded to traditional beliefs.

AFRICAN INDEPENDENT CHURCHES

Many of the indigenous African churches have their origins in the mainstream mission churches. Their independence has allowed them to integrate Christian teaching with traditional African ideas and values. They are usually Pentecostal, and emphasize the power of healing and exorcism. Many have a charismatic prophet as leader, such as the Kimbanguist Church in Zaire, founded by Simon Kimbangu, and the Harris Church in the Ivory Coast, named after William Harris. Some of the largest and best-known in Nigeria are the Aladura (or 'praying people') churches.

South Africa has perhaps the most successful independent tradition. Here, as elsewhere in Africa, many developed as a protest against white control of the historic churches.

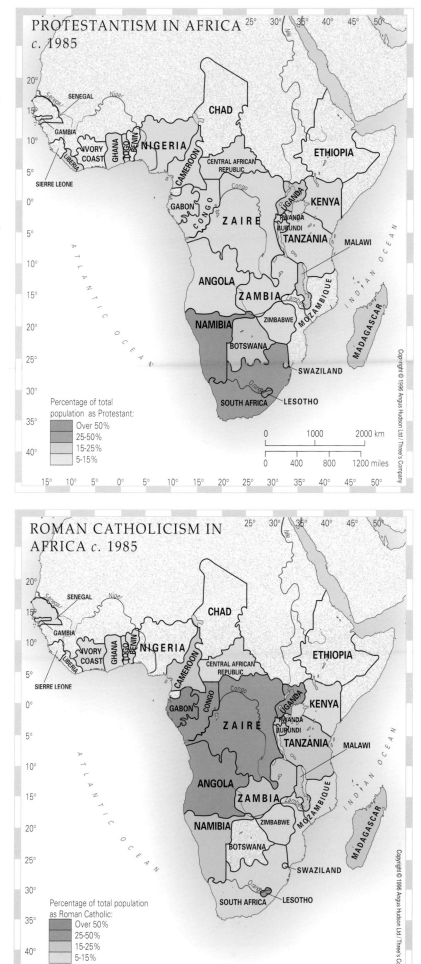

PROTESTANTISM IN AFRICA c. 1985

Percentage of total population as Protestant:
- Over 50%
- 25-50%
- 15-25%
- 5-15%

ROMAN CATHOLICISM IN AFRICA c. 1985

Percentage of total population as Roman Catholic:
- Over 50%
- 25-50%
- 15-25%
- 5-15%

Copyright © 1996 Angus Hudson Ltd / Three's Company

PROTESTANT MISSIONS IN LATIN AMERICA

Copyright © 1996 Angus Hudson Ltd / Three's Company

German Lutherans 1861
Baptists 1862
American Board of
Commissioners for Foreign
Missions 1872

MEXICO

Monterrey

CUBA

Episcopal Church of USA 1871
Anglicans 1741

Methodists 1807
Baptists 1923
Seventh-day Adventists 1923

Methodists 1834

HAITI
DOMINICAN REPUBLIC

Baptists, Lutherans, Presbyterians 1899
Methodists 1900
Seventh-day Adventists 1909

PUERTO RICO

Central
American
Mission 1896

Presbyterians 1872
Methodists 1873
Seventh-day Adventists 1893

Mexico

BELIZE

GUATEMALA

JAMAICA
Quakers 1671
Methodists, Moravians 1700s
Baptists 1783

HONDURAS

Presbyterians 1882
Quakers 1902

EL SALVADOR

NICARAGUA

Evangelical Alliance Mission (TEAM) 1906
Seventh-day Adventists 1910

Dutch Lutherans 1743
Scottish Presbyterians 1766
Seventh-day Adventists 1887

German Moravians 1735

Central American Mission 1896
Baptists 1900
Seventh-day Adventists 1900

COSTA
RICA

Jamaican Baptist
Missionary
Society 1887

PANAMA

VENEZUELA

Orinoco

Caracas

GUYANA

SURINAME

FRENCH
GUIANA

German Moravians 1849

Methodists 1815

Bogota

COLOMBIA

Presbyterians 1856
Evangelical Alliance
Mission (TEAM) 1906

Quito
ECUADOR

Amazon

Gospel Missionary Union 1896
Seventh-day Adventists 1905

PERU

B R A Z I L

Methodists 1877
Regions Beyond Missionary Union 1897
Seventh-day Adventists 1898

Lima

BOLIVIA

German Lutherans 1823
Methodists 1885
Scottish Presbyterians 1855
Baptists 1881

La Paz

Canadian Baptists 1898
Seventh-day Adventists 1898

PARAGUAY

Sao Paulo
Rio De Janeiro

CHILE

Asuncion

ARGENTINA

Baptists 1920
Methodists 1886
German Lutherans 1893

Parana

Methodists 1838
Waldensian Church 1856

URUGUAY

Santiago

Buenos Aires
Montevideo

Presbyterians 1845
Methodists 1877
Lutherans 1846
Seventh-day Adventists 1890

Methodists 1836
Lutherans 1843
Plymouth Brethren 1890s

PACIFIC OCEAN

ATLANTIC OCEAN

Patagonian
Missionary
Society 1844

Periods of early Protestant mission:
Before 1800
1800–1850
1850–1900
After 1900

0   1000   2000 km
0   400   800   1200 miles

30° 20° 10° 0° 10° 20° 30° 40° 50° 60°
100° 90° 80° 70° 60° 50° 40° 30°

148

CHRISTIANITY
IN LATIN AMERICA

MEXICO

CUBA

Baptists
Seventh-day Adventists

Assemblies of God

Anglicans

JAMAICA

HAITI
DOMINICAN REPUBLIC

PUERTO RICO

Pentecostal Church of God
Methodists
Seventh-day Adventists

Presbyterians

BELIZE

GUATEMALA

Assemblies
of God

HONDURAS

Moravians
Assemblies of God

Anglicans
Baptists
Seventh-day Adventists

Assemblies of God

Anglicans

Assemblies of God
Central American Church
Presbyterians

EL SALVADOR

NICARAGUA

COSTA
RICA

Moravians

Assemblies
of God

PANAMA

International Church of the
Foursquare Gospel

International Church of
the Foursquare Gospel

VENEZUELA

Orinoco

GUYANA

SURINAME

FRENCH
GUIANA

Assemblies of God
Baptists

United Pentecostal Church

COLOMBIA

Evangelical Missionary
Union Church
International Church of
the Foursquare Gospel

ECUADOR

Amazon

PERU

P A C I F I C   O C E A N

Assemblies of God
Seventh-day Adventists

B R A Z I L

BOLIVIA

Seventh-day Adventists
Evangelical Christian Union

PARAGUAY

CHILE

Mennonites

Parana

Pentecostal Methodist Church
Seventh-day Adventists

URUGUAY

Assemblies of God
Waldensian Church

A R G E N T I N A

A T L A N T I C   O C E A N

Christian Assemblies
Plymouth Brethren

Over 90% of population Roman Catholic
50%-90% of population Roman Catholic
More Protestants than Roman Catholic
Fast-growing Protestant minority, with percentage of
population that is Protestant
Pentecostal minority church } the largest named first
Protestant minority church

149

PROTESTANT MISSIONS IN LATIN AMERICA

CHRISTIANITY IN LATIN AMERICA

Protestant missionaries came to Latin America from the USA to revive Christianity in the nineteenth century at a time when North American Protestant values were attractive to the middle-class liberals who had steered the Latin American republics to independence. Since the ejection of earlier Roman Catholic missions, a shortage of priests had brought decline in the Christian faith. The Methodists and Baptists came to the Caribbean on the tide of the anti-slavery movement. The Assemblies of God and Seventh-day Adventists were two of the more aggressively evangelistic missions at the beginning of the twentieth century. By the outbreak of World War I, all the Latin American republics had established Protestant missions. However, with only half a million converts in the entire region, they represented only a tiny fraction compared with the residual Catholic population.

In 1970, about half of the Roman Catholic clergy were foreigners. Many supported indigenous political movements that strove for justice against repressive governments. With less dependence on their bishops, and often stipends paid by their missionary societies, foreign clergy were in an easier position to challenge the authorities. Increasingly, the indigenous clergy, and some bishops, notably Archbishop Romero of Salvador, openly denounced their governments from the pulpit. Reactionary persecutions of the Church followed. Between 1964 and 1978, 260 foreign missionaries were expelled from Latin American states, and over 450 priests arrested.

Similar authoritarian attitudes prevailed at first against Protestant missions. However, through the 1960s, relations improved and Protestant growth escalated, especially in poor urban districts. Latin America was, in truth, a mission region, with a great

majority of the population only nominally Catholic. The most spectacular Protestant growth has been among the Pentecostal groups, especially in Brazil, Chile, Mexico and Guatemala. Indeed, Latin America has been the most successful mission field in the world for the Pentecostal churches.

The most widespread Pentecostalist church is the Assemblies of God, whilst the Seventh-day Adventists are the most consistently successful of the evangelical groups.

Christian students in Campinas, Brazil, lead a service in a *favela* in the city.

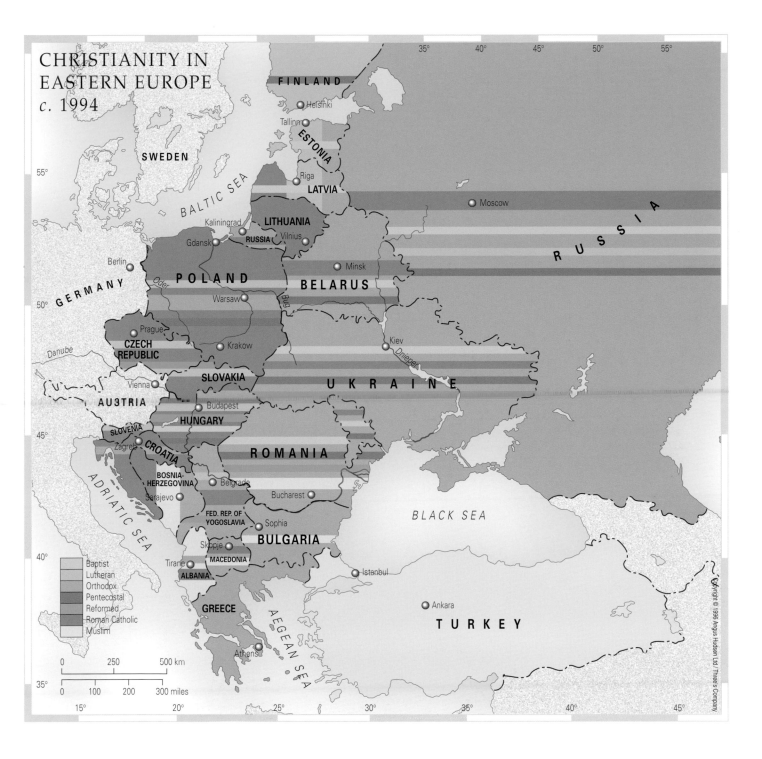

CHRISTIANITY IN EASTERN EUROPE c. 1994

Legend:
- Baptist
- Lutheran
- Orthodox
- Pentecostal
- Reformed
- Roman Catholic
- Muslim

0   250   500 km
0 100 200 300 miles

CHRISTIANITY IN EASTERN EUROPE

The main division in eastern Europe, between Roman Catholic and Eastern Orthodox, has persisted since the eleventh century.

By the 1920s most of the national Orthodox churches in the Balkans had come into being. Each church is independent but acknowledges the primacy of the Patriarchate of Constantinople. The traditional Protestant denominations have in several republics been overtaken by Pentecostals this century, though Lutheranism still holds sway in the far north. Roman Catholicism is still strong in central Europe, especially in Poland, where it is professed by over 90 per cent of the population.

In Estonia, Latvia and Bosnia, there is no majority confession. The main denominational allegiances are shown in equal parts.

PREDOMINANT RELIGIOUS AFFILIATION OF WORLD POPULATION *c.* 1990

75°
60°
45°
30°
15°
0°
15°
30°
45°
60°

NORTH AMERICA

SOUTH AMERICA

P A C I F I C   O C E A N

A T L A N T I C   O C E A N

Majority of population:
Christian
Muslim
Buddhist
Hindu
Buddhist, Confucian and Taoist
Buddhist and Shintoist
Jewish
Sikh
Animist

0   2000   4000 km

0   800   1600   2400 miles

150°   135°   120°   105°   90°   75°   60°   45°   30°   15°   0°

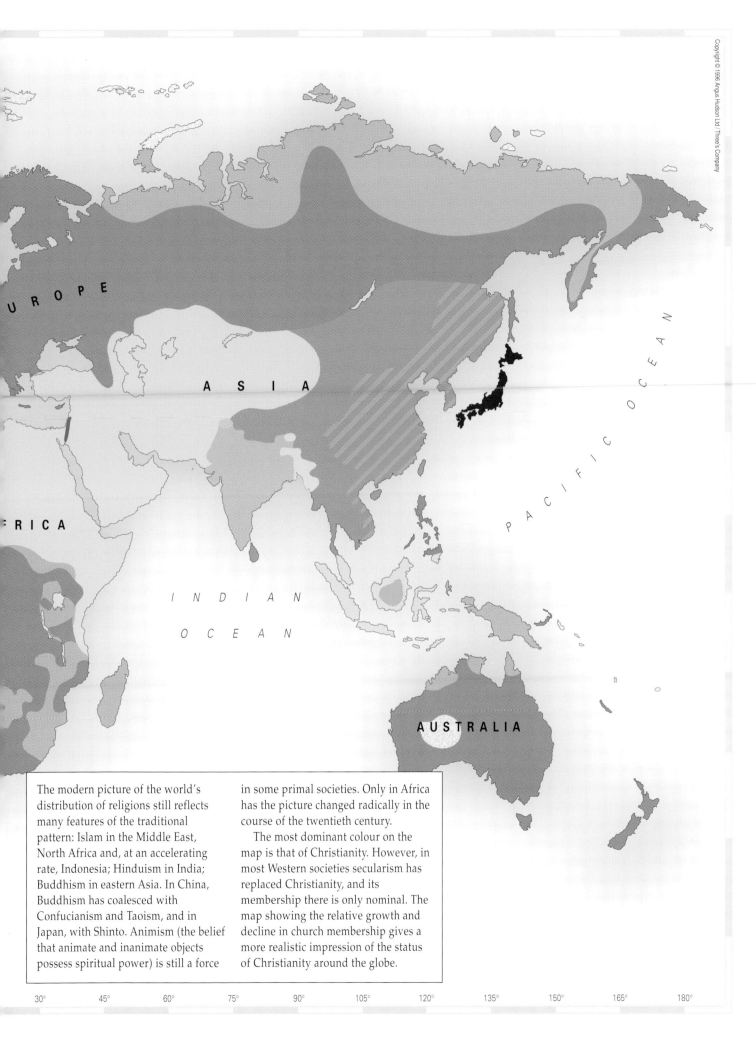

EUROPE

ASIA

AFRICA

AUSTRALIA

PACIFIC OCEAN

INDIAN OCEAN

The modern picture of the world's distribution of religions still reflects many features of the traditional pattern: Islam in the Middle East, North Africa and, at an accelerating rate, Indonesia; Hinduism in India; Buddhism in eastern Asia. In China, Buddhism has coalesced with Confucianism and Taoism, and in Japan, with Shinto. Animism (the belief that animate and inanimate objects possess spiritual power) is still a force in some primal societies. Only in Africa has the picture changed radically in the course of the twentieth century.

The most dominant colour on the map is that of Christianity. However, in most Western societies secularism has replaced Christianity, and its membership there is only nominal. The map showing the relative growth and decline in church membership gives a more realistic impression of the status of Christianity around the globe.

| 30° | 45° | 60° | 75° | 90° | 105° | 120° | 135° | 150° | 165° | 180° |

BRANCHES OF CHRISTIANITY IN ASIA

Majority denomination:

Syria	Greek Orthodox	Nagaland	85% Christian
Jordan	Greek Orthodox	Manipur	34% Christian
Iran	Armenian Apostolic	Mizoram	85% Christian
Georgia	Georgian Orthodox	Burma	Burma Baptist Convention
Armenia	Armenian Apostolic	China	Estimated over 10 million Protestants, and 6 million Roman Catholics (1990)
Azerbaijan	Russian Orthodox		
Kazakhstan	Russian Orthodox	South Korea	Presbyterian churches
Uzbekistan	Russian Orthodox		Other minority churches, each with over ½ million members:
Kyrgyzstan	Russian Orthodox		Roman Catholic Church, Korean Methodist Church
Qatar	Orthodox churches	Philippines	Minority church of over 3 million members: Philippine Independent Church
Bahrain	Anglican		
India	Estimated 16 million (1.91%) Protestants and 14.5 million (1.76%) Roman Catholics (1990) Other minority churches, each with over 1 million members: Church of South India Council of Baptist Churches of North East India Malankara Orthodox Syrian Church of the East United Evangelical Lutheran Churches in India Church of North India	Indonesia	Protestant Church in Indonesia Minority of over 2 million members: Roman Catholic Church
		Papua New Guinea	Evangelical Lutheran Church of Papua New Guinea Minority of over 1/2 million members: Roman Catholic Church

AUSTRALIA

Main branches of Christianity in those countries with significant Christian population:
- Eastern Orthodox
- Protestant
- Roman Catholic

Size of Christian population:
- Less than 1 million
- 1-10 million
- More than 10 million

CHRISTIANITY IN ASIA

After the 1966 Cultural Revolution in China Christianity was driven 'underground'. This gave rise to the secret house church movement, which spread rapidly.

With the relaxing of government control over religious worship churches have re-opened. However, estimates of present numbers of practising Christians are difficult to obtain and vary enormously. Some researchers have put the figure as high as 75 million Protestants and Catholics in 1992. In central Asia, Christianity tends to be confined to the Slavic immigrants, who are normally Eastern Orthodox; the most populous state being Kazakhstan. Islam thrives in many of the republics.

In southern Asia, India has sizeable Christian communities. Perhaps the most notable are those enclaves bordering Burma: Nagaland and Mizoram, where some 85 per cent of the population are Christian. Many of the boat people escaping the regime in Vietnam were Roman Catholic, though there remains a significant Christian community. Although in Indonesia the Church is stronger and officially tolerated, there have been Muslim reactions to Protestant evangelism, resulting in persecutions. In South Korea, on the other hand, the government has been completely favourable to the growth of the Church. Most there are Evangelicals. The Philippines still has one of the densest Roman Catholic populations in Asia.

INDEX

Page numbers in *italics* denote illustrations

159